T5-ACQ-946

BEAT THE MARKET
1985

BEAT THE MARKET 1985

by Jeffrey Weiss

VIKING

VIKING
Viking Penguin Inc., 40 West 23rd Street,
New York, New York 10010, U.S.A.
Penguin Books Ltd, Harmondsworth,
Middlesex, England
Penguin Books Australia Ltd, Ringwood,
Victoria, Australia
Penguin Books Canada Limited, 2801 John Street,
Markham, Ontario, Canada L3R 1B4
Penguin Books (N.Z.) Ltd, 182–190 Wairau Road,
Auckland 10, New Zealand

Copyright © Jeffrey Weiss and Cloverdale Press, Inc., 1985
Produced by Cloverdale Press, 133 Fifth Avenue, New York, NY 10003
All rights reserved

First published in 1985 by Viking Penguin Inc.
Published simultaneously in Canada

LIBRARY OF CONGRESS CATALOGING IN PUBLICATION DATA
Weiss, Jeffrey.
Beat the market.
1. Investments—United States—Handbooks, manuals,
etc. 2. Stocks—United States—Handbooks, manuals, etc.
3. New York Stock Exchange—Handbooks, manuals, etc.
I. Cloverdale Press. II. Title.
HG4921.W435   1985   332.64′273   85-645
ISBN 0-670-80572-6

Information either copyrighted by, originally published by, or directly attributable to the following sources appears on pages: 32–33, Shearman, Ralston, Inc.; 81–84, Lipper Analytical Services, Inc.; 84–85, Donoghue's *Money Fund Report;* 86, *Savvy* magazine.

Printed in the United States of America
by Haddon Craftsmen, Scranton, Pennsylvania

Without limiting the rights under copyright reserved above, no part of this publication may be reproduced, stored in or introduced into a retrieval system, or transmitted, in any form or by any means (electronic, mechanical, photocopying, recording or otherwise), without the prior written permission of both the copyright owner and the above publisher of this book.

For Sagaponack

I am deeply indebted to researchers Gene Brown, Nancy Dunnan, and Jay Pack for their energetic and enthusiastic efforts, and to the many other people who helped make this book possible.

CONTENTS

1. Beat the Market — 1
2. Anatomy of a Stock Transaction — 6
3. Creating Your Portfolio — 15
4. Buying a Ready-Made Portfolio — 52
5. Stock Market Timing — 64
6. Top Performers — 76
7. The Beat the Market Hot List — 87
8. Vital Statistics — 224
9. The Rules of the Game — 243

1
Beat the Market

BEAT THE MARKET

> If you bet on a horse, that's gambling.
> If you bet you can make three spades, that's entertainment.
> If you bet cotton will go up three points, that's business.
> See the difference?
>
> — Blackie Sherrode

There is a revolution afoot in America.

America has been galvanized by the concept of Easy Money. State-run lotteries, which opened to small, hesitant crowds only five years ago, now produce hour-long lines bottlenecking stores. Atlantic City's Boardwalk, in a state of advanced deterioration just a few years ago, now boasts some of the most expensive real estate in the nation. Horse racing, not long ago looked down upon as a pastime for the down-and-out, has emerged as the number-one spectator sport in America.

Gambling has taken a firm foothold in the America of the 1980s. The combination of hard times and raised hopes has made gambling an integral part of the entrepreneurial, capitalist spirit. Sixty percent of Americans now gamble. Surprisingly, today's gambler is younger, wealthier, and better educated than ever before.

After a decade of record inflation, unemployment, and bankruptcy, we are now more than ever delighted to read about the nurse's aide or the retired stevedore who strikes it rich with a lucky combination. It is not simply that we relish the individual's luck...we also envision ourselves in his or her position. Because maybe next time...

Yet the disadvantages of conventional gambling are considerable.

It is limited in locale—at least legally. If you live in Biloxi, you will need a jet, a good pair of legs, or a shady connection to find a green felt casino table.

In addition, winnings are taxable. This, of course, is a laughable point to many gamblers. Not so laughable is the fact that losses are *not* tax deductible. The average gambler loses 22 cents out of every dollar he wagers. Even more critical than this steady drain is the inescapable fact that the gambler who pursues his fortune at the roulette table or on the lottery line has no real means of improving his odds.

Beat the Market recognizes and hails the fortune-seeking dreams of today's Americans.

The aim of this book is to give each player the wisdom, the information, and the opportunity to pursue his fortune in a game in which the odds—at last—may be on his side.

- The game is legal in all fifty states.
- While winnings are, alas, taxable, every loss is tax deductible.
- The odds are completely dependent on the insight of the player.
- Most important of all, those odds can be improved—dramatically.
- It is the purpose of this book to better those odds.
- The casino is the New York Stock Exchange.
- The game is stock market investing.
- The object is to beat the market.

The comparison of New York's Wall Street with Atlantic City's Boardwalk is of course somewhat fanciful. Despite the sometimes feverish excitement—and haggard postmortems—common to both arenas, there are major differences.

The average investment has a value more than one thousand times as great as the average wager.

The conventional investment neither wins nor loses *instantly.*

The investor is generally building a portfolio of investments—rather than playing a series of isolated games.

For many, even the motivation is significantly different. Joe Kennedy spoke of that difference half a century ago:

> I think the primary motive in back of most gambling is the excitement of it. While gamblers naturally want to win, the majority of them derive pleasure even if they lose. The desire to win, rather than the excitement involved, seems to me to be the compelling force behind speculation.

Finally, and most compellingly, the difference between the individual who contemplates a $100 night at the crap table or a $10,000 campaign in the stock market is not one of scale or motivation or odds. The fundamental difference is that one is doomed to play out his lot with predetermined odds he can never hope to change.

BEAT THE MARKET

The longer the gambler plays, the more likely it is that his own results will exactly conform to the odds against him. Certainly he will have winning nights. On balance, however, he is fated to played out his allotted time with a seductive and heartless Lady Luck.

Even the average stock market speculator loses money on balance. He follows the crowd, buying in at market tops, swearing he'll never invest another dollar—on the precise day the market's skid stops. But it needn't be that way. There are no "house odds" on Wall Street. There are winners, and there are losers.

It isn't always easy to tell who will be a winner and who will be a loser on Wall Street. PhDs don't all make fortunes. The rich don't always get richer. And the old line, "If you're so smart, how come you're just a stockbroker?" underscores what many investors have learned the hard way: A friendly and confiding voice on the phone doesn't always cloak a font of financial wisdom.

In the end, the difference between the winners and losers is most often incremental—a little better corporate information here, a slightly more reliable indicator there. But the difference in their results is what this book is all about.

We want to make you a winner.

In *Beat the Market* we have collected

- the most valuable advice, the most pertinent information, and proven statistics for beating the market
- extensive information on the tried-and-true techniques of portfolio building
- a full-scale encyclopedia embracing some of the hottest stocks in America—complete with charts, statistics, and inside information
- a guide to purchasing ready-made portfolios, crafted by the most successful investors in America
- a hard-nosed look at stock market timing—with a dozen of the most valuable indicators explained, reviewed, and analyzed.

Finally—as if all this weren't enough—there is a real, risk-free opportunity for you to BEAT THE MARKET.

The rules are quite simple.

1. Give yourself $25,000 to invest in any of the stocks covered in this book.

2. Create your own portfolio—and send it in to us.

3. The best portfolio we receive is worth $25,000 to the person who designed it.

Perhaps no other book in history has provided such valuable information—or such a powerful incentive for using it.

Welcome to *Beat the Market!*

2
Anatomy of a Stock Transaction

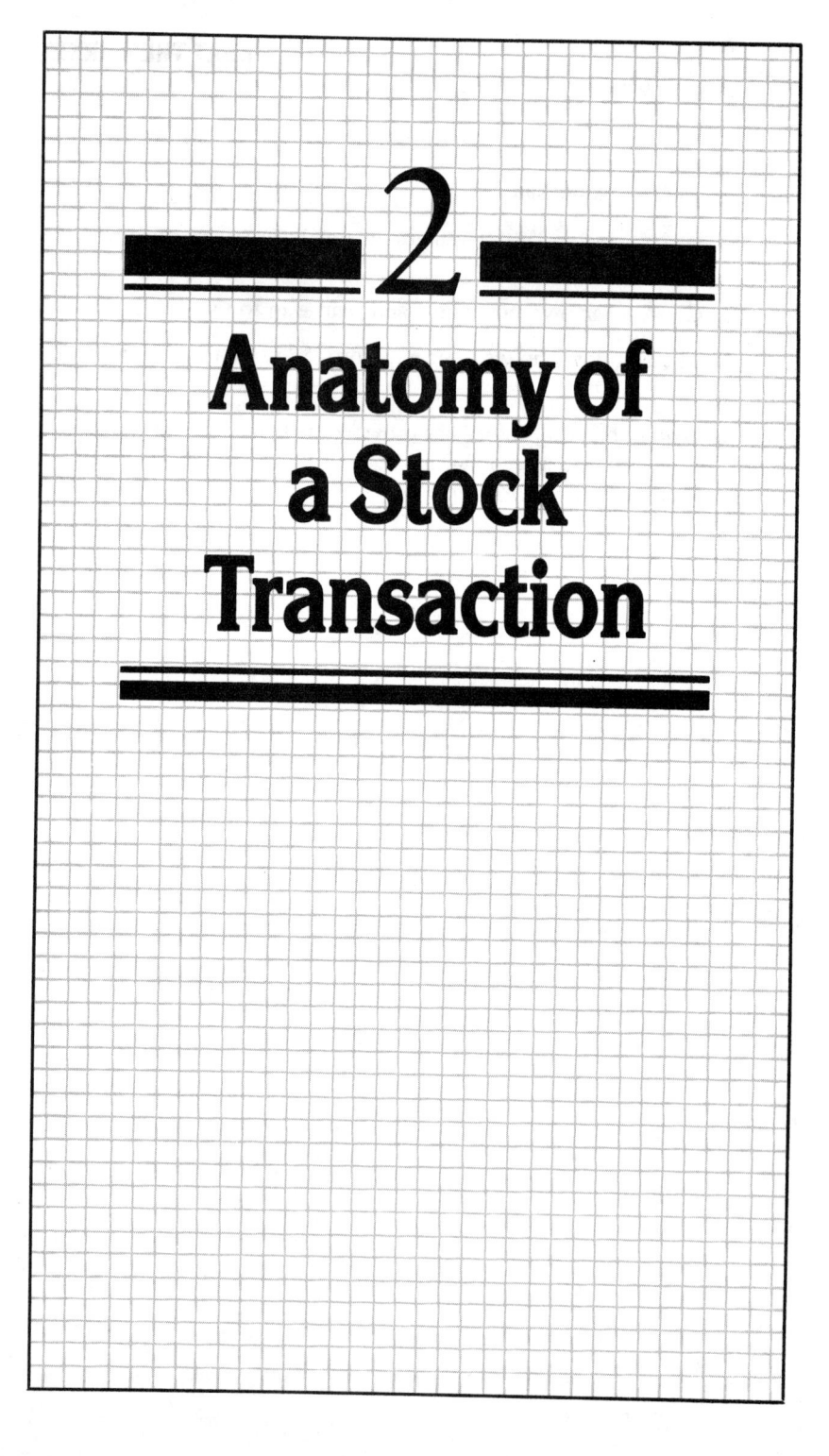

ANATOMY OF A STOCK TRANSACTION

Many individuals—even those with substantial savings—have traditionally avoided the stock market. For some, the attendant risks are simply not worth taking. For some, there is an unease verging on shyness about taking a first step into stocks. For others, the shadowy ghost of the 1929 panic still haunts the market. Finally, there are many who are inclined to invest who simply haven't taken the time or trouble to learn how it's done.

WHY INVEST?

The answer is quite simple. Let's look at some recent history.

In the year 1950, stocks had already recovered much of the lost ground and lost prestige that afflicted them throughout the Great Depression. Many who had been through the wrenching declines of that era had sworn off stocks completely. By 1950, particularly to anyone gazing back into the chasm of the early 1930s, stock prices were quite high. There may have been considerable doubts about the market's ability to sustain its gains.

The simple fact is that a stock selling for $35 per share in 1950 would today be worth—with dividends, but no new outside funds, reinvested—$1,350. And, as everyone knows, the intervening years have hardly been uniformly bounteous. Put another way, a thirty-year-old couple with the foresight and wherewithal to have invested $30,000 in 1950 would be retiring today as millionaires. And, the effects of inflation and the changing value of the dollar notwithstanding, a million bucks is still a bundle of cash.

In the thirty-five years since mid-century, American business has grown up and outward. The local company has become the nationwide company—and gone on to become the multinational. The international community has marveled at, deplored, and envied the profitability and power of these globe-straddling corporations.

Ownership of stock is one of the few ways for the American citizen to share actively in this profitability—and power. Every share of stock represents a minuscule, but real, fragment of a major corporation. In the end, there is no power in any corporation that does not derive from the power of the shareholders. Even the mightiest chairman of the board operates only at their discretion.

But, for all but the largest investors, the capacity of the individual to wield significant power within a corporation is minimal. Even someone with a 500-share block of IBM (worth more than $50,000) owns less than 1/1,000,000 of the corporation—small leverage, indeed.

ANATOMY OF A STOCK TRANSACTION

The only *practical* reason for purchasing stock on a small or intermediate scale is to share in the profits of the corporation.

WHAT IS STOCK?

Suppose you decide to start up a company but you need help financing it, since you don't have the $50,000 necessary to get going. You decide to sell shares in your company—1,000 shares at $50 each, the stock's offering price. The $50 price is the original market valuation.

Everybody who buys a share in your company is called a shareholder. If someone buys one share, he owns 1/1,000th of the company. If someone buys two shares, he naturally owns 2/1,000th of the firm. To signify ownership, each shareholder is issued a stock certificate indicating the number of shares he or she owns. For every share owned, the shareholder is entitled to one vote in the company's business affairs. A shareholder can vote either by appearing in person at the company's annual meeting or by signing a proxy, authorizing one of the company's officers to vote in his behalf.

Your stockholders invested in your company because they believe it has a good moneymaking product or service and that they will see a profit. In other words, shareholders hope to make money in one of two ways: through receiving dividends or through an increase in the value of their shares, called appreciation.

Dividends

Let's say in the second year of business your company is able to pay all its bills and taxes and have a small profit of $4,000. The company has two choices: It can put all earnings ($4,000) back into the firm in order to expand or improve its facilities; or the board of directors can vote to pay a cash dividend to the shareholders—either all of the $4,000 or part of it.

If the directors decide to pay out $2,000 in dividends, the other $2,000 is called "retained earnings." In this case there are 1,000 shares; each shareholder would receive $2 per share—a yield of 4 percent on the initial investment of $50 per share. Dividends are usually paid quarterly—once every three months. Dividends paid on common stock move up and down with the fortunes of the company, although directors try very hard to avoid cutting a dividend. Many companies allow you to reinvest dividends in the company stock without using a stockbroker. This is an excellent way to build your portfolio.

Appreciation

The other way your shareholders may make money is if the price of the stock they purchased goes up. The only way to test this is to put it up for sale. Companies that are trying to grow generally do not pay dividends; they attract investors who are more interested in seeing the price of the stock rise than in receiving dividends. A rise in stock price is called appreciation, a factor that is determined by supply and demand.

The Stock Exchange

Stock trading is customarily handled by one of the stock exchanges. The exchanges do not actually own the stocks; they simply provide a place where buyers and sellers can meet. If the stock trades on a public exchange, it is said to be "listed."

The largest exchange is the New York Stock Exchange (NYSE), also known as the Big Board. The American Stock Exchange (AMEX) lists a number of companies, many of them smaller in size. Regional exchanges handle local companies as well as a number of "dual-listed" companies that are already on the NYSE or AMEX.

There are also thousands of stocks that do not trade on any of the exchanges but instead are handled over-the-counter (OTC). On occasion, this means that they are bought and sold directly by the parties involved — without any intermediaries. More often, it means they are bought and sold with the assistance of dealers who specialize in over-the-counter stocks. Stockbrokers in turn buy and sell these stocks directly from the dealer and not through an exchange. Most OTC stocks are those of small companies. Your new company most likely would be traded OTC until it becomes large enough to qualify for listing on the NYSE or AMEX. The National Association of Security Dealers (NASD) oversees the OTC markets and has an electronic quotation system available to all brokers on their desk-top computers.

ANATOMY OF A STOCK TRANSACTION

HOW STOCK PRICES ARE DETERMINED

Stocks that are listed on an exchange or through the NASD are really sold in an auction. Buyers and sellers, through an intervening network of stockbrokers, floor traders, and specialists, reach an agreed-upon price. The price of a given stock at a given instant is a momentary reflection of an extraordinary universe of factors—from the prevailing sentiment in the entire market to the company's latest press release.

Every share bought must be matched by a share sold; the crudest means of matching the number of shares bought and sold is by changing the price. When buy orders outnumber sell orders, stock prices rise, because additional shares may be obtainable at higher prices: Shareholders unwilling to sell at 99 might be willing to sell if the price were to rise to 100.

It is the subtle fluctuation of this buy/sell imbalance that traces the course of a stock price during any business day. It is the larger fluctuation of this imbalance that charts the long-term course of a given stock. If a prolonged imbalance exists, the price of the stock will continue to move in the designated direction.

BUYING A STOCK

Once you decide to buy a stock, you must let your broker know, for unless you participate in a dividend reinvestment plan as described on page 8 or are buying shares directly from the handful of companies that allow this, he is the only person who can buy and sell stocks for you. You may use either a full-service broker or a discount broker. The former is set up to give you buy-and-sell suggestions, to provide research, and to monitor your portfolio. The latter offers no such frills and merely places your buy-and-sell orders—but with significantly lower commission charges.

One of the most critical determinants of your eventual success in the stock market may be your choice of broker. After all, it's your hard-earned dollars we're talking about—there's no room for second-rate people. Start by asking friends and colleagues at work for suggestions, just as you would if you were looking for a doctor or a building contractor. If you already have a banker or lawyer whom you like, he or she will probably be able to recommend a good broker.

ANATOMY OF A STOCK TRANSACTION

After you've gathered several names, call and make appointments with each one. Before actually conducting an interview, take time out to list your investment objectives and what type of portfolio you want to set up or add to. Be prepared to discuss these objectives as well as your age, family commitments, and net worth. Without adequate information, it is difficult for a broker to select the right investments for your portfolio.

During that first interview, be sure you get satisfactory answers to these questions:

- What is your training?
- How long have you been a broker?
- How long have you been with this firm?
- Do you handle clients in my income category?
- How would you allocate a sample portfolio of $10,000 for someone with my investment objectives? How much would you suggest I put in stocks, bonds, and cash equivalents?
- Are you conservative or aggressive, and why?
- How do you select stocks?
- Will you send me copies of your firm's research if I open an account?
- Will you give me names of several references that I may check?

Once you've opened an account with a broker, you can immediately begin buying and selling equities. Your broker, if you've made a wise choice, should spend time with you in constructing the best possible portfolio to meet your stated objectives.

At the end of a year, take time out for an annual review to determine if the broker has done a good job for you. Always keep in mind that a broker is a business advisor who must generate commissions—he is a salesman seeking to support himself while investing your money for you. You *don't* have to buy everything he is selling.*

---

*For a full discussion of how to deal successfully with a stockbroker, read *How to Talk to a Broker* by Jay J. Pack. New York: Harper & Row, 1985.

ANATOMY OF A STOCK TRANSACTION

When you place your order with your broker, you may specify one of three types:

1. Market Order: This is the most common, and, in most cases, the recommended, means of placing an order. A Market Order instructs the broker to make the trade at the current market price—whatever that price may be. It is possible, of course, that the price may change somewhat before your order is actually handled. But with a market order, you are sure of having your trade executed. And, to cut down on sudden surprises, always ask your broker for a current quotation as you're placing your order. Unless he is criminally slow, or unless you're trading into a bizarre situation, your trade should take place within a quarter of a point or so of the price you were quoted.

2. Day Order: This "limit" order instructs the broker to make a trade for you if a given stock reaches a given price anytime during the course of a business day. If that price is available to the broker, he must make the transaction. If, by the close of business, the order has not taken place, the order is torn up—it is *not* automatically reactivated the next day.

3. Good-Till-Cancelled (GTC) Order: This "limit" order instructs the broker to make a trade for you if a given stock reaches a given price from now until doomsday. In most cases, brokers set their own ninety-day limit on such orders.

It is worth noting that, at any time prior to execution, it is possible to call your broker and cancel either of the above "limit" orders. For example, U.S. Steel closed yesterday at 34⅝. You're interested in buying it, and you'd like to see if you can pick up 100 shares during a downswing. You could place a day order at 34. If the stock moves low enough to trigger your order, you've saved yourself some money. On the other hand, if it continues to drift around 34½ all day, you can call your broker, cancel the limit order, and buy in at the market.

However, the reason that limit orders are discouraged is quite simple. Suppose that you've not only picked the right stock, but also the right day—but you picked the wrong type of order. If U.S. Steel opens at 34⅝ and starts climbing, past 35, all the way to 36, you still don't own it—and, in trying to save yourself ⅝ of a point, you lost out on 1⅜. A good general rule is simply this: Once you've settled on a stock, go out and get it. The market order may cost you an eighth or a quarter, but it won't ever cost you a point.

ANATOMY OF A STOCK TRANSACTION

In buying shares of stock, the standard order size is a 100-share block, or a "round lot." Round lots are handled directly on the floor of the appropriate exchange. Any order for less than 100 shares (or for the extra 57 shares in an order of 157 shares) is called an "odd lot" and is handled indirectly through dealers who specialize in nonstandard orders. In general, there is a minor penalty (often an automatic ⅛ point charge per share) for trading in odd lots.

After you phone your broker, the trading desk then phones your order to their clerk stationed on the floor of the appropriate exchange. Some firms have booth space for one or two clerks on the floor of the exchange, whereas others have twenty to forty spaces in eight or nine booths. When the clerk on the floor of the exchange receives the order by phone, he writes it out and hands it to his floor broker, who is a member of the exchange. (Only members of the exchange are actually allowed to trade on the floor.)

The floor broker then walks to the appropriate trading post on the floor where this particular stock is traded. (The NYSE has over twenty trading posts, or stations.) All buying and selling is done around these stations. Approximately ninety stocks are assigned to each post. Indicators hung above the posts or counters show which stocks are sold in each section, and just below each one is a price indicator that notes the last price and whether it was up or down.

As the floor broker approaches the appropriate post, he looks at the monitor to see what the last sale was for the stock. He then aks the other brokers around the station, "How's Company XYZ doing?" Another broker may say, "Twelve and one-quarter to twelve and a half." Those are the best bid and offer prices at that moment, i.e., $12.25 to $12.50.

The broker waits to see if any better offers are made and eventually he makes a bid for you by saying, "One half for a hundred," which means he will pay $12.50 per share for 100 shares of Company XYZ.

Sometimes a broker receives no response to his bid, in which case he will have to raise it. The bidding continues until the floor broker feels he's obtained the best possible price, in which case he says, "Sold" or "Take it."

Orders can be placed only during trading hours: 10 A.M. to 4 P.M. EST, Monday through Friday, except holidays.

As soon as the transaction is completed, the two floor brokers involved—the one who sold and the one who bought—inform their offices, usually by wire or phone. Thereafter, your broker will call you to inform you of the transaction and the price at which the trade was executed. This confirmation will be followed up by a mailed, written confirmation.

ANATOMY OF A STOCK TRANSACTION

The final question to consider in a stock purchase is whether or not you actually want to take delivery of your stock certificates. If you choose not to, your broker will hold your stock for you in what is called "street name." Your ownership is in no way diminished, and the great majority of shares are, in fact, held in street name. In the end, this is a minor issue—the choice is up to you.

There are certain reasons why you might wish to request a stock certificate: for the simple pleasure of ownership, for security (in case your brokerage firm begins to disintegrate), or for collateral against a loan.

If you choose to hold your stocks in street name, you will be spared the concern about the certificate's safekeeping (a lost or stolen stock certificate is always traceable—but at a loss of time and money). You will also be spared the hassle of returning the certificate to the broker—particularly if you decide to sell your shares while vacationing.

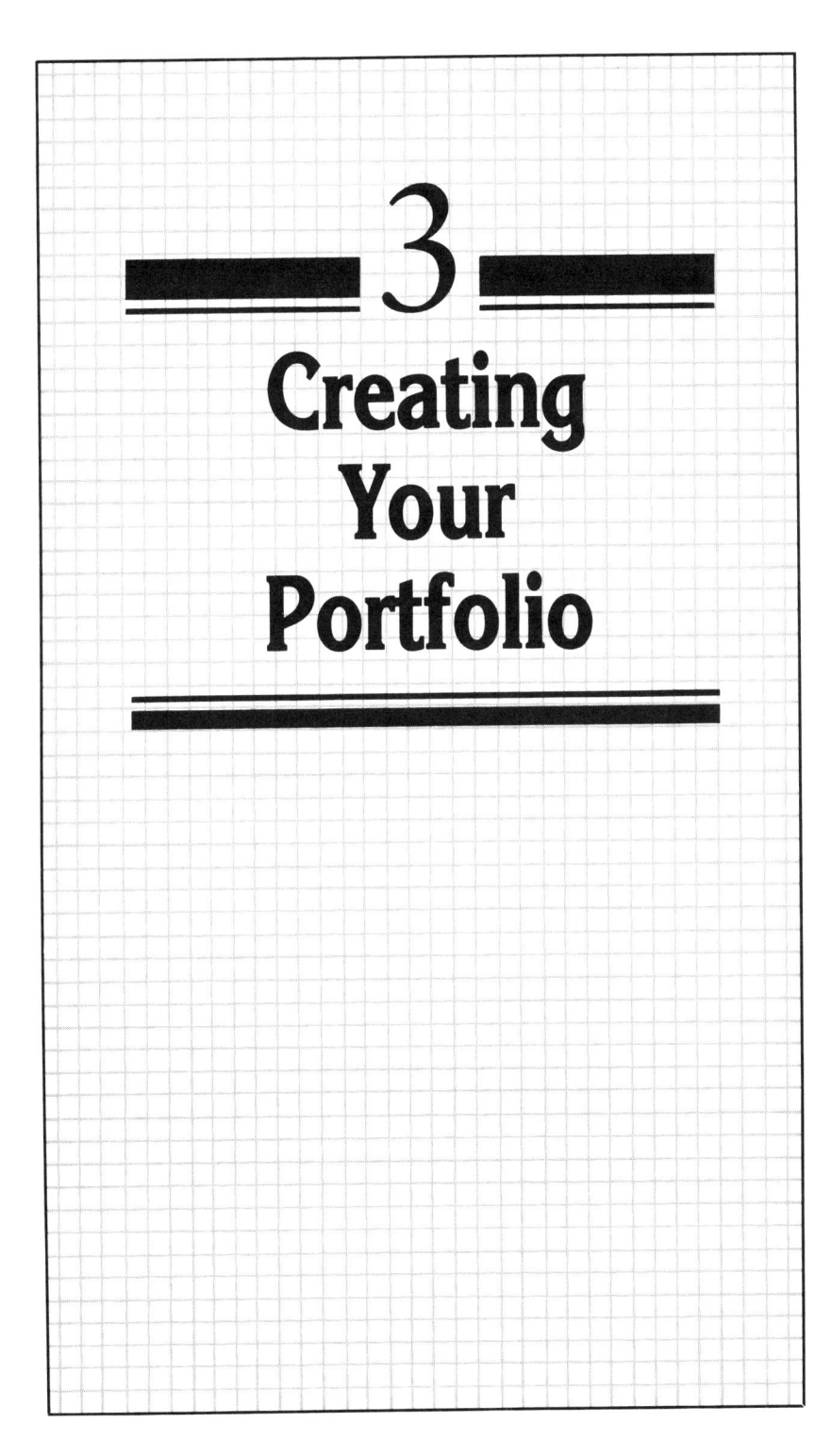

3
Creating Your Portfolio

CREATING YOUR PORTFOLIO

An investment portfolio is a concept that conjures up a polished boardroom table, pinstriped investment bankers, and multimillion-dollar stock transactions. Yet a portfolio need not involve this flashy scenario; nor, in fact, is it dependent at all on size. An investment portfolio is nothing more than an itemized list of investments. The moment you own two or more stocks, you qualify as the manager of a stock market portfolio.

No matter what the size of your portfolio, the principles of its construction and care are the same. It is never static; it changes daily, expanding and contracting as the value of each security fluctuates in price. That's why monitoring your portfolio on a regular basis is so essential to its well-being. But before we get into monitoring your portfolio, let's first learn how to build one.

The contents of any portfolio depend upon several things: your age, income, net worth, family responsibilities, and investment goals. This obviously means that no one portfolio is ideal for everyone. One size, unlike bathrobes, does not fit all!

THE THREE BIGGIES

Before putting your money down, you must give some consideration to what you want to get out of your investment. Fortunately, there are only three basic portfolio choices to deal with: income, growth, and balanced.

An income portfolio is one that consists of stocks with high yields or dividends, such as public utilities or closed-end bond fund investment companies.

A growth portfolio is not designed to take advantage of dividend income; rather it consists of stocks that should increase (or appreciate) in price. Candidates would be high-technology, medical technology, or blue chip stocks.

A balanced portfolio, quite obviously, has a mixture of both growth and income stocks.

The type of portfolio that's best for you will be dictated primarily by your personal financial needs. Do you have enough money to live comfortably right now but will need more when you retire? If so, you're a good candidate for a growth portfolio.

On the other hand, if your immediate need is for additional income (to put your children through school, for example), then you should work on setting up an income portfolio. Actually, most people tend to combine the two and run a balanced portfolio.

Regardless of your portfolio type, you certainly want to select winners—the best possible stocks to meet your objectives. If you are willing to assume a little risk, you could try several speculative issues; but if you're on the conservative side and have trouble sleeping at night, it is best to stick with those companies that have top-quality management and a strong financial outlook. Let's look at the issue of risk more closely.

THE RISK FACTOR

Most of us think of risk, when applied to the world of investments, as a situation in which we are likely to lose our money. That's a legitimate definition. It also implies, quite correctly, that some investments are lower in risk because we are unlikely to lose our money when we invest in them. These include savings accounts, CDs, bank money-market accounts, and government securities (i.e., U.S. Treasury issues). Others, such as start-up companies, speculative tax shelters, and index futures, are unquestionably very high in risk. Many investment vehicles, of course, fall in the middle. In planning a portfolio, you need to keep in mind that high-risk investments, when they pan out, will yield high—even speculative—returns, whereas low-risk investments always yield smaller profits along with smaller chances for loss. You've got to figure out how much risk you're willing to take and what portion of your portfolio you wish to devote to high- or low-risk stocks.

You'll undoubtedly discover that your feeling about risk is tied closely to your income level and perhaps to your age. It's not unusual for younger investors to asume more risk than those approaching retirement. Those with more disposable income feel more comfortable investing in riskier stocks.

These are the obvious characteristics of risk. Yet risk also has a less obvious side, a more subtle definition. In fact, there are virtually no investments that are risk free.

For example, U.S. Savings Bonds were once considered safe and profitable investments. Millions of patriotic, income-oriented investors supported the famous E-Series bond, despite its minuscule interest rate. Beginning in the late 1960s, however, inflation began to cut into—and then overtake— that rate of return. With an inflation rate over 10 percent, the tiny returns available through old-fashioned E-Series bonds had turned into losses of more than 5 percent per year.

Risk is relative. And, in the topsy-turvy investment climate of the late twentieth century, nothing is risk free. The only thing an investor can rea-

CREATING YOUR PORTFOLIO

sonably do is seek out situations in which potential rewards are commensurate with those inevitable risks.

Let's look at how two specific types of risk can affect your portfolio.

Stock Market Risk

All stocks, as we've already discussed, go up or down in price, whether you're watching them or not, whether you own 100 shares or 1,000. This movement in price relative to the overall stock market is called *volatility*. Wall Streeters love to express the volatility of a stock's price in terms of its *beta*. The Standard & Poor's index, which represents the average of the market, has a beta of one. So, if a stock has a beta of two, it has historically moved twice as much as the S&P index; therefore, it is that much riskier.

Beta numbers are listed with each of *Beat the Market*'s Top 200 Stocks.

When using the beta number, it's important to realize that it measures *only* that part of a stock's risk that relates directly to the stock market. Keep in mind that stocks also have inherent risks, separate from those that are market related. They operate quite independently of the rise and fall of the market; the beta, therefore, is only one way to measure one type of risk.

The most direct way to fine-tune your risk factor is to adjust your portfolio's average beta. Choosing stocks with higher betas increases volatility and risk. More defensive postures are achieved by reducing the average beta.

Another obvious and significant means of reducing stock market risk is through diversification. No stock is impervious to sudden, unexpected news; any stock can crumble almost overnight. Even the most far-flung network of corporation watchers might not pick up a product defect, a suspicion of cancer linkage, the death of a company president, or the failure of a critical supplier. Even the most astute and watchful investor should spread his risks across a range of industry groups (automobiles, chemicals, drugs, banks, etc.).

Finally, the most defensive posture is achieved by cashing in one's entire stock portfolio, then moving the funds to short-term income accounts. Money-market funds generally sell at a constant $1 per share, so that one can presumably never lose money...one simply earns income. Nonetheless, there is a broad range of money-market funds. Some hold portfolios of what are, in effect, the IOUs of foreign banks. It is argued by certain analysts that, in an international crisis, such funds are at risk—or at least may be pinned down through litigation or "frozen" assets. The same analysts urge their clients to seek out only those money-market funds that hold portfolios consisting exclusively of debt backed by the U.S. Treasury. Such funds can generally be recognized by the inclusion of "Federal" or "Treasury" in the names—although the prospectus of every money-market fund will detail how its millions are invested.

Interest Rate Risk

A number of stocks (or industries) fall into the category of "interest sensitive" and as such are markedly affected by changes in interest rates. These groups include the utilities, banks, finance companies, and the housing and building group.

Here's what happens to each when interest rates trend upward:

1. Utility companies have to pay more on monies borrowed for expansion or upgrading of facilities.

2. Banks and finance companies are forced to pay more on money deposited in their institutions as well as for money they borrow.

3. Building falls off because of higher interest rates.

In general, avoid these groups when interest rates are high or on the way up.

DEVELOPING A PERSONAL STRATEGY

The final consideration before actually buying stocks for your portfolio is to decide upon your timing policy. You should probably avoid the policy touted by lots of pros—"quick in and quick out"—unless, of course, you've got plenty of money to spend on commissions and plenty of time to spend overseeing your portfolio.

The typical investor should use a slightly more conservative approach. The three strategies that are most popular are: (1) buy and hold; (2) dollar cost averaging; and (3) market timing.

CREATING YOUR PORTFOLIO

Buy and Hold

The "buy-and-hold" strategy means making investments for the long haul and overlooking any short swings or changes in the market. That means you must be the type who doesn't get jumpy and sell out at the first sign of a decline. Buy-and-hold investors must be prepared to ride out any market declines. Your basic philosophy, if you adopt this strategy, is that the companies selected for your portfolio have inherent strengths that over the long run will bring in higher prices and/or increased dividends. Generally, the stocks listed as Blue Chips in the stock section of this book fall into this category.

The buy-and-hold strategy is ideal for building a portfolio of stocks attuned to long-term changes in the nation's economy. American demographic patterns alone suggest a number of significant intermediate- or long-term investment possibilities:

1. Companies that will capitalize on the developing baby boom among older, more affluent parents

2. Companies that will profit from the "graying," or aging, of the United States population

3. Companies that will be prime contributors to the growing "robotization" of American industry

4. Companies with natural resources that are likely to be in limited supply by the turn of the century.

First, clearly, a number of these trends are already well recognized, and therefore largely "discounted" by the price of the related stocks. Nonetheless, it is important to remember that many investors are in the market for the short term—and have not yet anticipated the full impact of future developments. Second, there might be trends that you envision, or that you sense because of your own vocational or avocational interests. If so, it might be worth your while to investigate those corporations that are best positioned to take advantage of such opportunities. A final note: If you were to conclude that there will be a copper shortage in the years ahead, you are far better off going for the pure play, i.e., investing in a company that deals solely, or largely, with copper (like Phelps Dodge) rather than in a company (like Atlantic Richfield) whose copper stake is a small percentage of its total investment profile.

Dollar Cost Averaging

This method of investing ranks as one of the most simple and successful strategies available to investors. In short, the investor designates a predetermined amount of money he can invest at regular intervals—perhaps $100 per month. The success of the system depends on a stock market that moves sideways or up over the long run, and on the self-discipline of the investor.

In practice, dollar cost averaging works much as a payroll savings plan does—forcing the investor to make a regular, fixed contribution. In fact, many mutual funds have investment programs whereby a predetermined amount of money is automatically transferred from the investor's checking account to his mutual fund account on the first of every month.

In theory, the advantages of dollar cost averaging are based on simple mathematics. Let us suppose that the investor has chosen the Sine Wave Fund as his primary investment vehicle. He has elected to invest $100 each month.

In the beginning, the fund is selling for $10 per share. He therefore is able to buy 10 shares. Thereafter, the fund climbs dramatically to $15 per share. At this point, he is able to buy 6.666 shares with the same $100. The find hits a financial wind sheer and shudders down to a mere $5 per share. At this point, the investor's $100 will buy him 20 shares. Finally, the Sine Wave Fund rebounds to its starting price of $10 per share, and that same $100 will purchase another 10 shares.

The results?

The investor has invested four times, at a total cost of $400.

The fund's share price rose $5 above its starting price, fell $5 below its starting price, and ended up exactly where it had begun. Common sense suggests that our investor should be even.

In fact, he now holds (add them up for yourself!) 46.666 shares, worth $466.66—a gain in excess of 16 percent on a vehicle that only moved sideways.

The beauty of dollar cost averaging lies in the fact that it mathematically forces the investor to buy fewer shares when the shares are expensive, and more shares when they are cheap. The order of the decline and fall doesn't matter. Volatility helps...as does a market trending upward. The only things that can undermine its success are a relentless, year-after-year market decline and the intervention of a nervous investor. In the real world, our hypothetical investor would probably have been so fearful, angry, frus-

CREATING YOUR PORTFOLIO

trated, and apoplectic about Sine Wave's crash from $15 down to $5 that he would have stopped investing at precisely the moment when he could have picked up the largest number of shares for the money. Discipline is the cornerstone of all investing; never, perhaps, is it more important than in the case of dollar cost averaging.

One of the few disadvantages of this system is the difficulty of investing an amount as small as $100 in the stock market. With minimum commissions set at close to $30, the transaction costs of investing directly in stocks are almost prohibitive. It is for this reason that so many investment analysts recommend that investors using the dollar cost averaging system make use of mutual funds.

Timing

The third major investment strategy depends on market timing. Market timers use everything from darts to charts, and from trendlines to hemlines (historically, the market does tend to rise and fall with the lengths of women's skirts). They watch the activities of the Federal Reserve Board, the sentiments of their fellow investors, and certain of the market's "internal" signals. Some follow so-called "supercycles," often lasting a decade or longer, while other timers move in and out on the same day.

All in all, market timers include a few of the most—and many of the least—successful investors. They tend to be an aggressive, speculative lot who are convinced, rightly or wrongly, that they can tell which way the market is going to move. Timing schemes, like betting systems, have come and gone through the years. The only certainty is that nothing works all of the time.

Nonetheless, there are certain indicators which have proven remarkably accurate in forecasting market trends—and which make more direct sense than the length of women's skirts or the fate of the New York Mets (who have won pennants *only* in years which were dismal for the stock market). Even so, there are two principal difficulties in putting these indicators to use. They are almost never in complete agreement. And even when they *are* pointing strongly in a given direction, it takes considerable discipline to believe—and act upon—the signal.

So important and potentially profitable are these timing indicators that we have given them their own chapter on page 64. You may not wish to use them but, for your own investment tactics and overall understanding of the market dynamic, it may at least make sense for you to know what they are forecasting.

CREATING YOUR PORTFOLIO

DETERMINING A STOCK'S QUALITY

Regardless of your choice of strategy, you want to select the best possible stocks. How can you tell which ones are right for your portfolio? The specific tried-and-true standards of measurement described below are critical tools.

Surprisingly, much of the material you will need in order to determine a stock's potential and its position in (or not in) your portfolio is easy to come by and often free of charge. Quarterly and annual reports from corporations, newsletters, research from brokerage houses, and financial sections of newspapers all provide enormous amounts of data—more than any one investor can reasonably wade through. The secret, of course, is knowing what to look for.

Here are the tools necessary to gauge the value of any security.

Earnings Per Share

Earnings per share (EPS) is one of the most critical yardsticks. It reduces the company's financial picture to one simple figure. Earnings per share is the company's net income (after taxes) divided by the average number of common stock shares outstanding.

You'll find this figure in the company's annual report, in Value Line, Standard & Poor, or material from a brokerage firm. When you read or hear that a company is growing at a certain rate, the earnings per share is the measurement.

Price-Earnings Ratio

The P/E is regarded by many as the most important analytical tool available and is widely used by analysts, brokers, and investors of all stripes. You'll find the P/E for publicly traded companies in the daily newspaper.

The P/E is determined by dividing the current price of a stock by its earnings for the last twelve months. This figure reflects the investment world's opinion of a stock in comparison with the market as a whole. For example, a high P/E such as 11 or 12 indicates market optimism on that stock, whereas a lower P/E, 5 or 6, means investors think less highly of that issue.

The P/E *cannot* be used in isolation—it must be compared to P/Es for the same company over a period of several years, and with P/Es of

23

CREATING YOUR PORTFOLIO

other companies in the same industry group. For example, if the P/E of your stock drops sharply and others within the same business are also dropping, it's not as dreadful as if your stock were the only one on the way down. It may signal a general market decline and/or a general industry decline.

Companies that are growing rapidly tend to sell at a high P/E, say 20 and up. Those with slower growth rates, or those companies whose earnings move up and down with the economy, generally sell at a lower P/E ratio.

Here's one way to use the P/E ratio effectively:

1. Find the five-year P/E for the Dow Jones average which is listed on Mondays in *The Wall Street Journal*.

2. Compare it with the five-year average P/E of the company you are considering.

3. If the company's stock is selling at a P/E that's lower than its own five-year average and also lower than the five-year Dow average, you need to determine whether the company is in trouble, or if you can get a good buy.

OTHER EVALUATION TOOLS

Although the methods we've discussed will prove enormously helpful in evaluating a stock's potential, they are not the end of your evaluation task by any means. The annual report and your calculator will widen your true feeling of the company and its stock.

The Balance Sheet

Let's start by looking at the balance sheet in the annual report. It gives you a picture of the company's financial position at the end of its fiscal year. You'll see that it indicates what the company owns (its assets), what it owes (its liabilities), and its capital. While studying the balance sheet, keep in mind that the better the firm's financial situation, the more likely management will be able to expand, advertise, support research, develop new products, and acquire other companies.

The first item to examine in the balance sheet is the current, or working, capital ratio. This is the ratio of current assets to current liabilities, but

CREATING YOUR PORTFOLIO

it is not given as such. You'll have to do a little digging to get it, but it's not hard. Both current assets and current liabilities are listed on the balance sheet; divide current assets by current liabilities to obtain the ratio.

Although there is no one perfect current ratio, look for a company with a 2-to-1 or 3-to-1 ratio; i.e., one in which current assets are twice or three times as large as current liabilities. A ratio that is much higher may signal increasing inventories or underutilization of cash. A lower ratio may signal eventual cash-flow difficulties. The exceptions are utility companies. Due to their steady stream of income, they can operate at a lower current ratio.

Debt

The second item to take into consideration is the company's debt in relationship to its total capitalization. This figure is important because it indicates the company's ability to raise cash. Generally, debt should *not* be over 40 percent of total capitalization.

You'll find the long-term debt figures in the balance sheet. (Long-term, incidentally, does not include the amount due within the next year—that's called short-term debt.) Long-term debt is the dollar amount the company must pay to those from whom it has borrowed money.

The debt figure alone is not sufficient—it must be viewed in relationship to the company's capitalization. Capital includes long-term debt plus "stockholders' equity" in the company; that is, all the funds invested in the business by both the lenders (i.e., the banks) and by the stockholders, plus earnings reinvested in the business. The term "stockholders' equity" refers to preferred stock, common stock, and retained or reinvested earnings.

Generally, it is easiest to determine the company's debt picture by using an equity-to-debt ratio. This can be calculated by taking the total assets of the company and dividing by the value of the company's outstanding bonds. A ratio of at least 5 to 1 is favorable.

Book Value

In many instances, book value is the key to finding tomorrow's takeover candidates. Theoretically, each company's book value is the dollar amount shareholders would receive if the company were suddenly to sell every one of its assets.

CREATING YOUR PORTFOLIO

Book value is a complex calculation based on hypothetical appraisals of thirty-year-old factories, fleets of Mac trucks, inventory of unsold pressure cookers, and anything else to which the company might lay claim. The total dollar amount is then reduced by the company's outstanding debts, and divided by the number of shares outstanding. In this way, a "hard" figure is elicited for the actual share-value of a company.

TAKEOVER STOCKS

Companies likely to be taken over by another corporation share a number of common characteristics. If you're interested in playing the takeover game, look for companies that have several of the following characteristics:

- low price in relation to book value
- tangible, concrete assets such as oil, gas, minerals, forests, or retail outlets
- higher than average liquid assets
- low debt
- small number of shares outstanding
- low price relative to earnings
- strong financial position in terms of the balance sheet
- ease of absorption—financial companies are more easily integrated than highly specialized companies like textiles
- history of takeover interest and previous bids
- a recent, unexplained stock price rise
- prospective bidders already own stock
- indicated interest in being acquired

Many of the leading takeover candidates have risen, not surprisingly, from among those companies in which actual stock price is significantly below book value. For example, a conservative estimate of the book value of the enormous Santa Fe Southern Pacific Corporation is $30 per share (although some valuations run nearly twice as high), made up largely of real estate, petroleum, and mineral holdings. The stock currently trades at around $25 per share. A group of investors could reasonably move in, buy out the company, sell off part, or all, of its holdings, and come out ahead.

Clearly, no individual investor is going to be able to undertake such a scheme. But profits can represent an even greater percentage of investment for the small investor who has purchased shares of a takeover stock before the takeover news hits the presses.

The reason for this is simple: When an organization decides to purchase the shares of a company, they want to get their hands on a tremendous number of shares as quickly as possible. The inducement they use is price. Generally, shareholders may be offered 20 to 25 percent more for their shares than they could get on the open market. In the example cited above, an investor group might offer $32 to $35 per share for Santa Fe-Southern Pacific stock, in order to be sure that investors—even those who would otherwise be reluctant—will "tender" their shares quickly.

Profit Margins

Profit margins are another crucial ingredient in determining a stock's quality. Profits are listed in the annual report, usually expressed as a percentage of sale. Often the heading will read: "% Oper. Inc. of Revs." This figure shows the proportion of sales being converted into profits. For a growth company it should be somewhere between 15 and 30 percent. Sales should, of course, keep up with growth in order to sustain the company's overall expansion. But if sales have been increasing much faster than earnings, it may mean that management needs to cut costs or divest itself of unprofitable divisions or subsidiaries.

When operating costs are growing faster than earnings, you'll hear your broker say that profit margins are being "squeezed." In this situation, the price of the stock generally falls. Look instead for a company in which earnings are rising faster than costs—in this case, you'll be dealing with "widening" profit margins.

It's a good idea to compare the company's profit margins from one year to the next as well as with the industry as a whole. This information

CREATING YOUR PORTFOLIO

is available in Value Line, from Standard & Poor, or from your broker. As you become more experienced, you may want to use the profit margin factor as a guide for when to sell a stock, i.e., when profit margins level off or begin to drop.

SELECTING INCOME STOCKS—ONE SUCCESSFUL STRATEGY

Beverly Jacobs, Vice President in Charge of Portfolios for the investment firm of A. Feldesman & Associates in Cleveland, has devised a successful strategy for picking income stocks. Jacobs's standards:

- The company must have ten consecutive years of uncut dividends.
- Its ratio of long-term debt to total capitalization must be 40 percent or less.
- The stock must have a yield of at least 6 percent. Any stock whose yield drops to 4 percent should be sold.

(Jacobs's firm has outperformed the Dow Jones Industrial Average and the Standard & Poor's 500 on an annualized rate over the last five years.)

HINTS FOR THE BEGINNING INVESTOR

1. Don't get fancy. Chances are you're not going to make a killing right away. Killings will happen to you now and again—if you're patient. But the world is filled with people who lost a small fortune trying to make a big one.

2. Don't buy stocks based on information or news that is already widely recognized. It is a chronic error of beginning investors that they buy on good news. As logical as this might sound, it is often a trap. In most cases, the real insiders had an inkling of the news and have al-

CREATING YOUR PORTFOLIO

ready pushed the price up. There is even a Wall Street axiom that says, "Buy on the rumor; sell on the news."

3. Buy a stock only if you can say why you feel it will be a worthy investment. There is a strong inclination among new investors to purchase the stock of those companies they feel good about—for no worthwhile investment reason. Most seasoned professionals learned the hard way that "good feeling" was an insufficient reason to purchase a stock.

4. Don't move in and out of the market so quickly that your commission costs become a significant drain. With an average commission cost even as low as 5 percent, your stock has to move 10 percent just to move even. Sometimes that will happen quickly—but not very often.

5. Set yourself a realistic investment objective. If you shoot for 50 percent per year, chances are you'll lose badly. But if you set yourself a strong, steady goal—such as twice what you would earn in a money-market account—you're far more likely to reach your goals. A steady gain of 18 percent per year—just 1½ percent per month—will double your money in four years. Invest for the long term.

6. Spread your risk. *No* company is exempt from sudden shocks and jolts. Stocks do drop by as much as 20 percent in a single day. Scattered across ten stocks, that averages out to only a 2 percent loss. But if you continue to invest in a single issue, sooner or later you'll find yourself reeling from the effects of stock shock.

7. Read about investing. Follow the financial news on a regular basis. Much of the value of a sound financial education is simply learning what *not* to believe, when *not* to buy, when *not* to sell.

8. When you feel you're really ready to invest, conduct one last careful experiment. Play with a shadow portfolio. The entire *Beat the Market* concept encourages that. In this case, it's just a game. But always, it's to hone your skills and improve your judgment without costing you a cent. Even better, play with several pools of imaginary cash, and invest them each on a different set of standards—buying rationale, holding period, investment objective. See which strategy works best for you, and follow it when you try for real.

CREATING YOUR PORTFOLIO

9. Always allocate a maximum amount you are willing to lose. Like the gambler with an unlimited line of credit, it is depressingly easy to pour money into a losing series of investments. If you've played out your cash allotment for the year, stop. You can get killed waiting for the killing. And you can lose a good nest egg dollar by dollar by dollar—throwing good money after bad.

10. When you lose, take it in stride. Self-examination to discover possible lessons is clearly worthwhile; self-castigation is not. Everyone loses. Anxiety, dread, recriminations—save those for other, more important things. And when you win, self-examination may be just as important. And be sure not to eat up your earnings in celebration!

**SELECTING EMERGING GROWTH CORPORATIONS—
ONE SUCCESSFUL STRATEGY**

Elliott Schlang, Editor of Prescott, Ball & Turben's *Great Lakes Review*, has a successful method for selecting emerging growth companies:

- Company must be medium sized with annual sales under $500 million
- Must not be largely held by institutions
- Must have a record of continuous sales and earnings growth above the inflation rate
- Must have a specialty or a priority product that insulates it from economic cycles
- Companies in which insiders have sizeable holdings are favored
- Non-union labor
- Domestic involvement which offers protection against foreign currency fluctuations
- A P/E ratio of about one-half projected earnings growth rate

SPECULATION

If you've decided to bite the bullet and go for a flier, long-term holdings won't do for you. You need stocks that will leap forward rather than walk slowly. Your choices include

- Stocks being issued to the public for the first time (i.e., new issues)
- Companies that may be bought by another company (i.e., takeover candidates)
- Stocks that have been severely depressed and look like they're about to turn around
- Companies that announce a new product or technological breakthrough

ELECTRIC UNTILITIES— AN INCOME PORTFOLIO

The first electric power lines in this country were installed by the Edison Electric Company in 1882 in New York City. At that time, long copper bars were used to conduct electricity rather than the thin flexible wire cable used today. When the first switch was turned on, some sixty Manhattan homes had electric light for the very first time.

Historically, electric utilities have appealed to the most conservative investor whose primary aim is income. Traditionally, utilities have offered very high dividend yields, often as high as 9 or 10 percent. So when the rate of inflation begins to approach double-digit figures, this is one stock group where the investor will still be seeing a healthy return—in terms of disposable income—on his or her money. Recently, however, new developments— in particular, financial pressures relating to nuclear plant construction—have led to investor concern. Almost exclusively, the troubled companies within this industry have been those engaged in nuclear power programs. Yet, apart from the no-nuke issue, the outlook for the utility stocks still remains quite favorable.

Obviously the safest group is the no-nuke group—those that have absolutely no nuclear exposure. Yet, because they are considered a "safe" investment, these no-nuke stocks pay below industry yields. It's the old trade-off

CREATING YOUR PORTFOLIO

we discussed before: the higher the risk, the higher the yield, and vice versa.

Below is a table of no-nuke utility stocks that can be safely added to the most conservative income portfolio.

NO-NUKE ELECTRIC UTILITY COMPANIES*

COMPANY	ENERGY SOURCES (PERCENTAGES)				
	Coal	Oil	Gas	Hydro	Purchased
Allegheny Power	63			1	36
Central Illinois Public Service	99	1			
Idaho Power	24			71	5
Interstate Power	97	1	2		
Iowa Southern	99		1		
Kansas Power & Light	67	31	2		
Louisville Gas & Electric	94		2	4	
Montana Power	99			1	
Nevada Power	85	9			6
N.Y. State Electric & Gas	74			2	24
Orange & Rockland		34	30	3	33
Potomac Electric	89	11			
Teco Energy	89	11			
Utah Power & Light	75	1		4	20

*Source: *Market Letter* of Shearman, Ralston Inc.

CREATING YOUR PORTFOLIO

ELECTRIC UTILITY COMPANIES
WITHOUT NUCLEAR CONSTRUCTION PROBLEMS*

COMPANY	Coal	Oil/Gas	Nuclear	Hydro	Purchased
American Electric Power	81		12	1	6
Atlantic City Electric	48	20	31	1	
Baltimore Gas & Electric	25	12	56	7	
Boston Edison		63	25		12
Carolina Power	69	3	28		
Cleveland Electric	90		10		
Commonwealth Edison	48	8	44		
Detroit Edison	86	7			7
Eastern Utilities		78	22		
Florida Power & Light		62	28		10
Gulf States Utilities	3	80			17
Houston Industries	18	74			8
Illinois Power	99	1			
Middle South Utilities	10	50	14		26
Niagara Mohawk	16	36	10	33	5
Pacific Gas & Electric		33		34	33
Portland General Electric	5		21	17	57
Puget Sound Power & Light	11			8	81
San Diego Gas & Electric		63	1		36
Texas Utilities	55	45			

*Source: *Market Letter* of Shearman, Ralston Inc.

CREATING YOUR PORTFOLIO

An income portfolio based on utility shares need not consist solely of no-nukes. Those utilities that have already completed their nuclear projects are often operative with lower costs than those utility companies using gas, oil, coal, or hydro power. The companies listed below, although relying to some degree on nuclear energy, have not been especially troubled by political or financing issues. But because they are "nukes," they do carry more risk and therefore pay a higher dividend rate than the no-nukes.

How to Get a Greater Charge from Your Electrical Company

A few years ago, in order to make investing in public utilities a bit more attractive to the general public, Congress created a special form of tax shelter through the Economic Recovery Tax Act of 1981. It allows investors who own shares of common stock in certain utility companies to delay paying taxes on their dividends until they sell their stock.

To participate in this tax shelter, you must have stock in a utility that has a qualified Dividend Reinvestment Plan, also known as DRIP or DRP. Your dividends must be put right back into the company. The law allows you to defer taxes on annual dividend income of up to $750 for individuals and $1,500 for married couples, as long as the dividends are reinvested in the same public utility company's stock.

There's even another little sweetener: some utilities will give a 5 percent discount on the stock purchase price when you buy more shares through this Dividend Reinvestment Plan.

The following are qualified public utility companies. In other words, when dividends paid by these companies are automatically reinvested in their common stock, they qualify for up to $750 ($1,500 on joint return) of tax exclusion. The companies listed below also offer a five percent discount of the purchase price of their shares when purchased through DRP.

American Electric Power	Duquesne Light
Boston Edison	Florida Power & Light
Central Maine Power	Florida Progress
Commonwealth Edison	Hawaiian Industries
Detroit Edison	Illinois Power

Kansas City Power & Light	Pennsylvania Power & Light
Kansas Gas & Electric	Public Service Colorado
Kansas Power & Light	Public Service Electric & Gas
Louisville Gas & Electric	Puget Sound Power & Light
Middle South Utilities	Southern California Edison
Minnesota Power & Light	Southern Company
Nevada Power	Southwest Public Service
New England Electric System	Teco Energy
N.Y. State Electric and Gas	Texas Utilities
Northern Indiana Public Service	Toledo Edison
Ohio Edison	Wisconsin Power & Light

GOING INTERNATIONAL—A FOREIGN-BASED PORTFOLIO

There are various situations in which diversification in foreign companies pays off for the investor. Although it takes a bit of doing, foreign stocks should, at one time or another, be part of your portfolio. If you feel a little uncertain about investing abroad, it may whet your appetite to know that during bear markets in the U.S., foreign markets tend to outperform ours.

Consider foreign markets

- when the U.S. stock market is down
- when a foreign economy shows signs of improving
- when U.S. inflation is on the rise

There are a number of advantages to building an international portfolio. First, nearly half the world's publicly traded stocks are registered outside the U.S., so unless you consider these issues, you're working with less than 50 percent of your total investment opportunities. Second, this type of portfolio provides you with some desired diversification. And third, it provides a hedge against domestic economic problems, such as inflation, depreciation of the dollar, or a decline in the U.S. stock market.

CREATING YOUR PORTFOLIO

The Risks Are There, Too

The key danger spots are fortunately all quite obvious: currency fluctuations, political upheavals, economic downswings, lack of liquidity, and changes in foreign and domestic tax policies. The negative ingredient you're most likely to feel is the first one, currency fluctuations. The strength of a country's currency has a severe impact on the success of a stock. For example, if you invest in a Japanese company and the yen appreciates against the dollar, your investment will be worth more when it is converted from yen to dollars. On the other hand, if the dollar rises, then the value of any foreign investment will decline.

How to Build an International Portfolio

American stockbrokers almost never make direct trades in foreign markets because most countries do not offer seats on their stock exchanges to foreigners. There's a way around that obstacle with an ADR, or American Depository Receipt. ADRs are issued by American banks acting as a depository of a foreign corporation held abroad. An ADR is actually a contract between the holder and the bank, certifying that a given number of shares of the foreign company have been deposited with the bank's foreign office or custodian.

Buying ADRs is very much like buying a U.S. stock through your broker. The main difference is that you receive a negotiable certificate issued by the custodian bank. That means you do *not* receive a stock certificate.

CREATING YOUR PORTFOLIO

FOREIGN CORPORATIONS WITH ADRs TRADED IN THE U.S.

Anglo-American South African	Kubota, Ltd.
Beecham Group	Makita Electronics
Blyvooruitzicht Gold	Matsushita Electric
Bowater Corporation	Minerals & Resources
Broken Hill	Mitsui & Company
Buffelsfontein Gold	Nippon Electric
Canon, Inc.	Novo Industries
G.J. Coles & Company	Pelsart
Courtlands, Ltd.	Pioneer Electronics
DeBeers Consolidated	Plessey Company
Dresdner Bank	President Brand Gold
Fisons, Ltd.	President Steyn Gold
Free State Geduld	Rank Organisation
Fuji Photo Film	St. Helena Gold
Hitachi, Ltd.	Sony Corporation
Honda Motor	Tokyo Marine-Fire
IDB Banking	Tubos Acero De Mexico
Imperical Chemicals	Vaal Reefs Mining
Imperical Group	Welkom Gold
Ita Yokada	Western Deep Levels
	Western Holdings

CREATING YOUR PORTFOLIO

ADRs of more than 700 companies are sold in the U.S. through banks and brokerage firms. Most are traded over-the-counter, although some are actually listed on the stock exchanges.

In order to buy an ADR, simply call your broker, who will charge you the standard commission for the transaction. The broker (or banker) will collect any dividends your stock earns from the foreign bank and then pass them on to you in U.S. dollars. You also pay for the ADR in U.S. dollars.

ADRs are only one way to build a foreign portfolio. Perhaps an even easier way to get your feet wet in international waters is through owning shares in a mutual fund specializing in foreign investments. As with any mutual fund, this approach provides diversification as well as professional management. Although the majority of funds are American owned, most have foreign consultants who periodically advise the fund's manager on specific companies, as well as on the political and economic climate of the country involved.

There are about fifteen international funds to select from. Most of the large families of funds also have at least one international fund. In 1983, the international funds as a group outperformed domestic funds; they rose an average of 32.08 percent versus a rise of 17.63 percent for the domestic funds.

The key international funds are:

Canadian Fund
1 Wall Street
New York, NY 10005
800-221-5757

First Investors International
120 Wall Street
New York, NY 10005
800-221-3847

G.T. Pacific
601 Montgomery Street
San Francisco, CA 94111
800-824-1580

Kemper International
120 South LaSalle Street
Chicago, IL 60603
800-621-1048

Merrill Lynch Pacific
165 Broadway
New York, NY 10080
212-692-8162

Putnam International
265 Franklin Street
Boston, MA 02110
800-225-1581

Scudder International
175 Federal Street
Boston, MA 02110
800-225-2470

T. Rowe Price International
100 East Pratt Street
Baltimore, MD 21202
800-638-5660

Templeton Foreign
405 Central Avenue
P.O. Box 3942
St. Petersburg, FL 33731
800-237-0738

Transatlantic Fund
100 Wall Street
New York, NY 10005
212-747-0440

Before signing on with any of these funds, write or call for the prospectus. Investment philosophies for the funds vary widely from conservative to very aggressive. Scudder, for example, selects a country first, an industry next, and finally the individual stock. First Investors, on the other hand, looks for undervalued stocks anywhere in the world, including troubled geographic areas.

For more information on mutual funds, see Chapter 4.

Foreign Trading Strategies

Unlike buying domestic stocks, foreign trading involves more than just picking a sound company with a solid balance sheet, suitable P/E, and a promising future. You also need to consider the political and economic stability of the country involved (in general, it is unwise to select a great company headquartered in a trouble-riddled country, unless you're a seasoned pro). Other important factors that you should assess before making a foreign investment are the inflation and unemployment rates of the country and the government's attitude toward business.

Then, purchase stocks in currencies that appear likely to rise against the U.S. dollar, and diversify geographically—investing in the companies of only one foreign country can be very risky. Recent political turmoil has jeopardized investments in Mexico, South Africa, and Latin America, for example.

CREATING YOUR PORTFOLIO

INVESTOR GUIDELINES FOR FOREIGN STOCKS

- Stick to a well-managed, diversified mutual fund. In that way you spread out your risk over a number of companies. (See list on pages 38–39.) Check *Barron's* or the financial pages of the newspaper for a listing and performance record of the funds.

- Know the mutual fund's posture: Is it conservative, moderate, speculative? Does it match your appetite for risk?

- As you become more experienced in foreign investing, consider specializing in one geographical area.

- Avoid investments or funds that are heavily involved in either Mexico or Brazil — or any other economically troubled country — unless you are willing to make a highly speculative investment.

- Think of foreign stocks as long-term holdings for the most part. Keep in mind that the standard of living in most foreign countries is slowly rising. Thus, their stocks will rise as well.

- Read at least one of the publications that specialize in world markets, such as *Barron's, The Economist,* or *The Wall Street Journal.* Also excellent are: *The Daily Financial Times of London, World Business Weekly,* and *Far Eastern Review.* There are also several good newsletters; Paul Koerner's bimonthly *Worldwide Investment Notes* is one (Worldwide Investment Research, Ltd., 7730 Carondelet, Suite 407, St. Louis, MO 63105). Check also *International Investment Letter* P.O. Box 9666, Arlington, VA 22209.

A PORTFOLIO FOR THE SOCIALLY CONSCIOUS INVESTOR

Are you an ethical person who believes in good causes? You can put your money where your heart is by becoming an "ethical" investor. Whatever your convictions, you can avoid companies that make weapons, refuse to hire women and minorities, or follow other production or labor policies that conflict with your values. Being an ethical investor is not a pipe dream, nor does it involve burning your draft card. Furthermore, you won't be alone.

CREATING YOUR PORTFOLIO

Public pension funds invested approximately 2 percent of their assets (or nearly $2 billion) last year in socially conscious investments. The trend has become popular enough, in fact, to support its own professional organization, The Social Investment Forum.

This movement started in the 1960s, when various groups and certain corporations began to target where they wanted their money spent—and where they did not. Manufacturers of napalm, M-15s, and other military hardware were avoided like the plague. More recently, the thrust has been against companies without adequate equal employment oppoortunities, with money in South Africa, or with funds invested in nuclear plants.

The easiest way to participate in socially conscious investing is through buying shares in mutual funds set up solely for this purpose. (Mutual funds are large, diversified portfolios of stocks and other securities. Each fund issues shares in its portfolio. The value of these shares and the dividends paid to those who buy the shares vary according to the current value of the combined stocks and their combined earnings.)

Even though their investment objectives vary (some are conservative, others aggressive, some for long term holding, others for quick appreciation), they all operate on the premise of investing where social results are positive.

Here is a partial listing of socially conscious mutual funds.

The Calvert Social Investment Fund

Managed Growth Portfolio
1700 Pennsylvania Avenue N.W.
Washington, DC 20006
800-368-2748

Minimum investment: $1,000

This fund applies comprehensive social criteria in selecting securities. It invests in companies according to their proven history of making high quality and environmentally responsible goods. Companies must be equal opportunity employers and provide safe workplaces. This fund is also extremely sensitive to issues of nuclear power, armaments manufacture, and investments in any coutry ruled by a repressive regime. It has grown from $2 million in assets in the first quarter of 1983 to roughly $8 million at present.

CREATING YOUR PORTFOLIO

The Trust for Balanced Investment

>Shearson/American Express
>666 Fifth Avenue
>New York, NY 10103
>800-223-6024

>Minimum investment: $1,000

This trust or mutual fund is chaired by Leonard Woodcock, former UAW president. Its special criteria are labor-management relations, human rights, equal job opportunities, and environmental protection. It will not invest in South Africa.

The Working Assets Money Fund

>230 California Street
>San Francisco, CA 94111
>800-543-8800

>Minimum investment: $1,000

This is the only money market fund dedicated to managing socially responsible investments. Although the fund is competitive with other money market funds in terms of safety, liquidity, and yield, it chooses its investments according to their social and environmental impact. The Working Assets Money Fund invests in money market instruments that help finance housing, small businesses, family farms, higher education, and certain types of energy. It avoids involvement with enterprises that pollute, build weapons, discriminate against minorities, produce nuclear power, or support repressive foreign regimes. The chairman of this money market fund is Jack T. Conway, former president of Common Cause.

Pax World Fund

>224 State Street
>Portsmouth, NH 03801
>603-431-8022

>Minimum investment: $250

This balanced stock and bond fund was started in 1971 by a group of Methodists. It continues today to place emphasis on non-war-related indus-

CREATING YOUR PORTFOLIO

tries. The fund will not buy companies involved in the liquor, tobacco, or gambling industries. During 1983, the fund's assets grew from $8.4 million to $13 million.

If you are concerned with building a socially conscious portfolio, yet want to select stocks yourself rather than using a mutual fund, you'll need to spend some time on research. One way to start is by reading the specialized newsletters in the field.

Two recommended ones are:

Good Money Newsletter

>28 Main Street
>Montpelier, VT 05602
>800-223-3911

This monthly costs $36 per year and suggests which companies should be considered for your portfolio and which ones should be avoided, and why.

Insight: The Advisory Letter for Concerned Investors

>222 Lewis Wharf
>Boston, MA 02110
>617-723-1670

Also a monthly, *Insight* costs $40 per year. The newsletter follows about 1,000 companies and will send you four equity briefs per month as part of your subscription. In addition, the letter presents a monthly stock market update as well as financial and social profiles on selected companies.

A suggested buy list of stocks from *Insights* includes the following corporations, which *Insights* believes meet the general criteria for being socially ethical businesses:

AFG Industries	Herman Miller
Betz Laboratories	Millipore
Community Psychiatric Centers	National Education
Digital Equipment	Pitney-Bowes
Gannet	Quaker Oats
Hershey	Ralston Purina

CREATING YOUR PORTFOLIO

Rainier Bancorp.

Robertshaw Controls

Santa Fe-Southern Pacific Railroad

Security Pacific

Sysco

Thermo Electron

Tucson Electric

Wang Labs—Class B

TAKING ADVANTAGE OF A WEAK DOLLAR

For decades, international currencies were held in a careful and relatively rigid alignment with one another. A dollar was worth a certian number of centavos, centimes, or centimos (as well as pistareens, ouguiyas, and quetzals). Fluctuations were considered dangerous and, in most cases, avoidable.

In the early 1970s, however, most such agreements went the way of 3 percent unemployment rates and $35 gold. So-called "market forces," which had been artificially suppressed by the previous agreements, were allowed tremendous leeway. Currencies skyrocketed and collapsed in relation to each other.

Almost at once, the U.S. dollar began a steep decline against the Swiss franc, the German mark, and other so-called "hard" currencies. It appeared for a time that the dollar had entered a perpetually unfavorable period, in which it could do little but slow its losses. Yet, nearly six years ago, the dollar began a reversal that has now carried it to historic highs against the British pound, the Italian lira, and to long-term highs against Swiss and Grman currencies.

The strength of the dollar has produced a tremendous imbalance of imports in the United States, as foreign goods have become relatively cheap. It has also suppressed the forces of inflation, as foreign workers, foreign products, and foreign oil compete for American market share.

There are some who insist that "the dollar is back," and that such strength will persist. Nonetheless, with five or six years of almost uninterrupted rallies, it may behoove us to look at the investment implications of a declining dollar.

In short, a declining dollar will likely be brought about by declining "real" interest rates. Real interest rates are those obtained after subtracting the effects of inflation (an 8-percent money-market fund is paying a "real" rate of 3 percent with an inflation rate of 5 percent, for example). Real rates

CREATING YOUR PORTFOLIO

in the United States are at historic highs, and have been responsible for attracting billions of dollars of foreign money to this country. When those real rates decline, those billions may drift elsewhere, thereby weakening the dollar.

The effects of a decline in the dollar will likely be a gradual run-up in the price of commodities (particularly oil and gold), as well as an overall boost in inflation. Domestic manufacturers that have weathered stiff foreign competition should begin to see easier and more profitable market conditions as imported products become more expensive.

Perhaps the subtlest but most significant effect of a weak dollar will be in those corporations with heavy overseas sales. For example, a company that has made an 800,000 pound profit in Britain has seen the value of that profit drop from nearly $2,000,000 to about $1,000,000 in six years, just because of the strength of the dollar. Should that situation reverse, and the dollar begin to decline, those identical earnings should appear to grow because of favorable currency translations.

There are a number of industries that depend on international sales for more than one-third of both their sales and earnings. These corporations manufacture either universally popular goods or items that are considered necessities. Most of their products also tend to be low in price.

The key industries that fall into this category are cosmetics, drugs, food, and household products.

Here's a possible breakdown for your portfolio:

Cosmetics/Household Products	Foreign Business
• Colgate/Palmolive	50+%
• Gillette	50+%
• Procter & Gamble	30%
• Revlon	30%

Drugs	Foreign Business
• Abbott Laboratories	23%
• American Home Products	28%
• Bristol-Myers	32%
• Johnson & Johnson	40%

CREATING YOUR PORTFOLIO

- Merck   43%
- Pfizer   52%

Foods   **Foreign Business**
- Coca-Cola   40%
- General Foods   25%
- H.J. Heinz   35%
- McDonald's   22%

Industrials   **Foreign Business**
- Caterpillar Tractor   46%
- Hoover   59%
- IBM   42%
- Minnesota Mining & Manufacturing   35%

Key factors about each company:

- *Colgate* is the second largest domestic manufacturer of detergents, toiletries, and other household products.
- *Gillette* leads the world in the razor and razor blade market.
- *Procter & Gamble* is the leading U.S. soap and detergent manufacturer. Sales are 2½ times its closest competition, Colgate.
- *Revlon* does business in 100-plus countries; more than half its sales are generated by its drug, diagnostic, and optical operations.
- *Abbott Laboratories* generates drugs, diagnostic tests, intravenous solutions, lab instruments, and artificial sweeteners. It is one of the few hospital supply companies to increase sales with new Medicare cost-control rules.
- *American Home Products* has posted higher earnings every year for the past 25 years, and has nearly zero debt.

CREATING YOUR PORTFOLIO

- *Bristol-Myers* products include Clairol, Bufferin, Excedrin, Ban, Drano, and Windex, which are all popular worldwide.
- *Johnson & Johnson* is a leading producer of first-aid products, baby care items, and contraceptives.
- *Merck* produces human- and animal-care items plus environmental products and specialty chemicals which are big sellers here and overseas.
- *Pfizer* takes a majority of earnings from drugs such as Feldene for arthritis and Procardia for anigina treatment. It is strong in research and new products.
- *Coca-Cola* is the world's largest soft drink company with 1,850-plus bottlers. Coca-Cola also owns Columbia Pictures.
- *General Foods* derives one-third of sales from its coffees: Maxwell House, Yuban, Maxim, Sanka, and Brim. Other items popular abroad include Post cereals, Jell-O, Birds Eye, Gaines, Kool-Aid, and Minute Maid.
- *H.J. Heinz* has had twenty consecutive years of increasing profits. Its soups, ketchup, pickles, vinegar, and baked beans remain big sellers.
- *McDonald's* operates or franchises almost 8,000 fast food restaurants. Although about 70 percent of the domestic units are run as independent stores, only 5 percent of foreign restaurants are.
- *Caterpillar Tractor* has been forced to close several production facilities even though it is the world's largest producer of earth-moving equipment. With nearly 50 percent of its business overseas, this company would greatly benefit from a weaker dollar.
- *Hoover* sells its vacuum cleaners and other products in 120 countries.
- *IBM* does well regardless of the dollar—but any decline would be gravy.
- *Minnesota Mining & Manufacturing* makes copying machines and other office products that are well-received overseas. MMM has very little long-term debt.

CREATING YOUR PORTFOLIO

PLAYING WITH NEW ISSUES

An interesting, albeit speculative, way to build a growth portfolio is to invest a portion of your assets in new issues—that is, in companies making their first public offering of stock. This is one of the most volatile, high-risk areas of investing and is subject to a boom-and-bust atmosphere as are few others. For example, in the first half of 1982, new offerings amounted to a scant $391 million. In the first half of 1983, new offerings amounted to $5.58 *billion*—a surge of 1,400 percent in a single year.

On rare occasions, these new issues are offered by old companies. For example, when Ford Motor "went public" in the mid-1950s, the company was clearly old-line and well established.

The average new issue, however, is far from a household name. The great majority of them have never made a profit. Sadly, a majority of them never will.

Regardless of long-term prospects, brokerage houses are keen to peddle these new issues for the parent company. Often, the brokers involved actually believe the corporation's hype. Just as often, they're willing to settle for the big-block commissions, and let the investor do his own believing. These brokers, or underwriters, generally sell new issues in partnership. Merrill Lynch will agree to sell one million shares out of a ten-million share new issue. Other brokerage firms will take a share they believe they can reasonably sell.

Certain brokerage firms specialize in offering new issues. Others will have little, or nothing, to do with the practice.

A firm that is active in new issues may publish a list of those about to be released. If the firm is smaller, you may need to let them know you'd like to be contacted regarding these new issues.

Investor losses on such new issues are astonishing. Yet it is only within the ranks of such new issues that tomorrow's IBMs and Polaroids come to light. The ability to distinguish now between a Zerocks and a Xerox can make the difference later between a barrel and a Brooks Brothers suit. It is a science—or an art—or an instinct—that few can lay claim to with any consistency. Nonetheless, there are individuals and organizations who do follow the new issues market, and even a few who can honestly profess repeated success.

There are several publications that advise readers on the availability of new issues:

New Issues, edited by Norman G. Forsback, 3471 North Federal Highway, Fort Lauderdale, FL 33306. Monthly, $95/year. Started in 1978.

New Issue Investor, edited by James Love, published by Standard & Poor.

Investments Dealers Digest, a weekly to which most brokers subscribe.

Forsback, in particular, has had a solid record of success. The fourteen new issues he recommended in 1978 had an average gain of 462 percent; the twenty-four of 1979, an average gain of 207 percent; twenty-nine in 1980 – 126 percent; thirty-three in 1981 – 81 percent; nineteen in 1982 – 117 percent; twenty in 1983 – 110 percent.

If a new issue is considered "hot," the small or modest investor often has a hard time getting any shares. If the issue is managed by underwriters who have both retail and institutional customers, retail investors will probably be allotted less than 30 percent. One-third to one-half will be reserved for the firm's top customers. However, if the firm managing the offering has a large retail base, such as Prudential Bache, you'll fare much better. Two others with large retail bases are L.F. Rothschild, Unterberg, Towbin (New York City) and Alex, Brown & Sons (Baltimore).

Two advantages to participating in new issues are that there are no commissions, and the underwriter will usually underprice the shares relative to the stock market. Brokerage firms do this to induce heavy buying, and so the shares will move up in price after the initial offering.

Guidelines for Selecting New Issues

- Use a reputable underwriter. According to Norman Forsback, the best ones over the past five years have been

    Alex, Brown & Sons
    Prudential Bache
    Hambrecht & Quist
    L.F. Rothschild, Unterberg, Towbin
    Robertson, Colman & Stephens

CREATING YOUR PORTFOLIO

- Find a company with a history of rising sales and earnings.
- Select an offering that is designed to expand the business, not to rescue a floundering company. See if the money is to be spent on new plant and equipment.
- Avoid new issues in which money is going to reduce debt or cover general expenses.
- Look for a company that has a unique product and is not surrounded by competition.
- Read the prospectus. This document, which must be filed with the SEC, will give you a picture of the company's history and the qualifications of the officers and directors.
- Study the company's balance sheet. Look for debt less than 40 percent of total capital, sales of at least $50 million, and a growth record of at least 20 percent a year for three years.

WHERE TO RESEARCH YOUR PORTFOLIO

If you intend to make your own buy-and-sell decisions, you'll need two things: a discount stockbroker and a good financial library. We talked about brokers on pages 10-14. Here is a sampling of the research materials you'll find useful for portfolio management. Most are available at your library or in your broker's office.

Standard & Poor's *New York Stock Exchange Reports* is a large looseleaf volume that lists each company on the NYSE. A similar volume is available for the American Stock Exchange and for over-the-counter stocks. Pages are updated periodically. You'll find listed for each firm a general summary of the company, the current outlook, any new developments, and ten-year tables showing income and assorted balance sheet data.

The Stock Guide, also published by Standard & Poor's, is a fairly small handbook, yet a serious investor should not be without it. It contains abbreviated basic data on 5,000 stocks. A similar edition is published on bonds. They both come out monthly, and your broker may give you one for free.

The Outlook is a weekly investment service—once again from Standard & Poor's. It runs a master list of recommended issues as well as sug-

CREATING YOUR PORTFOLIO

gested sample portfolios for investors with differing financial objectives.

For current subscription rates on all Standard & Poor's publications, contact the corporation at 25 Broadway, New York, NY 10004.

Mansfield Chart Service is a reliable, veteran producer of stock graphs. Of all of the available chart services, we chose Mansfield for inclusion in this book. Every stock graph herein is from Mansfield. To subscribe, simply contact: Mansfield Chart Service, 2973 Kennedy Boulevard, Jersey City, NJ 07306.

The Blue Book of 3-Trend Cycligraphs provides twelve-year price, earnings, and dividend charts of market averages for more than 1,000 companies. It is put out by Securities Research Company, 208 Newbury Street, Boston, MA 02116.

Better Investing is a monthly magazine published by the National Association of Investment Clubs. It analyzes stocks and provides up-to-date views of the investment scene. To subscribe, write: National Association of Investment Clubs, 1515 East Eleven Mile Road, Royal Oak, MI 48067.

Trendline's Current Market Perspective contains charts illustrating weekly price movements and a thirty-week moving average for about 1,500 stocks.

Value Line Investment Survey, which is updated weekly, covers 1,500 stocks according to industry. To subscribe to this definitive publication, write to: Value Line, Inc., 711 Third Avenue, New York, NY 10017.

You should also make a great effort to read one of the following on a *regular* basis: *The Wall Street Journal, Barron's, Business Week, Financial World,* or the business section of *The New York Times*.

There are many other resources besides those listed here. Your broker may suggest others, or you may find alternatives through your own research.

4
Buying a Ready-Made Portfolio

BUYING A READY-MADE PORTFOLIO

By this point, we've covered a broad range of the tips and techniques for building your own stock portfolio. Such an undertaking can be immensely invigorating, educational, and profitable.

Nonetheless, there *are* drawbacks and difficulties.

Time: The process of building a portfolio can be enormously time-consuming. An investor who spends five hours per week following the market, and then nets $1,000 profit for the year, has earned $4 per hour—less than the average shoe clerk. While such gains may improve over the years, and while it may be more fun to research companies than to peddle loafers, such statistics can be illuminating—and discouraging.

Diversification: For the small-to-moderate investor, real diversification is difficult to achieve. Yet placing all your eggs in one or two baskets can be risky—the canyons of Wall Street are littered with broken baskets.

Commissions: Commission rates are graduated to favor big-volume trades and, therefore, the large investor. For the small-to-moderate investor, commissions often take a disproportionate share of potential market profits. For someone investing $1,000, commissions for buying and selling can eat up as much as 20 percent of the original investment. Someone investing $100,000 may pay only 2 percent in commission. In concrete terms, if both market players invest in a stock at 100, the small investor won't break even until the stock hits 120. The large investor shows a profit at 102⅛ In my first year as an investor, for example, I managed to lose $1,796. I then totaled my commissions for the year. They came to $1,792. Commission leaks are subtle and steady—and accrue regardless of your market success. It appears that rowboats leak more readily than yachts.

An additional drawback to this inevitable commission leakage is that short-term protection from market reverses is expensive. If you owned shares in Lear Petroleum, and you felt that oil stocks were about to suffer a short-term setback, it might make perfect sense to sell out one week and buy back the next—except for the two additional commission charges. Even the most prescient investor is left in this dilemma: either face these inevitable charges, or weather a potentially more damaging storm.

Threshold: Another disadvantage of investing in your own stock portfolio has to do with a sort of invisible threshold. If you were to set up your own "payroll savings plan," investing $100 per month in the stock market, you would find such a course an exercise in frustration. First, the minimum commission charges (around $30) will eat up almost one-third of your available investment; second, you won't find much to buy on Wall Street with only $70.

Liquidity: A final disadvantage of investing in your own stock portfolio arises from limited liquidity. If you have $4,000 tied up in Tyco Labs, and you suddenly need $800, you will have to sell a block of stock, wait seven days for the settlement, and then request a check from your broker.

These obstacles and liabilities are real. No one should begin the construction of a stock market portfolio without recognizing their impact. For many, they will matter little. But for others, these disadvantages could raise serious questions about the wisdom of independent stock market speculation.

These *is* an alternative, however—an alternative in which every one of these problems is reduced or eliminated.

That alternative is the field of mutual funds.

WHAT IS A MUTUAL FUND?

A mutual fund is an investment vehicle in which multiple investors pool their money under the guidance of a single investment manager. That manager may be an individual or, as in the case of most of the larger mutual funds, an entire organization—though that organization is often led by a single individual.

Depending on the mutual fund, investment portfolios may consist of stocks, bonds, treasury bills, or gold bullion. Some funds put their money into a wide variety of investment vehicles. Others are intentionally restricted and may, for example, invest only in the stocks of corporations with heavy exposure in the areas of defense and aerospace.

Mutual funds are perhaps the most natural outgrowth of an individual's proven ability to invest wisely. John Templeton, for example, developed such a keen sense for stocks on the move that it seemed only natural for him to begin managing other people's money, as well as his own. Therefore, in September 1954, he set up a small mutual fund, Templeton Growth Fund. Templeton, like many mutual fund managers, made money proportionate to the size and growth of the fund. By letting Templeton handle their funds, investors made money. A lot of money. A single $20,000 investment made on Templeton Growth Fund's first day of business would today be worth in excess of one million dollars.

Clearly, not all mutual funds can claim a record close to Templeton's—or even in the same, profitable direction. More than a few mutual funds are *below* their original offering price. Sometimes it is bad luck. Sometimes it is an "off" season. Sometimes it is just plain mediocre management.

But there *are* some mutual fund managers who, year in and year out, run up impressive records — weathering market collapses with minor losses, and leveraging moderate rallies into disproportionately large gains. John Templeton (Templeton funds), Peter Lynch (Fidelity Magellan Fund), and a short list of others have demonstrated their ability to prevail against the nastiest surprises and the most persistent slumps Wall Street can throw at them.

Not surprisingly, then, the success of investing in a mutual fund is utterly dependent on the individual or organization managing it. Every such manager is entitled to an "off" season. But year in and year out, his or her performance ought to beat the market. There are certain individuals who manage to do this. Seek them out.

HOW A MUTUAL FUND OPERATES

In general, it is enough for most investors to know that a mutual fund's value rises or falls depending on its investment results — and that their own investments in that fund move accordingly. However, it is important to understand what you are buying with your money.

Share Price

The Utterly Fictitious Mutual Fund has a series of investments that are this morning worth exactly $1,000,000. At the same time, investors own exactly 100,000 shares of UFMF. Each share represents an equal portion of the fund's holdings. Therefore, each share is at this moment worth exactly $10.00 ($1,000,000 divided by 100,000).

A mutual fund's share-price is always equal to the fund's total investment holdings, divided by the number of shares outstanding.

The share-price changes once each day and is referred to as Net Asset Value, or NAV.

BUYING A READY-MADE PORTFOLIO

Buying Shares

Anyone wishing to buy shares of UFMF simply sends money to the mutual fund office. New shares are *created* (investors don't buy or sell to each other) in direct proportion to the amount of money invested. For example, if someone were to invest $1,000,000 in UFMF at today's price

- they would receive 100,000 shares
- there would now be 200,000 UFMF shares altogether
- UFMF would now have holdings of $2,000,000
- everyone's shares would still be worth $10 each.

Redeeming Shares

Whenever an investor wants to withdraw his money from a mutual fund, he simply notifies the fund that he wants to *redeem* his shares. The investor receives his money (the number of shares he owns multiplied by the current share price). Those shares then simply cease to exist.

For example, if an investor wished to redeem his 10,000 shares, he would simply notify the fund. Shortly thereafter he would recieve a check for $100,000. (UFMF shares would still be worth $10 each, since the remaining $900,000 now would be divided among 90,000 shares.)

Share-Price Changes

Needless to say, the value of a mutual fund's shares fluctuates according to its investment results.

Let us suppose that, over a given period, the number of UFMF shares remains constant at 100,000. During that time, however, UFMF's investments do very well, growing from a value of $1,000,000 to $1,200,000. The result would simply be that each share in UFMF is now equal to $1,200,000 divided by 100,000, or $12 per share. An investor who had purchased UFMF shares at $10 would therefore have a 20 percent profit.

The same principles work in reverse. Should UFMF instead have *lost* $200,000 on its investments, thereby reducing its holdings to $800,000, the share price would then drop to $800,000 divided by 100,00, or $8 per share. The investor who had purchased UFMF at $10, would therefore have a 20 percent loss.

ADVANTAGES AND DISADVANTAGES OF MUTUAL FUNDS

Throughout this book we have spoken of the techniques, trials, and tribulations of creating your own stock portfolio. Whether or not you ultimately make money in the market depends naturally on the effectiveness of your research, the quality of your judgment, and the fickleness of the market.

The reasons for managing your own stock market portfolio are compelling. The process can be immensely exciting and educational. An individual's portfolio can be more carefully tailored to his or her needs than any publicly traded mutual fund. And, if you possess that special combination of abilities—insight, an analytical eye, and self-discipline—you may be able to build a record good enough to put you in the ranks of the finest mutual fund managers.

Nevertheless, the arguments for putting at least a part of your assets into mutual funds are just as convincing. There are many mutual funds that reduce or eliminate all six of the previously mentioned drawbacks to building your own portfolio.

Time

Few individual investors have the time to undertake the kind of extensive research that goes into the creation of a modern mutual fund portfolio. Many investment managers fly around the world, meeting with corporate leaders, trying to determine business conditions and the likely profitability of individual companies. At the least, they pore over up-to-date, computerized readings on hundreds of companies. Most mutual funds employ teams of researchers, thus far outstripping the capabilities (if not the results) of any single investor. And a $1,000 profit on the ten minutes spent writing a check to the fund obviously represents a better rate of return than that same $1,000 earned after one hundred hours in research and planning.

Diversification

Even a ten-dollar investment in a mutual fund offers instant diversification. If the fund owns shares in forty corporations, so does every investor in it. Such diversification serves as a limit on risk—forty stocks almost

BUYING A READY-MADE PORTFOLIO

never move uniformly (the odds are two in one *trillion* that every one of forty stocks will move in the same direction). It should be noted, however, that diversification does have its downside: Where you limit risk, you also limit opportunity.

In addition, mutual fund investors are able to sell a portion of their holdings without affecting their diversity. Someone with $4,000 invested in Franklin Dynatech, an aggressive technology fund, still owns precisely the same proportion of every stock in the portfolio when he withdraws $800.

Commissions

Mutual funds come in two broad classes: load and no-load. The "load" simply refers to the payment of a commission fee. This fee is generally used to pay for the fund's expenses and management salaries. Load funds take their commissions as a one-time fee at the time of the investment. The size of this fee is often around 8½ percent. A dollar invested in a typical load fund therefore buys 91½ cents worth of the fund's portfolio, once the fee has been deducted.

A growing number of funds have chosen to go the no-load route, which means that little or no money is drawn off directly as commissions. As you can imagine, however, payments for expenses and investment management are just as great in no-load funds. They are simply hidden by reducing the mutual fund's share price. In both cases, however, mutual fund commissions are generally more reasonable than direct stock commissions

Many of the mutual funds available today are offered as part of a "family of funds." Boston's Fidelity Group, for example, offers more than thirty mutual funds. An individual who has invested in one fund may, with a single phone call, shift all or part of his investment to a different fund. Thus, it is possible to have $10,000 in a portfolio of health care stocks on Tuesday, to have that money exchanged for shares in a money market fund on Wednesday, and to be reinvested in a portfolio emphasizing high-yield municipal bonds (or those same health care stocks) on Thursday—without any additional commission costs. Such cost-free flexibility has proven a major selling point to many investors.

Threshold

The capacity to establish any sort of "payroll-investing plan" is sorely limited by the difficulty (and exorbitant commission costs) of investing $50 or $100 in the stock market. Many mutual funds, on the other hand, offer programs of systematic investment, in which $25, $50, or $100 can be automatically invested once or twice each month — directly from an individual's checking account.

By the same token, it is possible with many mutual funds to set up the converse system: automatic withdrawal. Many funds have programs in which investors receive a constant $200 withdrawal from their accounts on the first of each month.

Liquidity

Stock market investors must wait a minimum of seven days after a stock sale before they can touch their funds. Almost every major money market fund offers check writing, thereby enabling an investor to draw money (usually a $500 minimum) directly from their investments. This is a particularly valuable feature for investors in "families" of mutual funds. As in the aforementioned Fidelity example, an investor with 100 percent of his holdings in Fidelity Magellan Fund can send off a $2,500 check on Tuesday night, drawn on a Fidelity Cash Reserves account — even one with a zero balance. On Wednesday afternoon, he simply places a call to Fidelity headquarters, authorizes the transfer of $2,500 from Magellan into Cash Reserves, and the check clears — instantly.

The field of mutual funds is continuing to expand, especially in terms of specialization. Individual stock funds are adding "sister" money market, bond, and specialty funds. Finally, almost every successful family of funds is working to offer a broad and progressive range of investor services.

WHAT TYPES OF FUNDS ARE AVAILABLE?

As recently as 1965, there were only 170 mutual funds in the United States. Almost all of them were either general stock funds, general bond funds, or stock-and-bond funds. There was little diversity, and there was little specialization.

BUYING A READY-MADE PORTFOLIO

The change has been explosive. In just two decades, the number of mutual funds has quintupled. Their assets have swollen from 17 billion to half a trillion dollars.

Even more dramatic, however, is the tremendous range of mutual fund categories now available to investors. Even the briefest sampling underscores the diversity and specialization that characterize today's mutual funds. There are funds that deal solely in the stocks of North American gold-and-silver mining companies, in low-grade municipal bonds, in stocks of health-care companies, in Minnesota tax-exempt bonds, and in the stocks of Far Eastern companies. In addition, these mutual funds have propelled that remarkable stepchild of inflationary interest rates: money-market funds.

While there are still many mutual funds that operate independently, most mutual funds are now members of a "family" of funds, as in the case of the gigantic Fidelity Group. Within such a family, transfer of assets from one fund to another is generally effortless. Also, within such a family, there is likely to be greater diversity. Most such families have at least one stock market fund, one bond fund, one tax-free bond fund, and one money-market fund. But that is far from all, as is detailed in the list of mutual fund categories below:

I. Stocks

  A. General

      1. Aggressive

      2. Moderate

      3. Conservative

  B. Specific

      1. International (Far Eastern, Canadian, etc.)

      2. Technology

      3. Defense

      4. Energy

      5. Financial

      6. Utilities

BUYING A READY-MADE PORTFOLIO

      7. Health Care

      8. High–Income

      9. Tax–Managed

     10. Mining

II. Money–Market

    A. Treasury Bills

    B. Commercial / Bank–backed

III. Bonds

    A. Treasury

    B. Corporate

    C. Municipal

HOW TO FIND THE RIGHT MUTUAL FUND(S) FOR YOU

Virtually every major newspaper in America carries a listing of major mutual funds. Such listings generally show

- an abbreviation of the fund's name
- the net asset value (or NAV—the actual net worth of a share of the fund on that particular day)
- the offering price (the cost, including commissions, of a share of the fund on that particular day. A listing of "NL" (No-Load), means that the shares are sold without commission. In such cases the NAV price *is* the offering price.)
- The change in these prices from the previous day.

An example:

Fund	NAV	Offer Price	NAV Change
Templeton Growth	9.67	10.57	+.04

BUYING A READY-MADE PORTFOLIO

This represents a typical day's reading, drawn from the Mutual Funds section of *The Wall Street Journal*. Templeton Growth Fund's Net Asset Value stands at $9.67. Anyone purchasing a share of the fund would pay this price, plus the load commission, bringing the actual cost to $10.57, which is termed the "offering" price. The final column shows that the value of the fund's portfolio rose by four cents per share from the previous day's calculations.

It is possible to pick out large families of funds with specialized investment funds, and to find those funds that match your investment objectives (growth stocks, tax-free income, Treasury bonds, etc.).

In addition, however, there are mutual fund directories, which list everything from ten-year records and investment objectives to fund addresses and special features. Two of the finest examples are: *Donoghue's Mutual Funds Almanac*, the Donoghue Organization, Inc., P.O. Box 540, Holliston, MA 01746, and *The Investor's Almanac*, W&W Publications, 710 West Main Street, Arlington, TX 76013.

It is possible, of course, to select a mutual fund simply on the recommendation of a friend, or advisor. However, few people have really taken the time to survey the broad range of funds, and few people have identical investment objectives. It is important that you first determine your own needs, and that you then select the fund or funds that meet those most directly.

Further, within any category there is likely to be tremendous divergence in customer services and investment records. Past records, particularly with an eye to long-term results, should always be paramount in selecting a mutual fund. Other features of greater or less significance include

- investment minimums
- monthly automatic investment programs
- monthly automatic withdrawal programs
- telephone "switch" programs — allowing an investor to move from a stock fund to a money market fund, and back again, with a minimum of cost and effort
- check-writing privileges — most money-market accounts allow limited check writing, for easy access to funds
- bank wire investment and redemptions

HOW TO INVEST IN A MUTUAL FUND

Once you have settled on a particular fund or funds, you should request the fund's prospectus and application. A prospectus is a document listing the fund's largely self-imposed bylaws, detailing such things as

- the minimum amount of money an individual must invest in order to open an account
- the degree of risk the fund managers are allowed to take
- the fund's investment objectives (income, growth, tax reduction, etc.)
- the primary investment vehicles (stocks, bonds, etc.)

The prospectus and application are generally available from the fund's sales department. If you have access to one of the directories listed above, you can simply call the number listed directly. Otherwise, you can always call 1-800-555-1212 and see if the fund has an 800 toll-free number available for calling from your particular area.

Once you have received and reviewed a fund's prospectus and have decided to invest, simply fill out the application, enclose a check for the amount of your initial investment, and mail it to the fund headquarters—thereby joining more than seven million other Americans as mutual fund investors. Within ten days, you will receive a confirmation of your investment and be assigned an account number. Thereafter, whenever you buy or redeem shares, or whenever a dividend is paid, you will receive an additional confirmation in the mail.

5
Stock Market Timing

STOCK MARKET TIMING

Throughout *Beat the Market* we have focused on proven techniques for creating profitable stock market portfolios.

Year in and year out, the finest portfolios *can* beat the market — regardless of the slings and arrows of outrageous bear markets. John Templeton, mentioned in the last chapter, on Mutual Funds, opened Templeton Growth Fund in 1954. Nine bear markets later, he had increased an original investment dollar *fifty* times. Superior stock selection can make the difference.

Yet anyone who has weathered a truly calamitous bear market, and has seen the good ravaged with the bad, knows that superior stock selection is not always enough. Similarly, anyone who has experienced the heady ride of a bull market in overdrive must also sense that stock selection is not the only way to beat the market.

Quite simply, *timing matters*.

Let us take a tough, sobering look at that tough, sobering decade — the 1970s. On January 1, 1970, the most broadly based index of New York Stock Exchange stocks, the NYSE Composite Index, stood at 52.10. By January 1, 1979, the NYSE Composite Index stood at 55.41.

This tiny gain would have driven a $10,000 investment to $10,597. In other words, the investor who bought and held an average stock market portfolio achieved a whopping gain of less than 6 percent during a period in which consumer prices nearly doubled.

If we were to give that same investor that same, absolutely average portfolio — but added a keen sense of timing — results might have been significantly different.

By making just the following six transactions during this same timeframe, that money could have close to quintupled:

Start	January 1970	$10,000	Invest in Money Market Fund
#1	May 1970	$10,400	Buy NYSE porfolio at 39.44
#2	January 1973	$17,264	Sell NYSE portfolio 65.37 invest in Money Market Fund
#3	December 1974	$20,889	Buy NYSE portfolio at 34.50
#4	December 1976	$34,675	Sell NYSE portfolio at 57.50 invest in Money Market Fund
#5	February 1978	$38,836	Buy NYSE portfolio at 48.67

STOCK MARKET TIMING

#6	September 1978	$48,157	Sell NYSE portfolio at 60.38 and invest in Money Market Fund
End	January 1979	$49,563	

The difference, making on average only one transaction every eighteen months, is astonishing. The gain is no longer 6 percent — but just under 400 percent.

And if this same timing sensitivity had been applied to a powerhouse portfolio...

It is thus that stock market fortunes are made.

TIMING TOOLS

But stock market timing has proved frustratingly elusive for most investors. There have been countless surefire methods for pinpointing those moments when the tides of fortune turn. Many of them have proven quite effective — for short periods of time. Yet time, and the changing investment climate, have a way of undermining almost every such system that comes along.

That does not mean that there are no telltale signs of a market in transition. In fact, one of the most effective strategies for "timing" the market is to do the opposite of what most other investors are doing. This is based on the disheartening observation that when every last soul in the country "knows" which way the market is going to move, the market is most likely to move in the opposite direction.

The "contrarian" motto states simply, "The stock market will do whatever will surprise the greatest number of investors." There are a number of tools for objectively determining the expectations of investors. Twelve of them are listed below. The principal difficulty in using these tools is that even those investors who follow them tend to waver — and disbelieve their message — at precisely the wrong moment. Those rare few who follow them faithfully, and have the self-discipline to act on their implications, will beat the market.

STOCK MARKET TIMING

The Federal Reserve

The indicator is based on the conviction that the Federal Reserve Board, more than any other institution or individual in the nation, controls the health of the American economy. When the Fed is in an expansionary mood, allowing interest rates to fall and the money supply to rise, the stock market generally does well. When the Fed is in a more restrictive mood, the money supply constricts, interest rates rise, and the stock market tends to suffer.

The key barometer for Fed-watching is the *Discount Rate*, the rate at which the Fed lends out money to its member banks. In order to smooth out temporary aberrations, the rule states that anytime the Fed raises the discount rate three times in a row — without an intervening drop — the stock market will soon begin to suffer. This "three steps then a fall" rule has a converse: Whenever the Fed *lowers* the discount rate twice without an intervening rise, the stock market will soon begin to rise.

This rule is generally quite accurate for long-term trends (spanning several years) — assuming that you're not *too* particular about hitting exact tops and bottoms. The Fed signal often comes months before or after a major turning point. But it is strong and historically reliable enough that you should know whether it's betting with you — or against you.

The January Rule

This apparently simpleminded rule states: "As January goes, so goes the year." Some adherents even go so far as to claim that just the first week of January is an excellent forecaster for the year as a whole. How accurate can such a guileless indicator be? Surprisingly enough, if the first week of January shows a stock market gain, the chances are four to one that the year as a whole will also be up. Further, if all of January shows a gain, the chances are seven to one that the year will also show a gain.

The Presidential Cycle

The President of the United States, both directly and through the indirect use of the supposedly independent Federal Reserve Board, can exert enormous control over the health of the American economy. It has been painfully demonstrated that the U.S. economy apparently needs to undergo the cleansing, cooling effects of a recession on a fairly regular basis. Jimmy Carter, for ex-

67

ample, hoped to avoid a recession altogether—and ended up four years later with an economy screeching under the naked brake of a prime rate that exceeded the 20-percent mark.

Most other presidents have recognized the need for both a recessionary and an expansionary phase in the course of their four-year terms. Presidents have generally understood that the public has a short-term memory, have "crunched" the economy early, and have ridden into the election on the back of a vigorous expansion.

Because the stock market mirrors the strength and weakness in the economy, it might be logical to expect the first half of a president's term to be hard on the market and the latter half to be profitable. This thesis is perhaps more compelling than any other timing program. An investor who undertook a long-term campaign of selling his stocks three weeks before Inauguration Day and buying them back on or near the end of the second year of the president's term (the last week of October is ideal) would have accumulated enormous gains over the years.

In our earlier example, during the years 1970–79, the average buy-and-hold investor would have turned $10,000 into $10,597. During that same period, and using the identical portfolio, the investor who followed the presidential cycle would have netted $33,084.

Froth

The stock market is termed "frothy" when it has undergone a long rally and has moved into a dangerous speculative phase. Often it is easy for an investor to be swept up in the clamor and carried along on the rising tide. Such a situation developed in the zealous, profitable days of late summer, 1929.

One of the most telling changes signaling the end of a powerful rally is the percentage of money going into weaker, lower-priced stocks. How is it possible to tell when this is happening? Fortunately, *Barron's* covers a group of these weaker stocks, under the heading Low Price Stock Index. There is a weekly comparison of the percentage of money being invested in these more speculative stocks, as compared to money going into the more conservative Dow Jones Industrials—an invaluable indication of market "froth." This figure generally hovers around the 3-percent mark. A sudden, dramatic jump to a reading much above 6 percent should be enough to undermine and reverse your stock market enthusiasm.

While not every rally culminates in such a speculative blow-off, investors who continue to invest in a rally after such a signal are almost invariably punished.

Specialist Shorts

The conventional investment activity on Wall Street is the buying and selling of stock. An investor first buys, or "goes long," a particular stock. To complete the transaction, he must ultimately sell it, thereby closing out the investment.

Surprisingly enough, it is also possible for an investor to undertake a reverse strategy. An investor is allowed to sell, or "go short," a stock which he does not already own. To complete the transaction, he must ultimately buy it back, thereby closing out the transaction.

The technicalities are a little more complex, but the process is straightforward (if somewhat mirror-image). the "long" investor hopes to buy low and sell high, into a rising market. The "short' investor hopes first to sell high and then to buy low, into a declining market. A short sale, then, is simply a sale of stock that the investor has not yet bought (but must eventually buy back).

At the center of every transaction on the New York Stock Exchange is the specialist — a single individual charged with the responsibility for each particular stock. It is he who keeps track of potential buyers and sellers, plays marriage broker, and is mandated to maintain an "orderly market."

Orderly markets are not always easy to maintain, particularly when the market is swamped with buy or sell orders for a given stock. In such cases, the specialist maintains order by having to make up the imbalance out of his own personal account: if there are 100,000 more buy orders than sell orders at a given moment, the price will naturally rise, and if sufficient stock still cannot be found to meet the demand, the specialist must sell his own supply of that particular stock.

To the uninitiated, this seems like an untenable position for the hapless specialist. But in actual fact, specialists generally do quite well. In part, this is because of their steady transaction profits. In greater part, it is because the public is generally *wrong* on guessing the course of the stock market. Being forced to bet against someone who is usually wrong is one of the simplest ways in the world to guarantee yourself a profit.

STOCK MARKET TIMING

Specialist trading statistics are a closely guarded secret. No statistics are ever available regarding a specialist's activities in a particular stock. The only information of any value available to the public concerns the number of *Specialist Shorts*.

This means, as you might imagine, the number of shares sold by specialists that they did not already own. In a recent week, for example, specialists sold *13 million* shares that didn't belong to them. They are expected to. What is important, however, is not the act itself, but the investment implications of that act.

Every week, *Barron's* publishes the NYSE's two-week-old statistics on the total number of shares shorted by everyone in the world, and on the number of shares shorted by NYSE specialists.

The ratio of those two figures can be illuminating. When specialists are doing a relatively small portion of the total shorting (when specialist shorts divided by total shorts drops below 33 percent) this is generally bullish for the stock market. When, however, the public is swamping the market with buy orders, and the specialist is shorting stock right and left (when specialist shorts divided by total shorts equals 60 percent), the public is about to be fooled — and the specialists are about to make a killing. Look out below!

Short Interest

Of less direct value, but still worth watching, is the Short Interest. Once per month, the NYSE releases statistics on the total number of shares sold short in each stock. More significant, however, is the total number of NYSE shares sold short — and its relation to the average number of shares traded each day.

The logic is indirect, but compelling. Every share once sold short will eventually have to be bought back. If a buying panic were to take place, and the short-sellers chose to buy their stock back all at once, how dramatic would the effect be? One measure is simply to divide the total number of shares shorted by the average number of shares traded each day. Historically, when the ratio has gotten much above two to one (in other words, when it would take two entire days' trading just to account for repurchasing shorted stock) the market has often been close to an important bottom. If for example, at the end of September, there are some 200 million shorted shares outstanding (still awaiting buy-back), and the average number of shares traded during that month is 80 million shares per day, the Short Interest Ratio would be 200 million divided by 80 million, or 2.5. This figure is quite high and suggests widespread anticipation of a market decline — exactly the environment out of which many rallies arise. Such "terminal pessimism" is often loosely timed, and occasionally completely misleading: besides, the statistics themselves are out-of-date. Nonetheless, a soaring short ratio can be a fairly reliable indicator (particularly in conjunction with other indicators) for determining long-term buying opportunities.

Odd-Lot Shorts

Blocks of stock bought or sold in multiples of 100 shares are termed "round lots." Blocks of less than 100 shares are termed "odd lots." As you might expect, odd-lot investors are generally those with the least money and the least expertise.

This is particularly true of that brazen bunch who risk house and car shorting stock (losses incurred when shorting stock are theoretically unlimited, since a stock shorted at 25 must still be bought back at 200, 300, or 1,000. In addition to the risk they take, odd-lot shorters are notoriously wrong about the direction of the market. When they are shorting like crazy (5,000 shares shorted in a single day), chances are good for a market rally. When they have given up shorting (500 shares shorted in a single day), the market may be vulnerable.

This is a short-term indicator, published daily (with two-day-old statistics) in almost any major newspaper. It is not so reliable that a major investment program should be launched on the basis of a single day's figures. Nonetheless, if statistics continue inordinately high or low over several days, it should give you a strong sense of where the "dumb" money is going. By investing accordingly, at least over the short term, you're playing the specialist's game: betting against someone who is usually wrong.

Put/Call Ratio

The most dramatic change in stock market investing in the past ten years has undoubtedly been the creation and emergence of a massive options market. Now even small investors can play out the moves of the big-ticket stocks. Options on 100 shares of IBM, for instance, can sometimes be purchased for as little as $6.25 each. Yet risks are high, and nowhere in the investment community, outside of commodity trading, are the odds as heavily stacked against the trader.

Nonetheless, the activities of these options players are clearly docu-

STOCK MARKET TIMING

mented. An option player generally purchases a *call* if he thinks the market is about to rally. He purchases a *put* if he expects it to decline. The ratio of puts to calls is therefore yet another statistic measuring market sentiment. Like almost every other such indicator, it reveals that extremes are almost always wrong.

In order to determine the volume of puts and calls traded, look at the very end of the weekly options listing. When the ratio of puts to calls drops dramaticaly (when put volume divided by call volume is less than 30 percent), this underscores excessive optimism. When the number of puts traded nearly equals the number of calls (when put volume divided by call volume is greater than 90 percent), this signals excessive pessimism. This is a short-term indicator, very reliable at extreme levels.

Reversal Days

A major reversal day signals the climax — and conclusion — of a stock market move. They are rare, but when they occur, they can serve as powerful indicators of an enduring change.

The market has been moving up for several months. Profits are growing, market enthusiasm is growing, cautionary statements have all but disappeared. In the morning, the stock market opens explosively, the Dow is up 10 on dizzying volume. By noon, it is up 18, and by 2:00 it is up 25. The feeling on the street is of uncontrolled ebullience. The pessimists cave in and buy. The optimists mortgage the house to add to their holdings. The last of the holdouts has invested the last of his dollars. Thus turns the tide. By 3:00, the market is up only 6 points, and, in a staggering final hour, the market closes down 12. Those who invested during the heady early hours may wait days or months for the rally to revive, unwilling to accept what has happened. The reversal — a major whipsaw on major volume — has been concentrated and complete.

Similarly, after days and days of disheartening declines, the market opens with a wrenching collapse. The Dow is off 12 points almost at the opening. By noon, usually amid rumors of a bank collapse or a war or tanker blown apart in the Straits of Hormuz, the Dow plummets to a 27-point loss — on top of the accumulated losses of the weeks before. The last optimist sells out, vowing never again to bother with the goddamned stock market. The last likely seller has sold the last of his holdings. In the midst of that apparent crisis, with doom and a foregone conclusion, the smartest money begins to come in. By 3:00, the market's loss has been pared to a mere five points. By the close, the market is up 10. Most investors, shaken by their losses, embarrassed by their ill-timed surrender, and determined to stay in money-market funds forever, will ignore the resultant rally—until it reaches it exciting, irresistible final stages.

Major reversal days appear only a handful of times in a decade. To those immersed in the euphoria—or the doom and gloom—objectivity is long gone. To those who can recognize such days as the climax and conclusion of a long-term trend, the opportunities for profit are enormous.

Graphs and Technical Analysis

In recent years, there has been a widespread revival of interest in the study of stock graphs and charts. Technicians with pencils, rulers, and bizarre terminology (pennants, breakouts, head-and-shoulders) pore over stock graphs to plumb the nature of the price movement.

Part of the popularity of this particular timing procedure arises from the fact that it is one of the few indicators that can be applied to individual stocks. And there *are* certain recurrent formations that increase the probability of a rally or a decline.

A **pennant formation** is creased when a stock's price moves, for instance, from 60 back down to 50. The next rally carries it only as high as 58. The decline drops it back just to 52. Ideally, the next rally might stop at 56, and the next decline at 54. We see therefore a narrowing of price, forming a visual pennant. Some compare this to the compression that takes place in an automobile cylinder, just before ignition. It is folklore—backed by moderate real-world probabilities—that the first move out of that pennant formation will persist. Buy or sell on an upside or downside penetration.

A **breakout** occurs when a stock's price has been moving in a narrow channel for a period of time. Most often, technicians look for cases in which a line connecting highs is parallel with one connecting lows. Any significant penetration of either line—particularly on rising volume—is statistically quite likely to persist. The longer the preceding channel, the more powerful the resultant breakout is likely to be.

A **head-and-shoulders** formation is created when a stock price rises, for example, to 60, then backs off to 55. The 60 peak becomes the left shoulder. The next rally carries the price to 70, before backing off once again to 55. The 70 becomes the head. If the price then rises to the 60 area (forming the right shoulder), then drops below 55 (breaking the "shoulder

STOCK MARKET TIMING

line"), it is common technical judgment that the rally has aborted — and that *significantly* lower prices lie ahead.

No brief explanation can reflect the more thoughtful (and occasionally zany) aspects of technical analysis. What does seem clear is that a few, easily identifiable formations *do* prove statistically reliable, from an investment point of view. Most of the esoteric formations, if they can be seen from any perspective other than hindsight, are not.

Psychology

Let us look back for a moment at that phrase from the reversal day—"The last of the holdouts has invested the last of his dollars." There *does* seem to come a point in any rally when the doubts, the frustrations, the nervous hopes seemed suddenly resolved. The market is beautiful. Investors are proud. They tote up their gains on the back of an envelope and begin to sense a future in which they might really begin to add to their winnings, might really begin to make it in the market.

The rally is over.

When you least expect it — at that one point when you just won't believe that the rally can possibly end *now* — it is over. This is not idiosyncratic, though investors the world over suffer the same euphoric blindness. Make it a hard-and-fast rule that on the day when you find yourself gleefully totaling your gains, sell out your holdings.

Correspondingly, there comes a time in an extended decline when demoralization seems to crystallize — when you begin to sell off even those stocks you were going to hold on to "no matter what." This private surrender often occurs with eerie simultaneity within the investment community. If you find yourself *finally* caving in, chances are thousands of others are as well. At such climactic moments, the moment is likely to turn.

One of the surest, and most difficult, means of enhancing your own market timing is to recognize that: first, most investors are probably feeling the same way you are; second, most of them are inclined to react the same way; and third, most of them will lose money.

Face up to your own, emotion-bound reactions. They won't always be wrong — but will be often enough to make you a fortune betting against them.

Investment Advisors and the Press

Even the smartest investors are generally filled with uneasy doubts, once they are committed to a particular course of action. Buying into a rumor-filled panic and selling into a wave of optimism require tremendous courage. Such investors speak little about their actions: They are either too secretive or too uncertain. Certainly, they do not find much agreement in the world around them.

Those who feel no hesitation about telling everyone else where the market is headed are likely to be much more brazenly self-assured. Often, however, such self-assurance, such lack of hesitation, arises from exactly that sort of widespread euphoria or discouragement *against* which markets make their most dramatic moves.

Thus, a reading of the popular press is likely to do little more than reaffirm an individual's emotional reactions. Even those investment advisors who make a living telling other people when and what ot buy are beset by the same subjective blindness.

There are some noteworthy exceptions listed below — investment advisors who, year in and year out, can beat the market impressively. But the sad, dismaying fact is that even the great majority of these men and women who do this for a living are wrong most of the time. This is not simply a cynical generalization. The Market Vane organization conducts a weekly survey of the nation's investment advisors and publishes the results. An investor who bet directly against these pundits, who bought in precisely at the moment when the greatest number of them were finally bearish, and who sold out when the greatest number were finally bullish, would have timed his moves perfectly — and made a fortune in the progress.

6
Top Performers

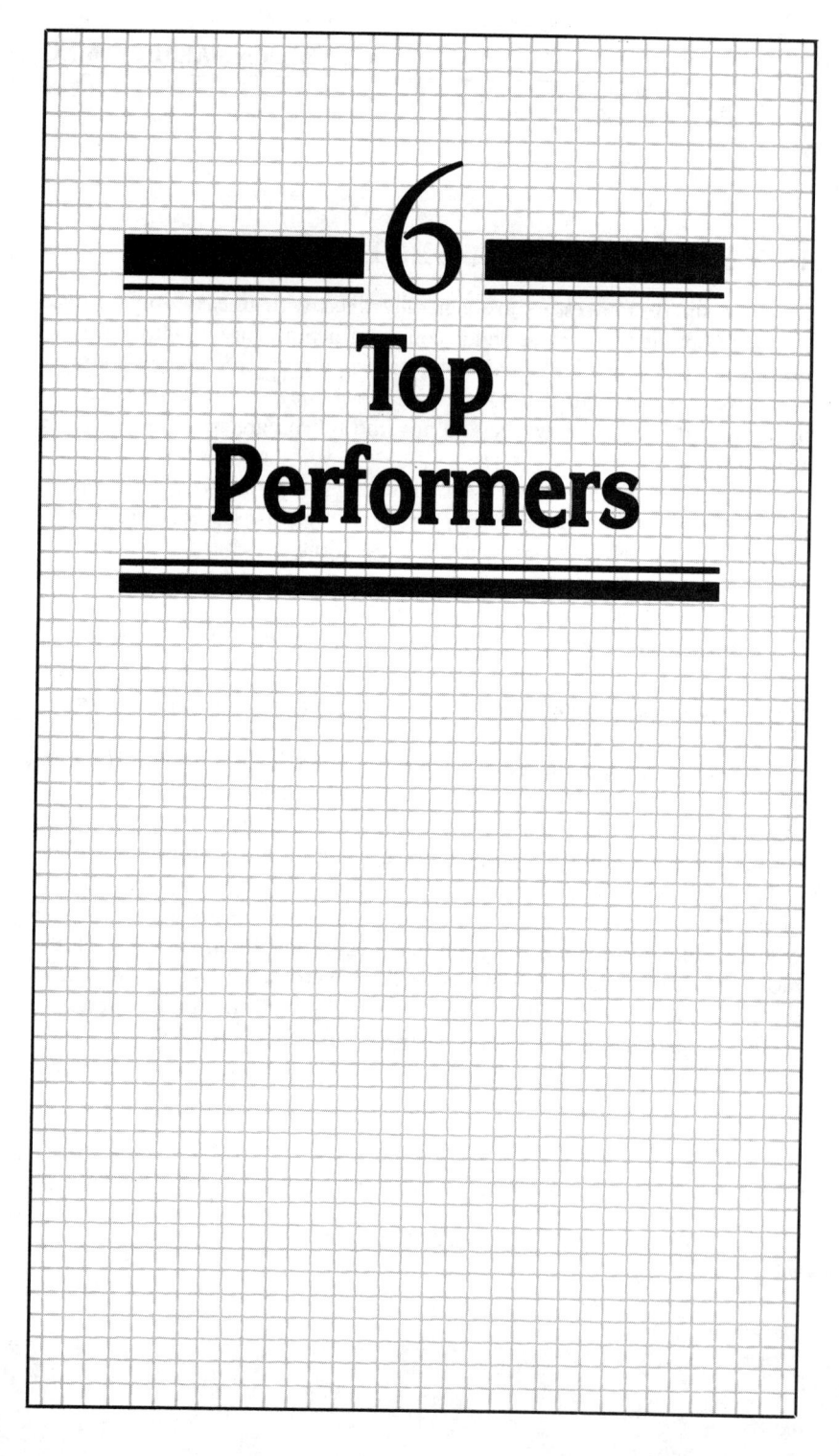

There may be no more telling indicator of the likely success of an investment program than its past results. Despite the omnipresent warning that past results cannot guarantee future performance, any investment that has consistently weathered good times and bad — and come out on top — deserves attention.

We have therefore compiled lists of current investment "Top Performers" in a variety of areas over a variety of periods — concluding in the final months of 1984. While the one-year ratings change regularly, those encompassing five- and ten-year spans suggest tried-and-true leadership. *But remember: Past results cannot guarantee future performance.*

Listed on pages 78–80 are sample results of an investment of $1,000 in an assortment of vehicles. The list is hardly exhaustive: cocoa futures, the Danish stock market, and seventeenth-century Flemish paintings don't show up. In addition, currency translations, income considerations, and the various submarkets of the foreign exchanges have been left out. What remains is nonetheless both intriguing and instructive. And, for those who rode the British market, confirmation of their foresight... for those who opted for savings accounts, particularly during the past year, assurance that safe is sometimes smart... and for those whose portfolios had a silver lining, a distinctly sobering sigh. All results are tracked through the first week of 1985.

SAMPLE $1,000 INVESTMENT RESULTS: LAST 5 YEARS

British Stock Market	$2,321
Dow Jones Transportations	$2,219
Japanese Stock Market	$1,874
AMEX Market Value	$1,664
French Stock Market	$1,656
NYSE Composite	$1,574
German Stock Market	$1,568
Dow Jones Industrials	$1,452
NASDAQ Composite	$1,439
Dow Jones Utilities	$1,373
Canadian Stock Market	$1,355
Passbook Savings Account	$1,307
Best Grade Corporate Bond	$ 982
Japanese Yen	$ 955
Swiss Franc	$ 613
Gold	$ 595
British Pound	$ 523
Silver	$ 217

SAMPLE $1,000 INVESTMENT RESULTS: LAST 3 YEARS

British Stock Market	$1,813
Japanese Stock Market	$1,600
German Stock Market	$1,570
French Stock Market	$1,511
Dow Jones Transportations	$1,466
Dow Jones Industrials	$1,376
NYSE Composite	$1,352
Dow Jones Utilities	$1,348
Best Grade Corporate Bond	$1,269
AMEX Market Value	$1,265
NASDAQ Composite	$1,255
Canadian Stock Market	$1,244
Passbook Savings Account	$1,174
Japanese Yen	$ 868
Silver	$ 785
Gold	$ 722
Swiss Franc	$ 686
British Pound	$ 610

SAMPLE $1,000 INVESTMENT RESULTS: LAST 1 YEAR

Japanese Stock Market	$1,242
British Stock Market	$1,238
French Stock Market	$1,183
Dow Jones Utilities	$1,113
Passbook Savings Account	$1,055
German Stock Market	$1,055
Best Grade Corporate Bonds	$1,043
NYSE Composite	$1,011
Dow Jones Industrials	$ 956
Canadian Stock Market	$ 953
Dow Jones Transportations	$ 930
AMEX Market Value	$ 910
Japanese Yen	$ 903
NASDAQ Composite	$ 882
Swiss Franc	$ 861
Gold	$ 800
British Pound	$ 794
Silver	$ 707

BEST MUTUAL FUND (Equity): 10 YEARS*
(Percentage increase)

1. Fidelity Magellan Fund	1923.24%
2. Twentieth Century Growth	1400.67%
3. Evergreen Fund	1393.47%
4. Pennsylvania Mutual	1384.83%
5. American Capital Venture	1338.92%
6. Twentieth Century Select	1320.86%
7. Quasar Associates	1261.79%
8. American Capital Pace	1257.24%
9. Lindner Fund	1246.30%
10. Oppenheimer Special	1165.00%
11. Sequoia Fund	1102.43%
12. American Capital Comstock	1046.23%
13. Fidelity Destiny	1020.56%
14. Value Line Leverage Growth	953.84%
15. Nicholas Fund	942.55%
16. Sigma Venture Shares	912.10%
17. Mutual Shares Corp	892.79%
18. Weingarten Equity	873.60%
19. Security Ultra Fund	860.28%
20. Pioneer II	841.64%
21. Fidelity Equity-Income	824.99%
22. Amcap Fund	820.73%
23. Acorn Fund	804.57%
24. Kemper Summit Fund	797.32%
25. Leverage Fund of Boston	794.11%

*Source: Lipper Analytical Services, Inc.

BEST MUTUAL FUND (Equity): 5 YEARS*
(Percentage increase)

1.	Fidelity Magellan Fund	322.38%
2.	Lindner Dividend	232.69%
3.	American Capital Pace	225.41%
4.	Phoenix Stock	221.02%
5.	Phoenix Growth	210.98%
6.	Lindner Fund	208.56%
7.	Lehman Capital Fund	203.78%
8.	United Vanguard Fund	198.67%
9.	NEL Growth Fund	197.19%
10.	Janus Fund	195.24%
11.	Loomis-Sayles Capital	193.23%
12.	Twentieth Century Select	189.78%
13.	St. Paul Growth	187.26%
14.	St. Paul Capital	182.16%
15.	IDS Growth Fund	178.75%
16.	Tudor Fund	178.53%
17.	Mass Capital Development	176.86%
18.	Nicholas Fund	174.06%
19.	Vanguard Quality Dividend I	173.22%
20.	Weingarten Equity	168.52%
21.	IDS New Dimensions	165.43%
22.	Fund of America	164.78%
23.	Fidelity Equity-Income	163.72%
24.	International Investors	160.09%
25.	St. Paul Special	158.62%

*Source: Lipper Analytical Services, Inc.

BEST MUTUAL FUND (Equity): 1 YEAR*
(Percentage increase)

1. Prudential-Bache Utility	27.95%
2. Greenspring Fund	24.42%
3. Sequoia Fund	22.69%
4. Selected American Shares	18.88%
5. Mutual Qualified Income	18.52%
6. Mutual Shares	18.09%
7. Federated Stock Trust	15.64%
8. Nationwide Growth	15.57%
9. Lindner Dividend	15.36%
10. American Leaders	14.11%

BEST MUNICIPAL BOND FUND: 1 YEAR*
(Percentage increase)

1. Hutton National Municipal	12.95%
2. Hutton New York Municipal	12.24%
3. Oppenheimer Tax-Free Bond	12.05%
4. DMC Tax-Free Income Trust Pennsylvania	11.09%
5. Dreyfus New York Tax-Free Exempt Bond	10.58%
6. Steinroe Tax-Exempt Bond	10.08%
7. Eaton Vance Municipal Bond	9.41%
8. National Security Tax Exempt	9.38%
9. Kemper Municipal Bond	9.28%
10. First Investors Tax Exempt	9.23%

*Source: Lipper Analytical Services, Inc.

BEST FIXED-INCOME FUND: 1 YEAR*
(Percentage increase)

1. Mutual of Omaha America	11.73%
2. Federated GNMA Trust	11.54%
3. Newton Income Fund	11.50%
4. Fund for U.S. Government Securities	11.37%
5. Retirement Plan American Bond	11.15%
6. IDS Selective	10.59%
7. Vanguard Fixed Income GNMA Portfolio	10.58%
8. Kemper U.S. Government Securities	10.58%
9. Columbia Fixed Income	10.57%
10. Companion Income Fund	10.51%

BEST GENERAL-PURPOSE MONEY-MARKET FUND: 1 YEAR†
(Percentage increase)

1. Kemper Money Market	10.27%
2. MoneyMart Assets	10.26%
3. Transamerica Cash Reserve	10.23%
4. Financial Daily Income	10.18%
5. First American Money Fund	10.17%
6. Cash Management Trust of America	10.15%
7. Lehman Cash Management	10.13%
8. SAFECO M.M.M.F.	10.13%
9. Mariner Cash Management Fund	10.11%
10. Vanguard Money-Market Trust Prime	10.10%

*Source: Lipper Analytical Services, Inc.
†©1984 Donoghue's *Money Fund Report* of Holliston, MA 01746

BEST FEDERAL MONEY-MARKET FUND: 1 YEAR†
(Percentage increase)

1.	American Treasury Shares	10.20%
2.	Cardinal Government Securities Trust	10.03%
3.	Hutton Government Fund	9.82%
4.	UMB Money Market Fund Federal	9.82%
5.	Lehman Government Fund	9.81%
6.	Mariner Government Fund	9.80%
7.	Alex, Brown Cash Reserve/Government Series	9.76%
8.	Mariner U.S. Treasury	9.74%
9.	Vanguard Money Market Trust Federal	9.74%
10.	First Variable Rate	9.74%

BEST TAX-FREE MONEY-MARKET FUND: 1 YEAR†
(Percentage increase)

1.	Daily Tax-Free Income Fund	5.75%
2.	First Investors Tax-Exempt Money Market Fund	5.71%
3.	Lexington Tax Free Money Fund, Inc.	5.68%
4.	Calvert Tax-Free Reserves Money Market	5.68%
5.	NEL Tax-Exempt Money Market Trust	5.67%
6.	Federated/NY Tax-Free Trust	5.60%
7.	T. Rowe Price Tax-Exempt Money Fund	5.59%
8.	Vanguard Municipal Bond Fund Money Market	5.56%
9.	Nuveen Tax-Exempt Money Market Fund	5.54%
10.	Midwest Group Tax-Free Trust Money Market	5.53%

†©1984 Donoghue's *Money Fund Report* of Holliston, MA 01746

BEST INVESTMENT ADVISORY LETTERS*

The Value Line Investment Survey
711 Third Avenue
New York, NY 10017

$365/year (52 issues)
Trial: $37/10 issues

The Outlook
Standard & Poor's Corporation
25 Broadway
New York, NY 10004

$175/year (52 issues)
Trial: $29.95/3 issues

Dow Theory Letters
P.O. Box 1759
La Jolla, CA 92038

$225/year (26 issues)
Trial: $5/3 issues

Granville Market Letter
P.O. Drawer 23006
Kansas City, MO 64141

$250/year (46 issues)
Trial: $85/3 months

Growth Stock Outlook
Box 9911
Chevy Chase, MD 20815

$95/year (24 issues)
Trial: $40/3 months

Holt Investment Advisory
290 Post Road West
Westport, CT 06880

$180/year (24 issues)
Trial: $25/6 issues

New Issues
Institute for
 Econometric Research
3471 N. Federal Highway
Fort Lauderdale, FL 33306

$150/year (12 issues)
Trial: $55/6 months

Professional Tape Reader
P.O. Box 2407
Hollywood, FL 33022

$250/year (24 issues)
Trial: $30/3 issues

Smart Money
The Hirsch Organization
6 Deer Trail
Old Tappan, NJ 07675

$98/year (12 issues)
Trial: None

Zweig Forecast
747 Third Avenue
New York, NY 10017

$245/year (18 issues)
Trial: $50/3 months

*Source: *Savvy* Magazine, December 1983

7
The Beat the Market Hot List

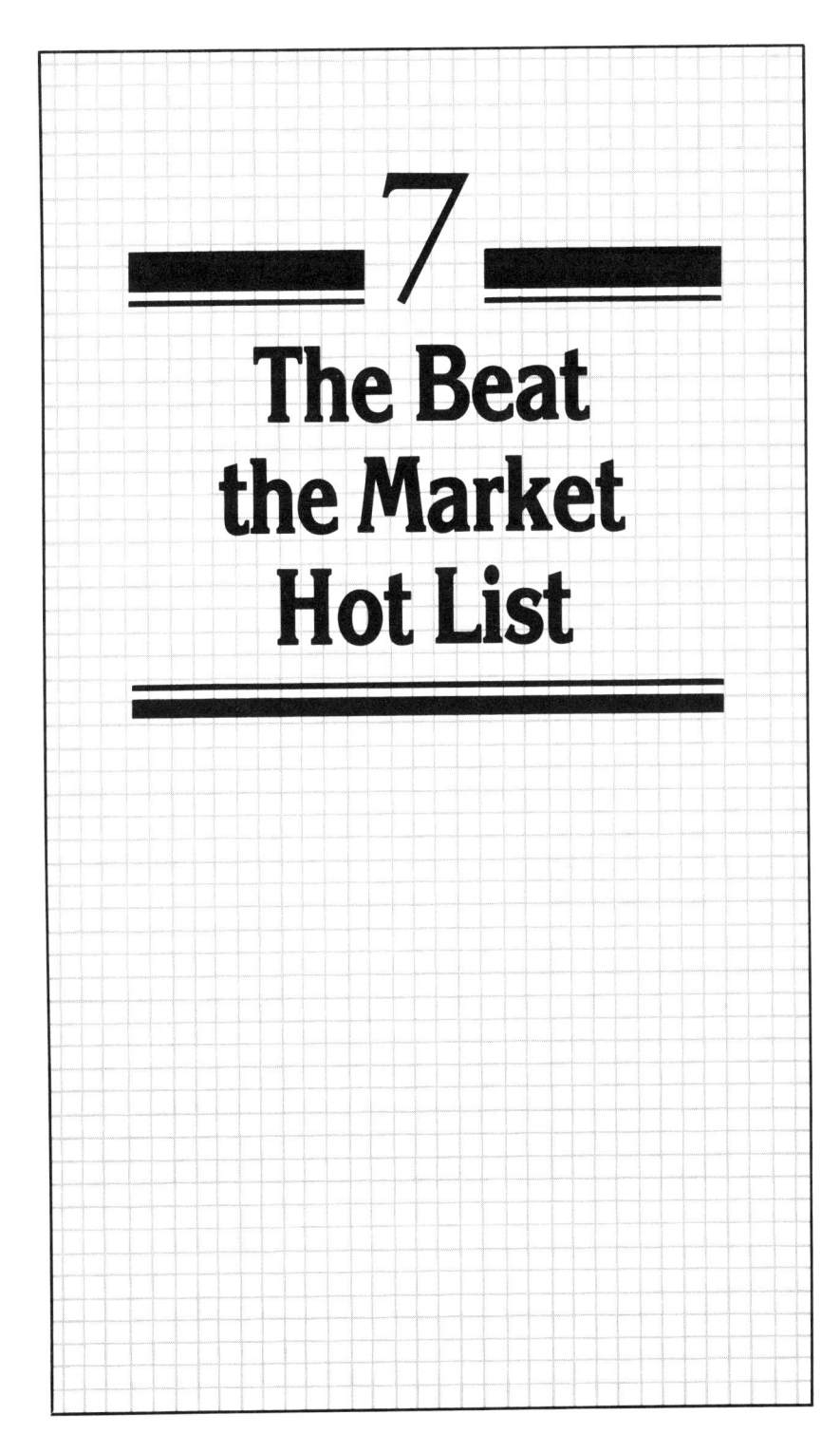

A Guide to Stock Symbols

TCKR: Ticker symbol. For example, the ticker symbol for the Advest Group is ADV. The reading ADV 7s11 means that 700 shares of Advest were traded at $11 per share.

HIGH: Highest price at which the stock traded in the past year.

LOW: Lowest price at which the stock traded in the past year.

PRICE: Price of the stock as of December 1984.

EARN: Earnings per share (in dollars) during the latest twelve-month period. A "d" means that there was a deficit. For example, Advest's reading of d0.05 means that Advest lost five cents per share during the latest twelve-month period.

P/E: Price-to-earnings ratio, determined by dividing the most recent price by the most recent earnings figures. A "d" indicates that there is no P/E for the stock, because the company didn't have any earnings — it lost money.

DEBT: Value of the company's long-term debt (in millions of dollars).

YIELD: Percentage returned to the investor through dividends.

(All figures current through December 1984.)

BLUE CHIPS: The market's "old reliables" — tried-and-true market giants, such as IBM, Procter & Gamble, and AT&T. Their dividends are relatively generous (about five percent at this writing), and their price stability makes them relatively secure... if a trifle unexciting.

SPECULATIVE: Stocks of new companies on the rise, of mid-sized companies in transition, or of older companies in trouble. Frequently, a single, unanswered question overhangs the stock — and Wall Street is betting against the company. Many times, Wall Street proves to be correct in its pessimistic valuation. Yet, when it is wrong — as when Chrysler was hammered down to $3 per share in the face of possible bankruptcy — there are potentially enormous profits. High risk, and on occasion, high reward.

WILD MIX: Stocks that may not have attracted — but deserve — considerable interest. They include many of the market's most intriguing sleepers, overlooked by the crowds but deserving more serious attention — as well as a number of stocks from industries that have fallen on relatively hard times, but might spring back to life: Deere in farm machinery, Evans Products in mobile homes, and Amax in metals.

Guide to Stock Graphs

To those who are already familiar with stock charts, the graphs on the following pages will be largely self-explanatory. However, for those new to the game, here is a brief explanation of the information they contain.

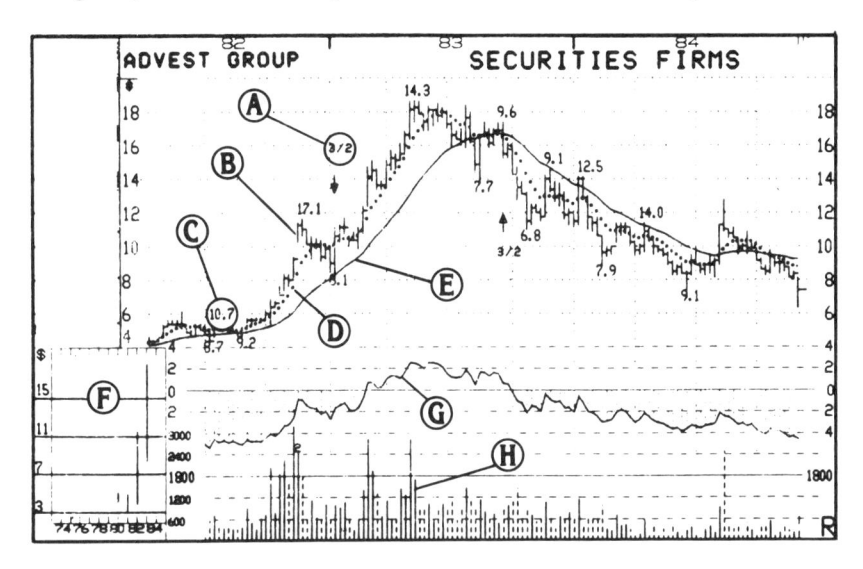

A: A relatively rare symbol, indicating that a stock split occurred at this point in time. In this case, 3/2 designates that 3 shares were created for every 2 already owned.

B: The daily price range of the stock. The vertical line stretches from the high to the low, with the cross-hatch designating the closing price.

C: The price-to-earnings ratio at important turning points.

D: A dotted line showing a weighted 10-week moving average (shows the trend without the day-to-day distraction).

E: A solid line showing a weighted 30-week moving average (shows a longer trend without the day-to-day distraction).

F: The stock's annual price range, generally over the past ten years.

G: The stock's performance ratio (a comparison of the strength of this stock with that of the average stock).

H: The number of shares traded each day (solid lines show up-volume, days on which the stock rose; dotted lines show down-volume, days on which the stock fell).

89

ADVEST GROUP

The main firm of this holding company "on the cutting edge" of the financial services boom is Advest, Inc., a regional brokerage company/investment banker whose activities and products span the entire financial services line. Operations are concentrated in the Northeast. Advest provides real estate services through Billings & Co. and sells fixed income securities through T.E. Desmond Co. The group has been growing via the acquisition of other firms — just last year, for example, Advest added the J.S. Barr & Co. and Vercoe & Co. brokerage houses as well as the investment firm of Burgess & Leith. And the company is now looking to get into the savings bank business, too.

AIR PRODUCTS AND CHEMICALS

Last year the sales of this company's commercial gases rose like a hot air balloon. The ballast that was jettisoned to achieve this ascent was the high interest rates that had been the bane of the recession of the early 80s and a built-in limitation on the activities of Air Products' customers. Investors should be alert to the possibility of high interest rates returning in mid-decade. Meanwhile, Air Products is working on a big contract that involves the company in the construction of an Exxon gas processing plant. Air Products also produces industrial chemicals. Stearns-Catalytic World, its building and engineering services division, currently seems to be stuck in a rut.

ALEXANDER'S, INC.

Alexander's owns eight department stores in the New York City area and manages seven others, most of which are also in or near the Big Apple. The stores, the biggest of which is 418,000 square feet, are oriented toward women's soft goods; men's merchandise accounts for only about 25 percent of their sales. Alexander's sells quality merchandise — much of it house brand or clothing obtained at discount — at a low price and with few frills. Alexander's is partners with Macy's in the huge Kings Plaza shopping center in Brooklyn. Takeover talk was the order of the day last year — and it was serious. Should such a move come to fruition, the new owners' most valuable asset would be the ground on which the stores stand.

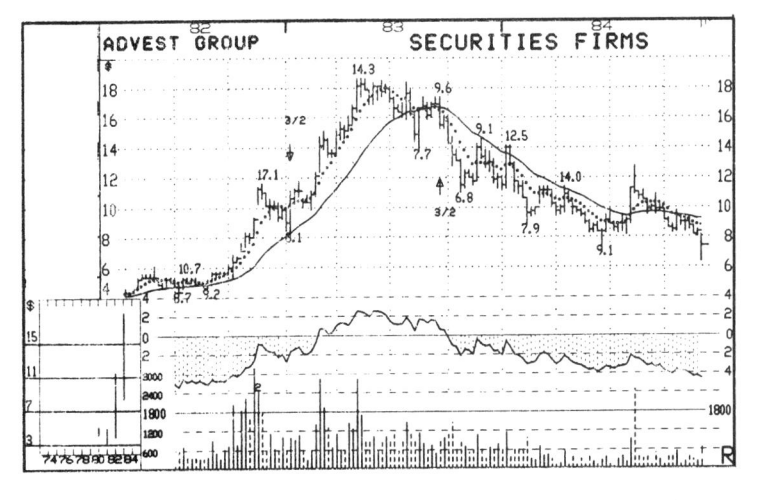

TCKR: ADV
HIGH: 14 1/8
LOW: 6 7/8
PRICE: 7 1/2
EARN: d0.05
P/E: d
DEBT: 28.1
YIELD: 1.6

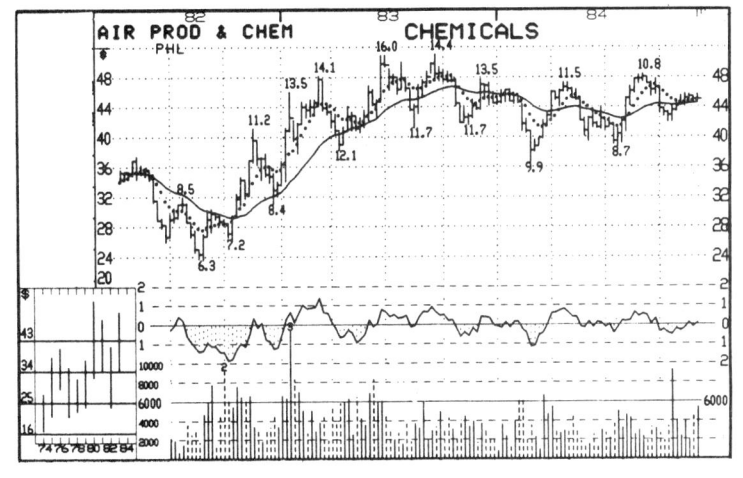

TCKR: APD
HIGH: 48 3/8
LOW: 36 1/2
PRICE: 46 3/8
EARN: 4.55
P/E: 10
DEBT: 403
YIELD: 2.6

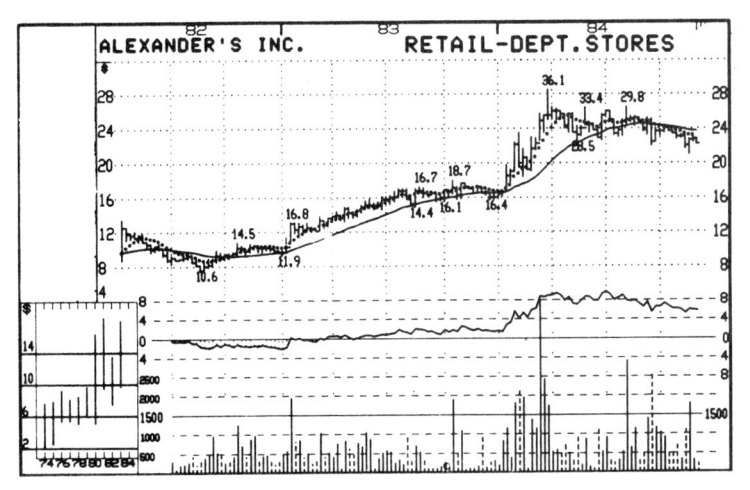

TCKR: ALX
HIGH: 28 1/2
LOW: 15 3/4
PRICE: 21 1/8
EARN: 0.89
P/E: 24
DEBT: 69.2
YIELD: —

91

ALLIED CORP.

Allied has a knack for achieving high visibility: For a number of years it was literally visible as the owner of the building at Broadway and 42nd St., in New York City, formerly known as the Times Tower. Then, in 1983, it purchased Bendix, which increased its aerospace industry earnings by 50 percent. That acquisiton also gave Allied vicarious connection to the most colorful management story in years—the working relationship between Bendix's William Agee and Mary Cunningham, which had been front-page news two years before. Buying Bendix was a powerful way of saying that Allied—originally Allied Chemical—was no longer just a chemical and oil company. Other recent acquisitions are Bunker Ramo and Fisher Scientific. Its auto product brands include Autolite, Fram, and Prestolite. Allied participates in the North Sea oil business and last year acquired an interest in a natural gas venture in Indonesia.

ALLIED STORES

Allied owns close to 600 department and specialty stores, with at least one in almost every state. Department stores include: The Bon, Block's, Donaldson's, Jordan Marsh, Joske's, Maas Brothers, Pomeroy's, and Stern's. Among the company's specialty store chains are: Ann Taylor, Bonwit Teller, Brooks Brothers, Catherine's Stoute Shoppe, Garfinckel's, Miller & Rhoads, and Plymouth. Stressing upscale clothing, where profit margins are highest, Allied last year was scheduled to open twenty five stores, including four department stores. Capital spending will average $125 million a year over the next few years.

ALLIS-CHALMERS

Allis-Chalmers makes big machines that lift, pump, spin, crush, grind, and filter. Cement-processing machines, dynamos, diesel engines, tractors, and lift trucks are among its products. Customers include coal mining companies, utilities, and the construction industry, and Allis-Chalmers also makes filtration machinery for air quality control. Hurt by the depression in the farm equipment industry, Allis-Chalmers has been pushing sales of small front-wheel-drive tractors. Lift trucks have been doing well, and the company's fluids-handling division could get a boost from more government activity to combat water pollution. But several years of losses, high debt, tight competition, and the fact that what they produce is business cycle-sensitive means that management's job is really cut out for them.

ALLIED CORP.

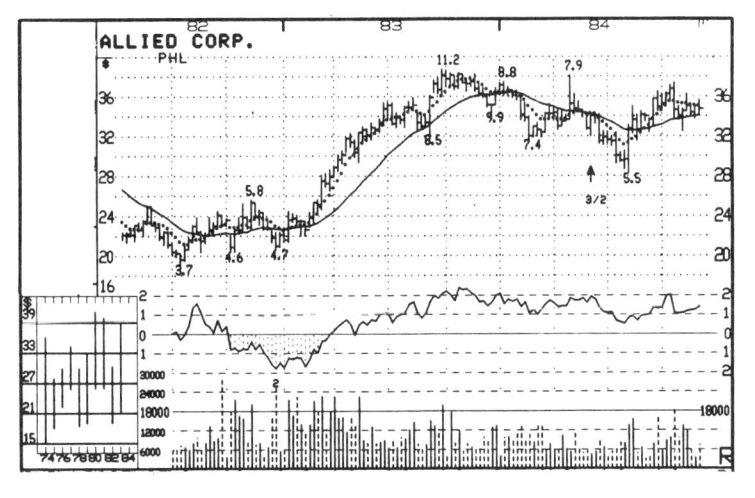

TCKR: ALD
HIGH: 37½
LOW: 28¼
PRICE: 35
EARN: 5.07
P/E: 7
DEBT: 1775
YIELD: 5.1

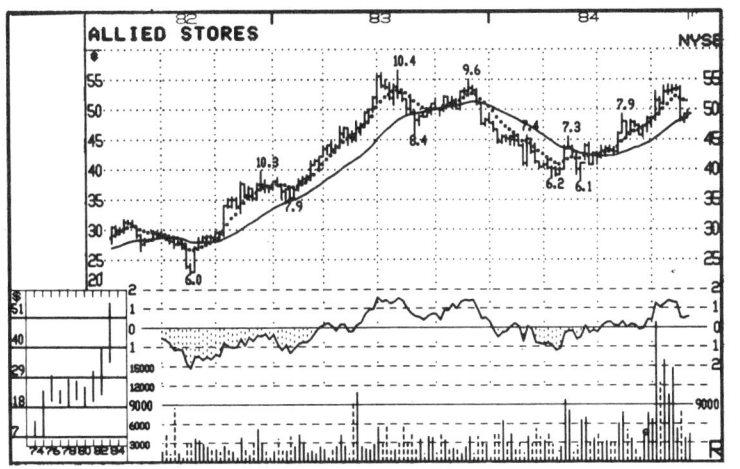

ALLIED STORES

TCKR: ALS
HIGH: 56½
LOW: 38
PRICE: 51⅝
EARN: 6.25
P/E: 8
DEBT: 752
YIELD: 3.9

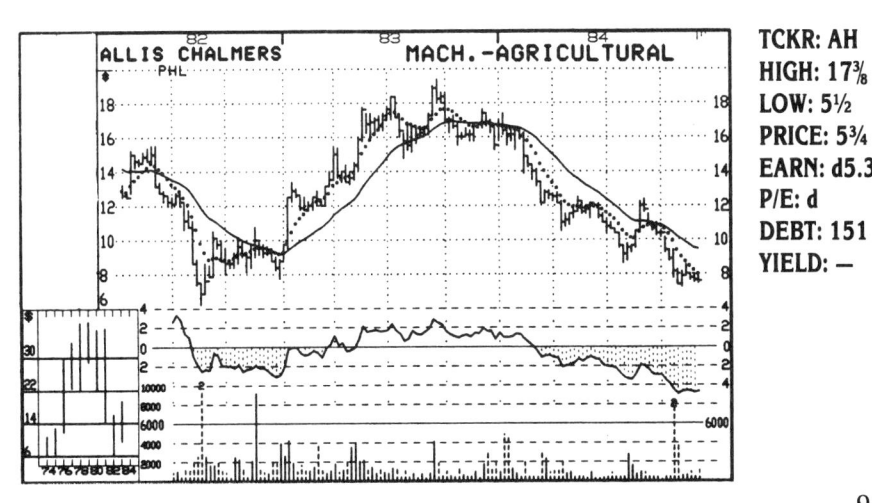

ALLIS CHALMERS — MACH.-AGRICULTURAL

TCKR: AH
HIGH: 17⅜
LOW: 5½
PRICE: 5¾
EARN: d5.37
P/E: d
DEBT: 151
YIELD: —

AMAX, INC.

Amax makes more molybdenum (or "moly," as it's quaintly called in the industry) than any other company in the world. What have you got if you've got molybdenum? An important component of steel and alloys, for starters. You've also got trouble, since a malaise settled over the moly market some time ago. In fact, the market was so depressed that Amax temporarily closed its two moly mines in 1983. Fortunately for Amax's management, employees, and stockholders, though, there's more to their operations than just this silver-gray metal. There is, for instance, aluminum, which is rapidly taking moly's place as Amax's main product. Burgeoning use of that supple substance in the auto and soft drink canning industries bodes well for Amax. The company also produces coal.

AMERICAN BRANDS

The fifth largest cigarette producer in the U.S., American Brands sells tobacco products in Britain through its successful Gallaher subsidiary. Cigarette brands include Carlton, Lucky Strike, Pall Mall, and Tareyton. But American Brands is trying to kick the habit by using cigarette money to diversify its product mix: The company has been buying into the food, hardware, insurance, liquor, office supply, security devices, sporting goods, and toiletry areas. Acquired companies so far include Acushnet, James B. Beam, Jergens, Master Lock, Pinkerton's, Swingline, and Sunshine Biscuits. American also owns the Franklin and Southland insurance companies.

AMERICAN CAN

Although its packaging preeminence has been maintained by the introduction of the solderless can, this company has lately been trading cans for cash. In the last three years it's plunked down $800 million worth of can-generated profits to buy into the financial services bonanza. And in 1983 alone, American Can jettisoned nineteen operations in an asset redeployment that would have pleased even General Patton. Since then, profits from financial services — which run the gamut from insurance to stocks and bonds — have exceeded those from the packaging division of the company. Diversification has also extended to clothing and consumer electronics. American Can's plastic products are expected to continue to flouish.

AMAX INC. — METALS MISC.

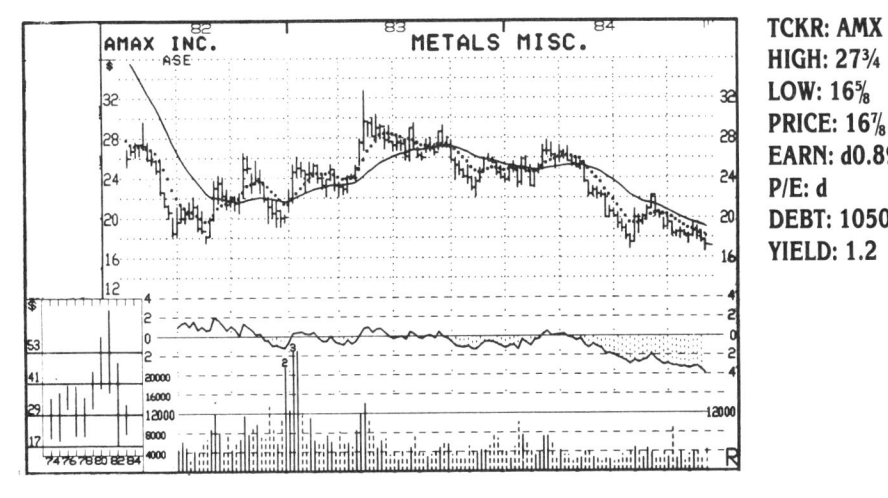

TCKR: AMX
HIGH: 27¾
LOW: 16⅝
PRICE: 16⅞
EARN: d0.89
P/E: d
DEBT: 1050
YIELD: 1.2

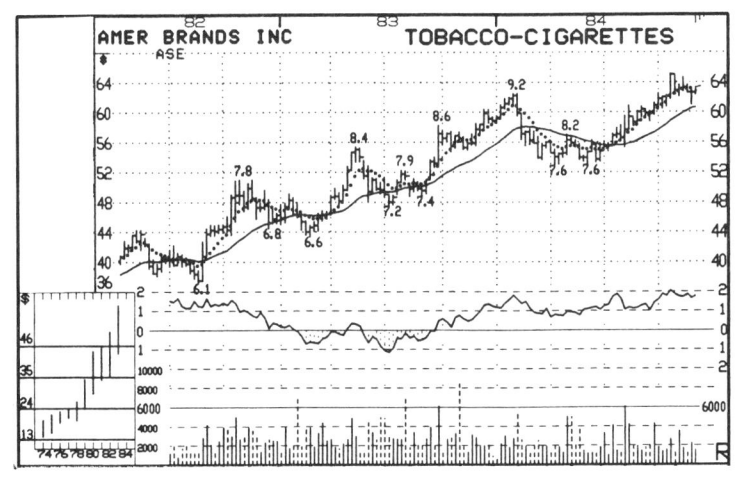

AMER BRANDS INC — TOBACCO-CIGARETTES

TCKR: AMB
HIGH: 65⅛
LOW: 52⅞
PRICE: 64⅛
EARN: 7.16
P/E: 9
DEBT: 685
YIELD: 5.8

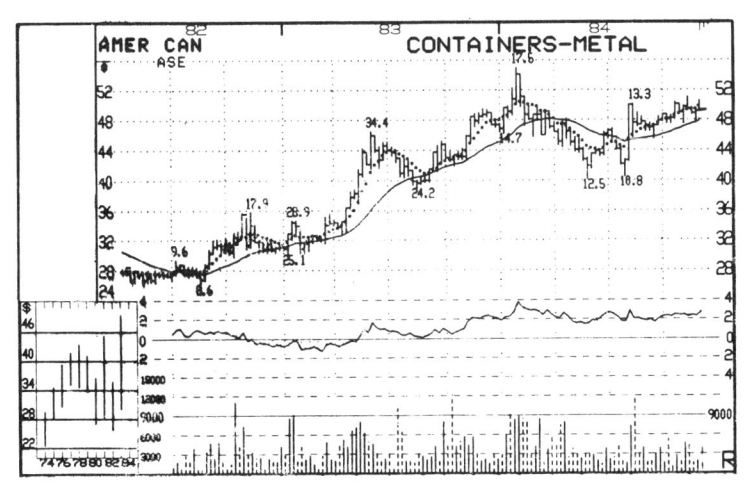

AMER CAN — CONTAINERS-METAL

TCKR: AC
HIGH: 55
LOW: 40⅛
PRICE: 51⅛
EARN: 4.61
P/E: 11
DEBT: 910
YIELD: 5.7

95

AMERICAN EXPRESS

Do you known *them*? That ubiquitous charge card (currently in about eighteen million American wallets) has extended the career of Karl Malden and paid for innumerable business lunches. But American Express is a lot more than plastic credit and distant sunsets these days. Travel now accounts for less than half its business, although it has been the healthiest part of the company of late. Currently, American Express means cable television (one half of Warner-Amex), Shearson, and Lehman Brothers Kuhn Loeb, which was acquired in 1984. Another recent acquisition is Investors Diversified Services; and there's also the Fireman's Fund, which is now a major component of American Express. Although the flame flickered a bit in this insurance behemoth in 1983, management has since rekindled the spark.

AMERICAN HOME PRODUCTS

Although as a company it deliberately maintains almost no profile at all, the brand names of American Home Products are commonly found in supermarket shopping carts: Black Flag, Chef Boyardee, Easy-Off, Gulden's, Jiffy-Pop, and Saniflush. American Home has divested itself of its housewares division, but still owns Brach's candies. Increasingly, however, other American Home Products are turning up in the medicine cabinet. Nonprescription names include Advil (its entry in the ibuprofen, a new non-aspirin pain reliever, market), Anacin, Dristan, and Preparation H. Inderal, American Home's profitable high-blood-pressure prescription drug, is no longer patent protected, but so far it has survived industry competition.

AMERICAN STANDARD

Fifteen years ago, in the heat of an acquisitions mania, American Standard acquired the Mosler Safe Co., whose head, William A. Marquard, took the helm at the new parent firm and righted the acquisitions-heavy conglomerate before it turned turtle and sank. Construction and mining operations have been tossed overboard, and the company's focus has narrowed. Building products, including plumbing fixtures, brakes, gears, and signaling equipment are its strong suits today, in addition to commercial printing, graphic arts equipment, and security devices. Last year American Standard divested itself of the business forms business and, with the acquisition of Trane Co., got into air conditioning. Trane's success is heavily dependent on a high rate of commercial construction. About 40 percent of American Standard's sales are made abroad.

AMER EXPRESS — SERVICES

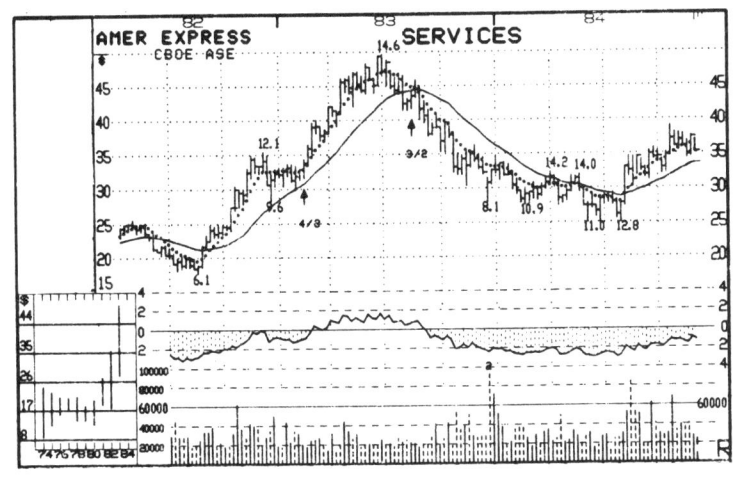

TCKR: AXP
HIGH: 39
LOW: 25
PRICE: 35⅞
EARN: 1.92
P/E: 19
DEBT: 3346
YIELD: 3.6

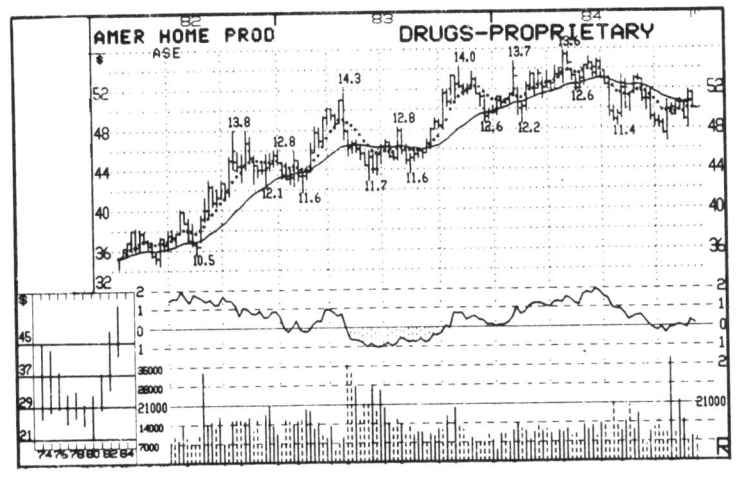

AMER HOME PROD — DRUGS-PROPRIETARY

TCKR: AHP
HIGH: 55¾
LOW: 46¾
PRICE: 50⅞
EARN: 4.33
P/E: 12
DEBT: 64.4
YIELD: 5.2

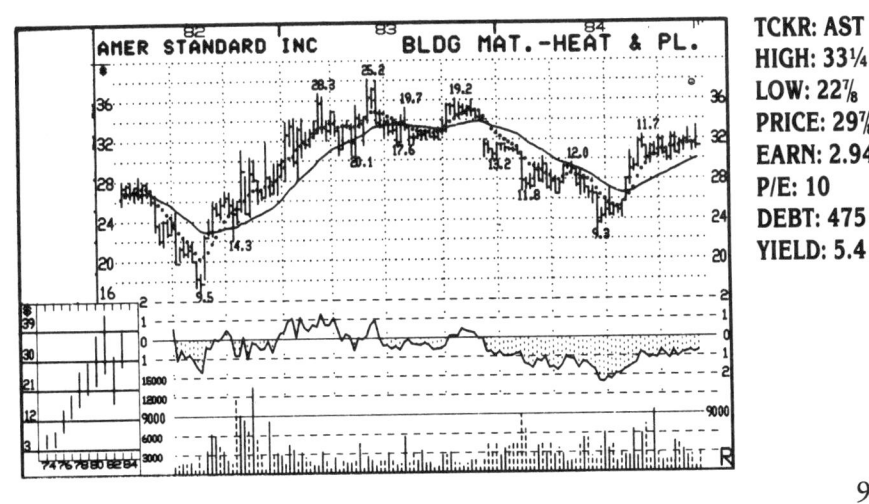

AMER STANDARD INC — BLDG MAT.-HEAT & PL.

TCKR: AST
HIGH: 33¼
LOW: 22⅞
PRICE: 29⅞
EARN: 2.94
P/E: 10
DEBT: 475
YIELD: 5.4

AMERICAN STORES

This retailing giant (third in the country in grocery store chains, first in drugstores) took its present shape and style in 1979, when the Skaggs chain bought the larger American Stores. American's 1984 purchase of the Jewel firm increased its holding to about 2,000 stores, including Acme Markets, Alpha Beta Stores, Buttrey supermarkets, Jewel T Discount Groceries, Osco drugstores, Rea and Derrick Stores, Save-On-Drugs, and Skaggs drugstores. The key to American Stores' success seems to be the frequent combination of drug and food operations under one roof.

AMR CORP.

AMR is a holding company whose *raison d'être* is American Airlines. Recent figures put American second in the U.S. in total revenue passenger miles, but it has also felt the profit squeeze that hit the airline industry a few years ago. AMR hasn't paid a dividend since 1980, but it has been aiming to do something about that. American's traditional hubs have been Dallas and Chicago, but Denver should soon become a third. Part of the burden of increasing profitability has been placed on the workforce through a new two-tiered wage system designed to lower labor costs and employ many new workers. AMR also owns AA Development, which has real estate holdings and shopping centers, and AA Energy, which is in the oil and gas business. Flagship International, their high-altitude catering service, will feed you pie in the sky.

ANALOG DEVICES

This company specializes in supplying the vital link between computers and the processes they control in industries that have been automated. These devices are connected to sensors — thermometers, for example — that measure what is going on at any given time in an industrial operation. The devices collect data and transform it into computer-readable information. The computer can then make corrections in the process based on that information — an activity known as feedback. Analog is number one in this field. Its products range from integrated circuits that are part of measuring devices, to the complete devices themselves. Approximately 40 percent of its sales are to foreign customers.

AMER STORES CO

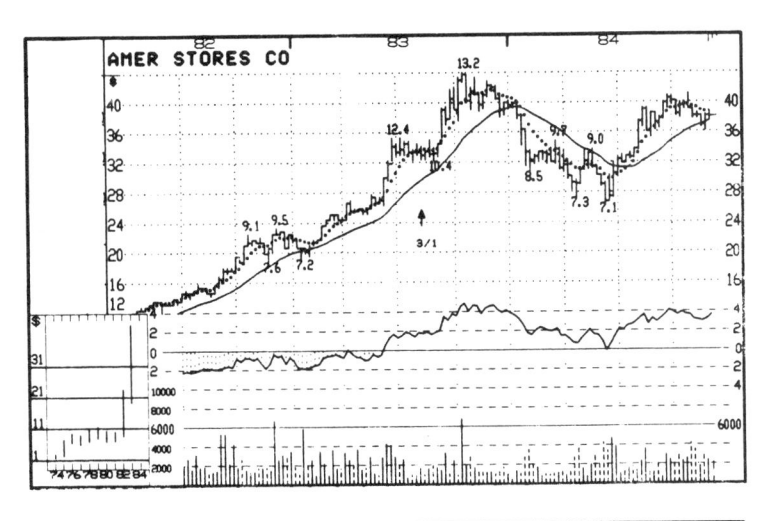

TCKR: ASC
HIGH: 41⅛
LOW: 26½
PRICE: 36¼
EARN: 3.98
P/E: 9
DEBT: 842
YIELD: 1.8

AMR CORP.

TCKR: AMR
HIGH: 41¼
LOW: 24¼
PRICE: 33⅝
EARN: 6.45
P/E: 5
DEBT: 1532
YIELD: —

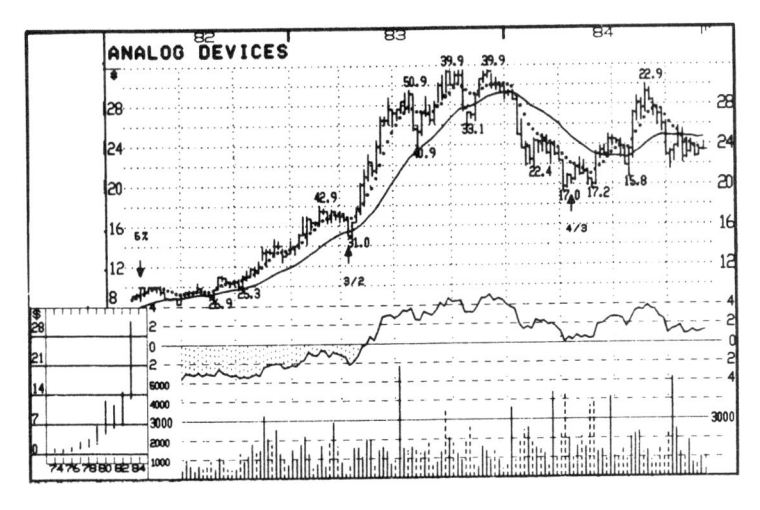

ANALOG DEVICES

TCKR: ADI
HIGH: 30¾
LOW: 19⅝
PRICE: 22½
EARN: 1.25
P/E: 18
DEBT: 28.2
YIELD: —

APACHE CORP.

The Apaches were a tribe of fierce, independent warriors in the Southwest — but this company shares only the name and location of those Indians. Apache Corp.'s forte is setting up and directing the operations of limited partnerships in oil and gas exploration and production; currently it is involved in thirty-six such enterprises. It also provides managerial services to other oil firms. Apache, which owns 7.1 percent of Apache Petroleum, is involved in a joint operation with Shell Oil in the Gulf of Mexico. Apache has been pushing natural gas sales lately, but that's against a backdrop of declining prices in a market tightened with renewed competition from oil heat. Apache also manages California tree farms and Wyoming ranches, and it packs and processes fruit as well.

APPLIED MAGNETICS

This company has sought to make it as a member of the computer supporting cast with IBM-compatible products. Its specialty is the recording head mechanism in the disk and tape mass storage devices that feed data and programs to computers. The advent of the personal computer market was an enriching opportunity for Applied Magnetics, but recently disappointing sales of those machines have caused inventory to pile up. Two years ago, Applied Magnetics began to sell recording heads for use with thin-film storage media, a move that should create substantial revenues in the late 1980s. Increased capital spending, however, could cut into those profits. Stock hit a four-year low in 1984, and things would have been worse had it not been for a one-time tax break.

ARROW ELECTRONICS

Arrow is number two in the country in the distribution of electronic parts and computer components. How did it get that way? By being everywhere. Arrow now has about fifty facilities from which it distributes its bits of silicon and ceramic to approximately 25,000 customers. This part of the business brings in about 90 percent of Arrow's revenues and an even larger percentage of its profits. Arrow also sells electrical parts, 50 percent of which are used in the construction industry. Arrow's kind of business requires a steady cash flow. Its subsidiary, Schuylkill Metals Corp. — a lead refiner specializing in the recovery of lead from batteries — was supposed to boost cash flow. But instead of keeping things flowing, Schuylkill has hung heavily on company operations, weighing down the balance sheet like... well, like lead.

APACHE CORP.
CBOE

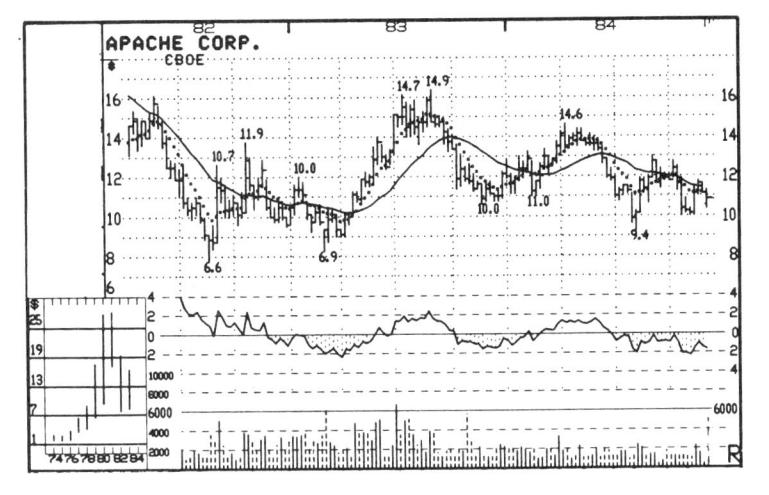

TCKR: APA
HIGH: 14⅝
LOW: 9¼
PRICE: 10⅞
EARN: 0.97
P/E: 11
DEBT: 99.7
YIELD: 2.6

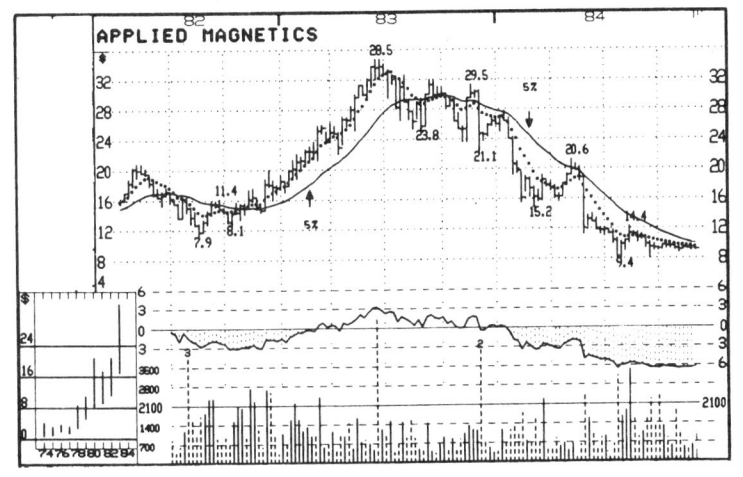

APPLIED MAGNETICS

TCKR: APM
HIGH: 29⅛
LOW: 8
PRICE: 9
EARN: 0.80
P/E: 11
DEBT: 2.62
YIELD: 13.5

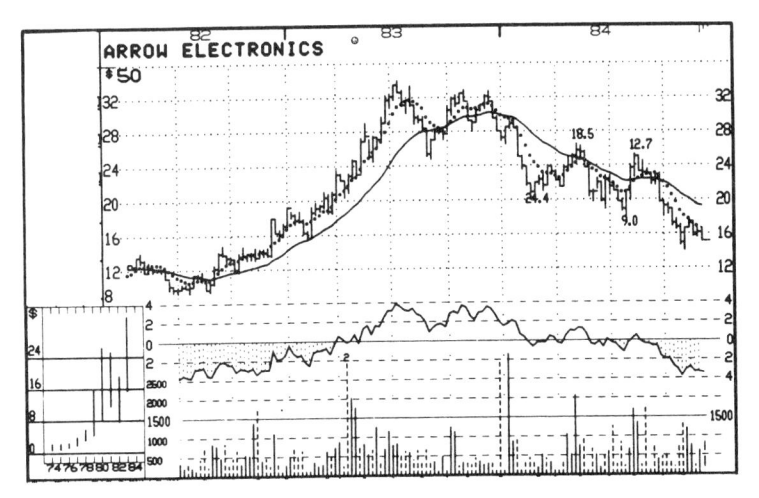

ARROW ELECTRONICS

TCKR: ARW
HIGH: 31⅜
LOW: 13½
PRICE: 13½
EARN: 2.11
P/E: 6
DEBT: 173
YIELD: 1.5

ATHLONE INDUSTRIES

Athlone's specialty is specialty metals, which were nothing special in the profit department last year. Its Green River Steel and Jessop Steel produce a variety of steel products, many of which are used by the machine tool industry. Aerospace companies are also important customers. And its Reynolds Fasteners is a nuts and bolts operation—literally—that sells mainly to the building and auto industries. But the company also has a sporty side. It sells sporting equipment and casual apparel through Dudley Sports, Gelfo Manufacturing, Henschel, LeeMar, and Sea Fashions.

AMERICAN TELEPHONE & TELEGRAPH

Can a shotgun divorce bring health and prosperity to this giant? Separation from the twenty-two local Bell companies has enabled AT&T—American Telephone and Telegraph—to get into computers. Time will tell how much IBM, traditional leader in the field, has to worry about the competition. In areas more familiar to followers of its stock, AT&T itself will have to fight off competition. First, it will have to retain long-distance customers in the face of wooing from MCI, Sprint, and the like. Second, it will have to blunt the challenge of firms that would like to sell you a new phone. AT&T's advantage here is that although the familiar Western Electric name has disappeared, AT&T equipment is still known for its high quality. Meanwhile, the company is doing well with its new PBX (private branch exchange) switchboard systems.

AVNET, INC.

If that TV technician fiddling with the new antenna on your roof is installing a Channel Master, it came from Avnet. But that's only where the company is most visible. Avnet is a company of parts. Its main exposure is in the distribution of electronic components, including circuits used in computers, a market that continues to exhibit a voracious appetite for more, more.... Avnet, with one-fifth of that market, is the largest and most profitable distributor of its kind in the country. It also distributes auto parts, electric motors, and instruments that control and measure for a variety of industries. Last year Avnet divested itself of American Precision, which sells clutch components for cars and trucks.

ATHLONE IND.

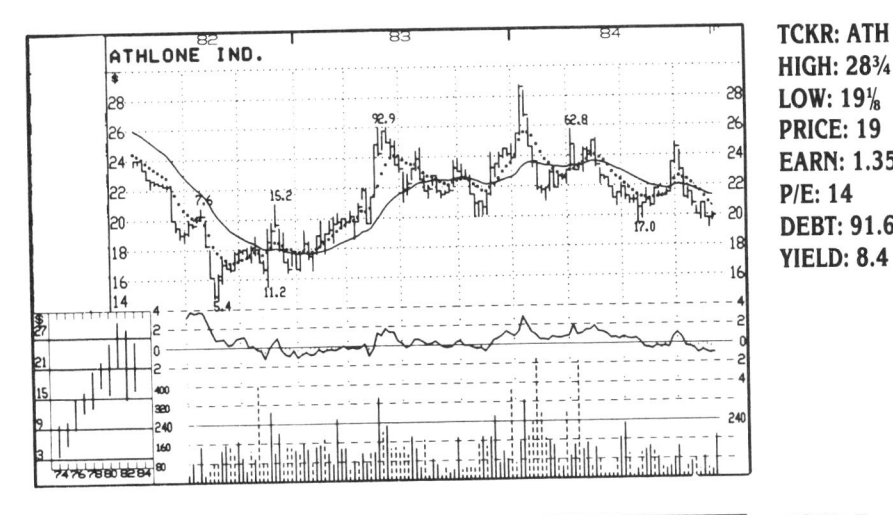

TCKR: ATH
HIGH: 28¾
LOW: 19⅛
PRICE: 19
EARN: 1.35
P/E: 14
DEBT: 91.6
YIELD: 8.4

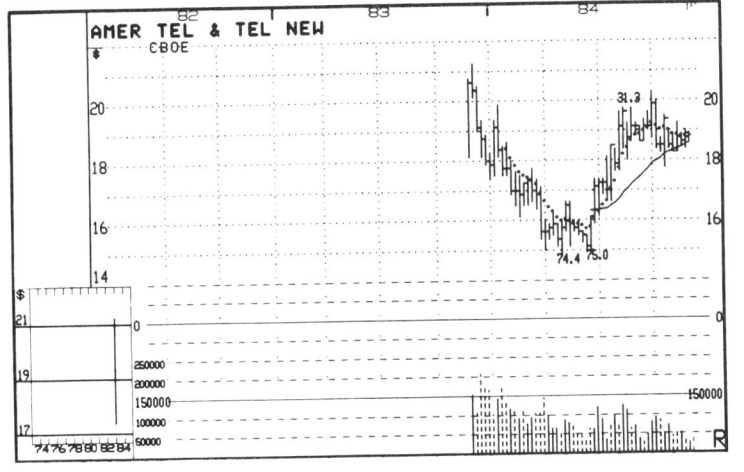

AMER TEL & TEL NEW
CBOE

TCKR: T
HIGH: 20¼
LOW: 14⅞
PRICE: 18⅝
EARN: n/a
P/E: n/a
DEBT: 8974
YIELD: 6.4

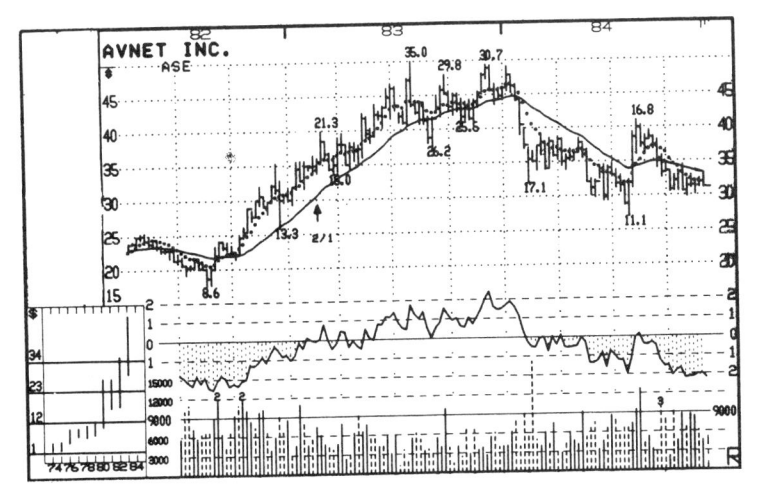

AVNET INC.
ASE

TCKR: AVT
HIGH: 49⅛
LOW: 27
PRICE: 32⅜
EARN: 2.47
P/E: 13
DEBT: 114
YIELD: 1.5

BAKER INTERNATIONAL

Call Baker if you want cementing shoes and collars, tooth-type rock bits, shaft-sinking equipment, or underreamers. And call them too if you have an oil well that needs rehabilitating. Oil field and gas services and mining equipment are Baker's forte; its Reed Tool company is strongly positioned in the drill bit market. Drilling, well completion, and oil production account for about one-third of Baker's sales. The strong performance of the last two years is due primarily to management's ruthless trimming of excess capacity and employees. Half of Baker's total sales are generated abroad. Debt retirement is currently one of its major priorities.

BASIX CORP.

If you don't want to invest your money in them, you can throw it at them. Basix (it used to be Basic Resources) owns Automatic Toll Systems, which takes quarters, dimes, and nickels at automated toll gates in close to 20,000 highway traffic lanes across the country. Basix also owns Winko-Matic Signal Co., which produces traffic control systems. Packard Press, a publisher of corporate and legal information, is also a Basix company, one in which the parent firm has been making substantial improvements. Basix also owns CRA, Inc., which leases and sells computer systems. And Basix is in the oil and gas business through R.J. Brown, which services offshore operations.

BAXTER TRAVENOL LABORATORIES

If you were in the hospital recently, you may have consumed one of this company's products through a tube: It produces intravenous solutions, as well as many kinds of blood- and urinary-related hospital equipment. Baxter Travenol is also a prominent manufacturer of kidney dialysis machines; and last year it purchased Extracorporeal, Inc., Johnson & Johnson's dialysis operation. Business has been healthy for Baxter, but it is currently being choked somewhat by hospitals emphasizing cost control in response to Medicare's tighter payment policies. Not that Baxter can't profit from that, since it also sells computer software to hospitals to help them function more efficiently. In 1983 it acquired JS/Data, Inc., and Stony Brook Systems. Baxter is also partners with Genentech, in an effort to develop new diagnostic tools.

BAKER INTL — OIL WELL EQUIP.

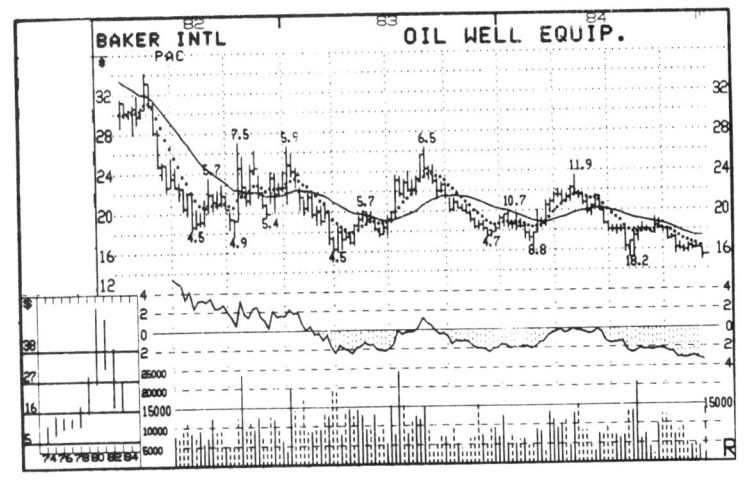

TCKR: BKO
HIGH: 23½
LOW: 15
PRICE: 16½
EARN: 0.84
P/E: 20
DEBT: 471
YIELD: 5.6

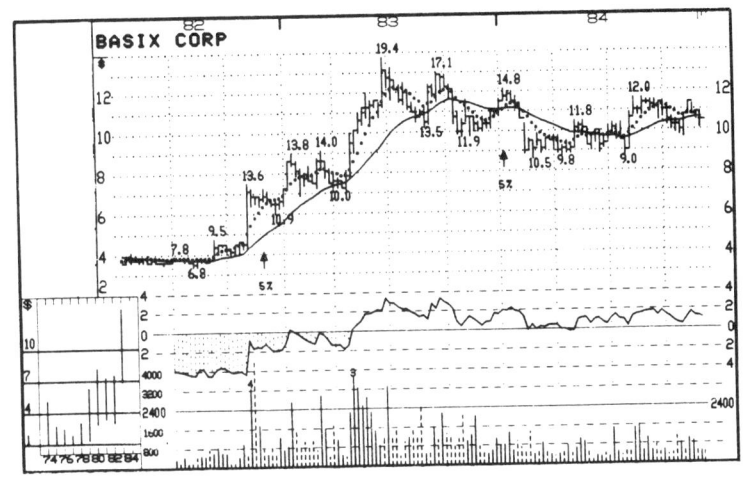

BASIX CORP

TCKR: BAS
HIGH: 12¼
LOW: 8⅝
PRICE: 10
EARN: 1.00
P/E: 1
DEBT: 56.1
YIELD: 1.2

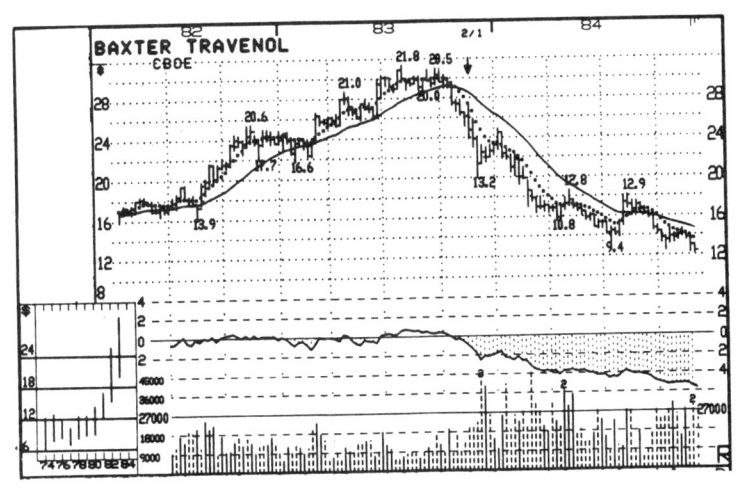

BAXTER TRAVENOL

TCKR: BAX
HIGH: 24⅞
LOW: 11¾
PRICE: 12⅞
EARN: 1.28
P/E: 10
DEBT: 289
YIELD: 2.6

105

BEATRICE CO.

There's a good reason why this company, established in Beatrice, Nebraska, in 1894, is no longer called Beatrice Foods: About 25 percent of its revenues are now generated by non-food businesses. Currently, Beatrice bottles Coca-Cola, distributes Cutty Sark and Mouton Cadet in the United States, and sells products and services under names such as Avis, Culligan, Danskin, Eckrich, Hunts, Jensen, La Choy, Max Factor, Meadow Gold, Playtex, Rosarita, STP, Samsonite, Shedd's, Stiffel, Swift, Swiss Miss, Tropicana, and Wesson. Last year, as if this multi-everything firm didn't have its fingers in enough pies, it swallowed Esmark for $2.8 billion. Can it digest such a meal? Only time will tell. Meanwhile, Beatrice is embarking on a new advertising campaign to promote the Beatrice name, and is taking a hard look at its assets to see what can be sold off to replenish the company coffers.

BEKER INDUSTRIES

Beker makes phosphate-based fertilizer and animal feed. Like those of farmers, Beker's prospects depend on several factors beyond their control. These include legislation providing for government payments for acreage reduction, the prospects for agricultural exports (which are partly a function of the strength of the dollar), and the weather. Beker's phosphate comes from Florida and Idaho. Last year it formed Conda Partnership, a joint venture with Western Co-operative Fertilizers Ltd., a Canadian firm, to exploit the Idaho deposits. Beker is also half-owner of Commodities-Trading International, which began trading last year.

BEVERLY ENTERPRISES

If anybody in Beverly's business benefits from economies of scale, it's Beverly itself. This company presides over the largest nursing home empire in the United States: approximately 850 institutions (more than 200 in Texas and California alone), containing about 100,000 beds. More than half its facilities are leased, and about two-thirds of its revenues come from Medicaid. Occupancy rate is in the area of 90 percent. Given this country's demographics, Beverly's growth position is not surprising: Building and buying are the by-words. Currently, about 200 institutions a year are being added. Beverly Enterprises, in a smaller way, is also represented in the home health care business and in retirement communities.

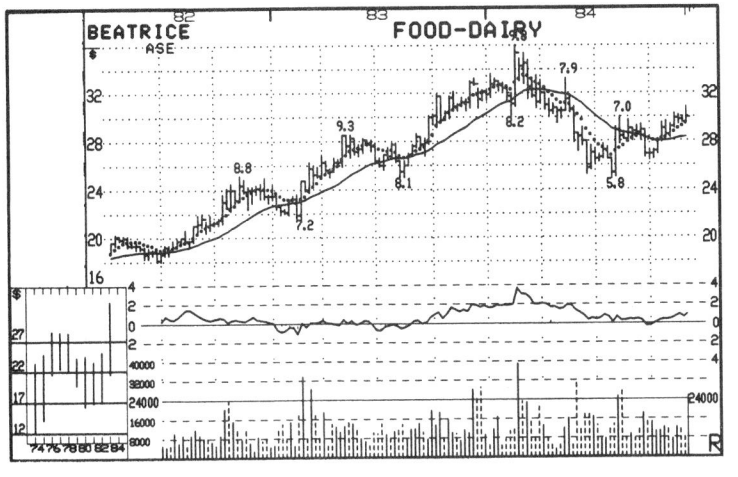

BEATRICE FOOD-DAIRY

TCKR: BRY
HIGH: 36
LOW: 24 7/8
PRICE: 29 1/2
EARN: 3.30
P/E: 9
DEBT: 2944
YIELD: 5.8

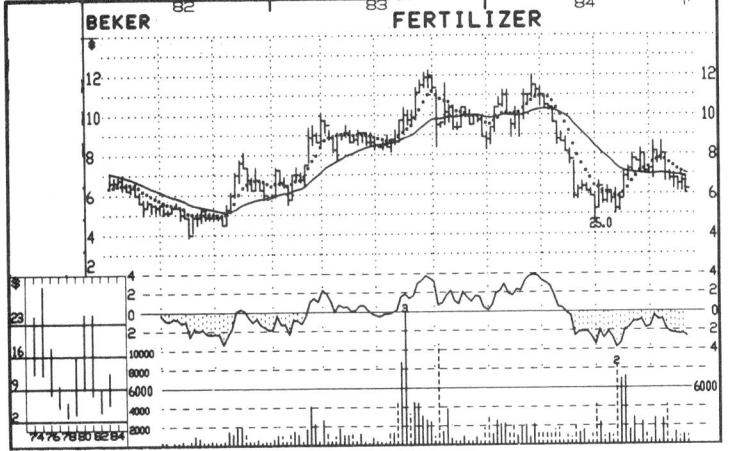

BEKER FERTILIZER

TCKR: BKI
HIGH: 12
LOW: 4 3/4
PRICE: 5 1/2
EARN: d0.01
P/E: d
DEBT: 126
YIELD: —

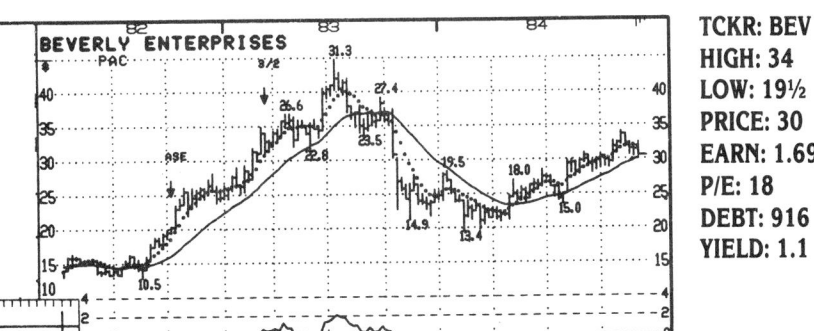

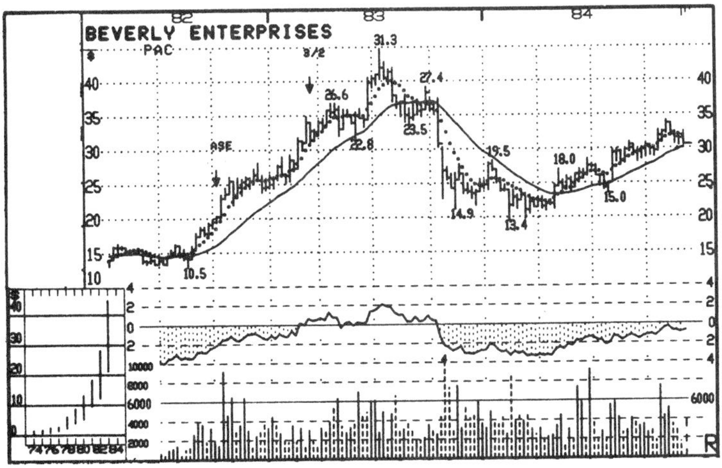

BEVERLY ENTERPRISES

TCKR: BEV
HIGH: 34
LOW: 19 1/2
PRICE: 30
EARN: 1.69
P/E: 18
DEBT: 916
YIELD: 1.1

BIG THREE INDUSTRIES

This company is a major vendor of industrial gas in the Southwest. It also sells industrial equipment to a variety of manufacturers and to the oil industry through Bowen Tools, Dia Log, Nowsco, and Ransome-Tempil. Big Three specializes in providing welding services and equipment to the oil industry. In fact, it amounts to 10 percent of Big Three's business, but that part of the business is currently down. Big Three Industries' symbol on the New York Stock Exchange is BIG. BIG's cogenerating gas plant at Bayport, Texas, is just now being completed at a cost of $100 million, and that may help it live up to the nickname. Meanwhile, the company has been actively buying back its own stock.

BORDEN, INC.

Gail Borden, the company's founder, invented the dehydrated meat biscuit, for which he was given a gold medal by England's Queen Victoria. The company's subsequent food products (which actually began with Borden's condensed milk) have been considerably more appealing. At one time, Elsie the cow was the symbol for the predominantly dairy-oriented Borden line. But she hardly fits today's Borden, which is also in the chemicals business in a big way, deriving about one-third of its profits from that field. Not that Borden has deserted food — you can buy its food products under many brand names (in addition to Borden's): Cremette, Bama, Cracker Jack (500 million boxes a year), Campfire, Drake's, Eagle, Kava, Luxury, None Such, Old London, ReaLemon, Snow's, Wise, and Wyler's.

BRISTOL-MYERS

Buspar is not an elegant name, but the folks at Bristol-Myers hope it will be doing beautiful things for them in the near future. Buspar is a nonsedative tranquilizer that does not preclude drinking for the person who takes it. Nuprin is Bristol-Myers's version of ibuprofen, the new nonaspirin product which is currently gaining popularity as an over-the-counter analgesic. Cancer-fighting drugs also loom as important pharmaceuticals for this company. Nonprescription products sold by Bristol-Myers are Colace, Comtrex, Excedrin, Enfamil, Keri Lotion, Natalins, Peri-Colace, Sustagen, and Vi-Sols. It manufactures grooming aids under the names Ban, Clairesse, Clairol, Final Net, Nice 'n Easy, Short & Sassy, and Tickle. Household products are Drano, Renuzit, Vanish, and Windex.

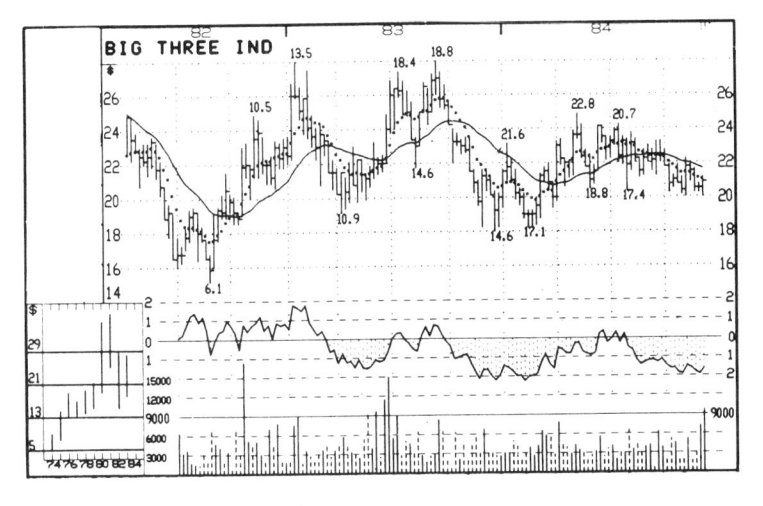

TCKR: BIG
HIGH: 24⅞
LOW: 18
PRICE: 21
EARN: 1.25
P/E: 17
DEBT: 198
YIELD: 3.8

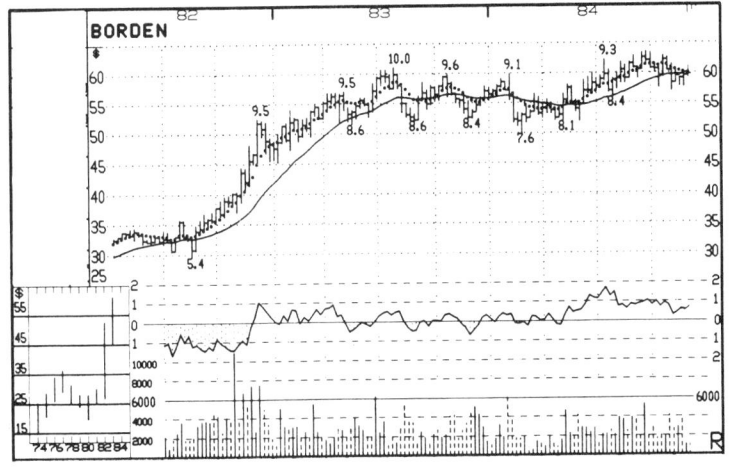

TCKR: BN
HIGH: 63½
LOW: 49⅞
PRICE: 62¼
EARN: 6.73
P/E: 9
DEBT: 358
YIELD: 4.4

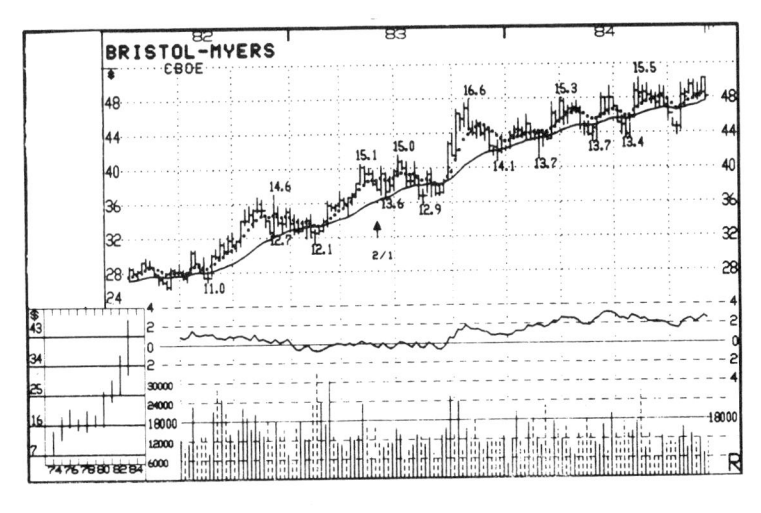

TCKR: BMY
HIGH: 50⅜
LOW: 40¾
PRICE: 48½
EARN: 3.35
P/E: 14
DEBT: 90.6
YIELD: 3.3

BROWN GROUP

Brown makes shoes for men and women (two-thirds of company sales are women's models) under the brands Air Step, Buskens, Connie, De Liso, Fanfares, Footworks, Levi's Shoes and Boots, Life Stride, Marquise, Naturalizer, Palter, Regal, and Wildcats. And there's Buster Brown: Look for them in there, too. "Connie," "Fanfares," "Naturalizer," and "Regal" are names of Brown's retail chains, too, as are B&F, De Young, Faflik, Famous Footwear, Shoeland, and Wetherby-Kayser. In addition, the company operates several specialty apparel retail chains, including more than 300 Cloth World outlets. Brown also makes a variety of sporting equipment. In recent years, management has been pacing the floor over competition from shoe imports. So far, the response has consisted of installing computer-assisted production systems, cutting costs substantially.

BROWNING-FERRIS INDUSTRIES

This company takes it away—waste, that is. Solid or liquid, from any source, Browning-Ferris will find a way to remove and possibly recycle it. The company can often collect residential garbage more cheaply than municipal sanitation departments, thus garnering Browning-Ferris many contracts. Commercial and industrial solid wastes, however, constitute the bulk of the business—business stretching over four continents. Two years ago Browning-Ferris bought CECOS International, which substantially increased its exposure in the chemical wastes area. Down the road a piece, some big profits may be in the picture from a recently launched joint project with Air Products & Chemicals: plants that burn waste and produce energy at the same tme.

BURLINGTON NORTHERN

It's the biggest rail system in the United States, operating over almost 30,000 miles of track in half of this country and Canada. Coal shipping operations have recently felt a competitive push, but since 80 percent of Burlington's profits still come from rail shipments, the company can be expected to make sure that the coal situation doesn't get out of hand. This company may have been working on the railroad, but it has not fallen prey to tunnel vision. Its Meridian Land and Timber Co. presides over almost fifteen billion tons of coal deposits, BN Transport is its trucking services firm, and its Plum Creek Timber Co. owns 1.5 million acres of forest. In 1983, Burlington purchased El Paso Co., which got the railroad into the oil and gas business. Burlington stock was split 2-for-1 last year.

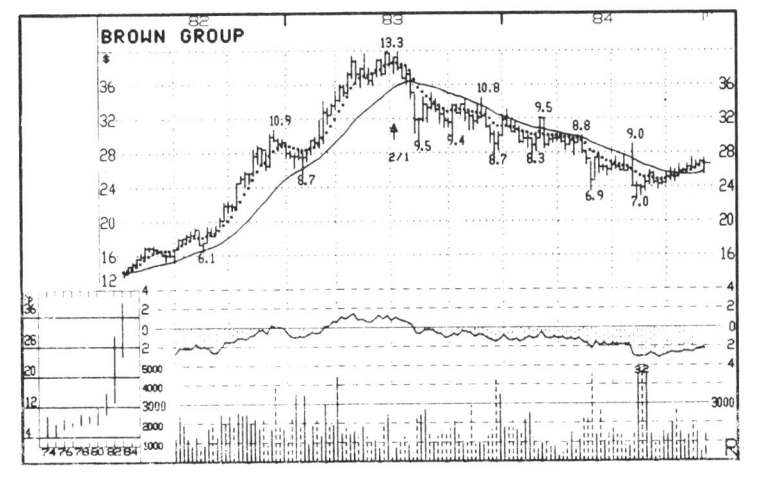

TCKR: BG
HIGH: 33
LOW: 22¾
PRICE: 26⅛
EARN: 3.23
P/E: 8
DEBT: 68.8
YIELD: 5.2

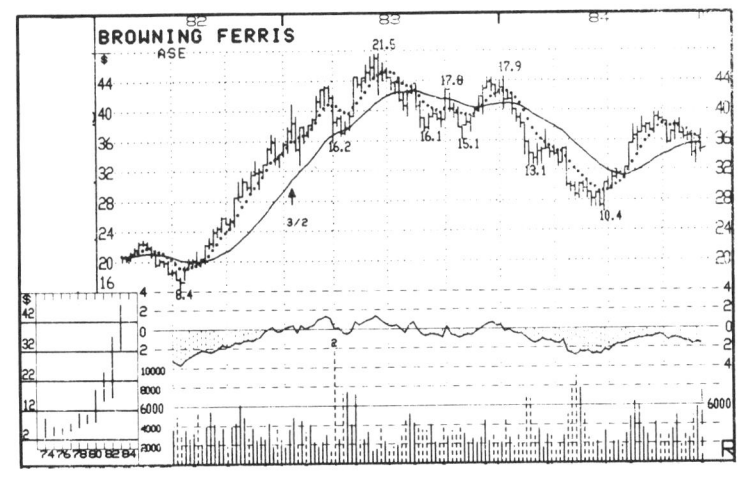

TCKR: BFI
HIGH: 44½
LOW: 26½
PRICE: 33⅞
EARN: 2.54
P/E: 13
DEBT: 116
YIELD: 3.2

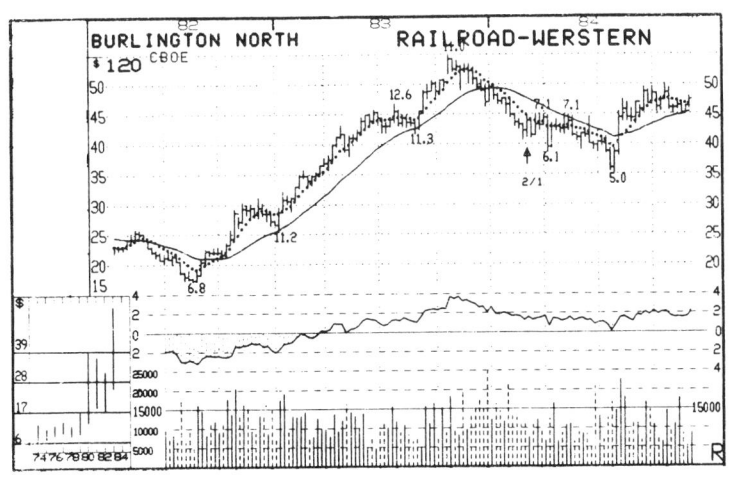

TCKR: BNI
HIGH: 50¾
LOW: 35
PRICE: 46¾
EARN: 7.07
P/E: 7
DEBT: 2250
YIELD: 2.1

111

C 3, INC.

This company may sound like a character from *Star Wars*, but 95 percent of its sales come from helping the United States government with its computer problems. C3, which has an excellent track record of garnering good government contracts (last year management feasted on one that could ultimately bring in as much as $73 million), takes currently available computer equipment and configures it with other hardware and customized software for particular applications. C3 also trains employees, maintains the systems, and manufactures computers through their Micro Products division. In both 1982 and 1984 C3 was briefly suspended from government contracts while various alleged improprieties were investigated.

CENTEL CORP.

Centel, which used to be Central Telephone & Utilities Corporation, provides phone service to over 200,000 customers in the Midwest, Florida, Nevada, North Carolina, Texas, and Virginia. It also sells electricity to 150,000 customers in Colorado and Kansas. From this solid base Centel has been branching out into business communications, security systems, and cable television (it now has about 250,000 subscribers, many of whom pay for premium channels). Cellular radio telephone is a field that could provide future growth for Centel. The company is cash rich and ready to take advantage of any potential acquisitons that might come over the wire.

CHRIS-CRAFT INDUSTRIES

This company has a minor oil and gas operation, and its plastics division turns out a variety of products which account for about one-fourth of Chris-Craft's sales and profits. But Chris-Craft's profit picture looks best when viewed through a cathode ray tube, because the company's main business is television. Through controlling interests in BHC, Inc., and United Television, Inc., it has five VHF stations and one in the UHF range. Chris-Craft's earnings almost doubled last year because United Television's profits were consolidated with its parent company's. Also in 1984, through a complicated exchange of stock, Chris-Craft acquired a 25 percent interest in the troubled Warner Communications; losses from the Warner interests may mean tax credits for Chris-Craft.

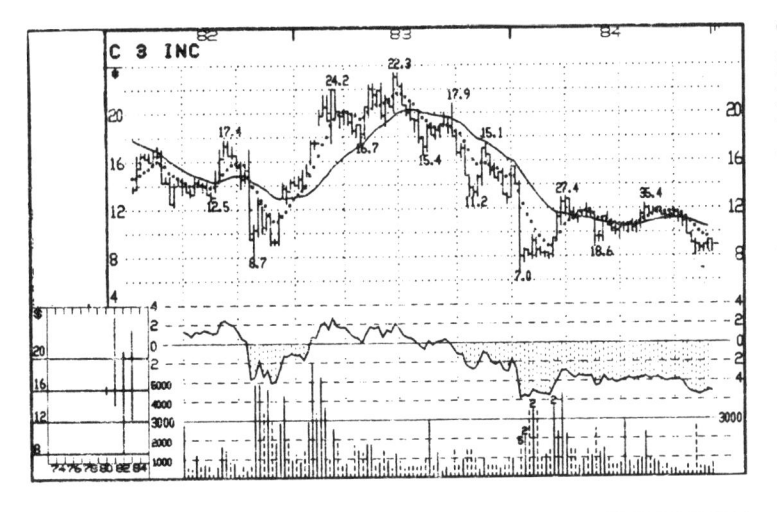

TCKR: CEE
HIGH: 15½
LOW: 6¾
PRICE: 7⅞
EARN: 0.27
P/E: 29
DEBT: 1.63
YIELD: —

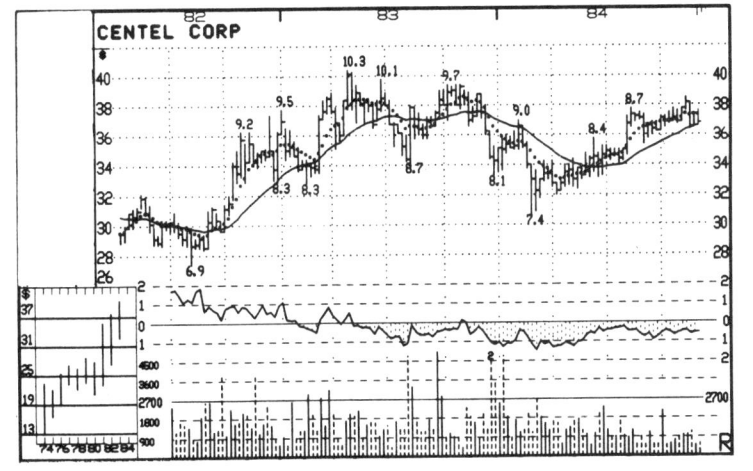

TCKR: CNT
HIGH: 38½
LOW: 30⅝
PRICE: 36⅜
EARN: 4.38
P/E: 8
DEBT: 785
YIELD: 6.4

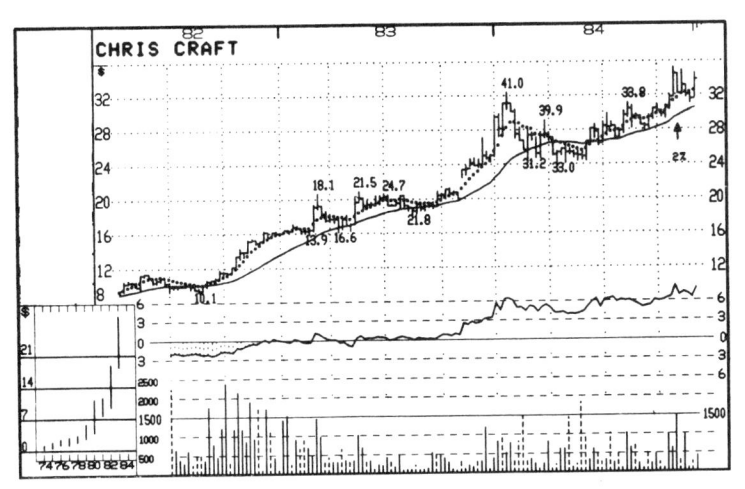

TCKR: CCN
HIGH: 35¼
LOW: 24⅝
PRICE: 33⅜
EARN: d1.84
P/E: d
DEBT: 259
YIELD: 1.4

CIRCUS CIRCUS ENTERPRISES

Party! Party! is this firm's business. The house specialty for its Nevada hotels and casinos is a sure-fire gimmick — free circus acts to draw the crowds. That and cheap food attract a large middle-class clientele, which gives them the volume Circus Circus depends on. There is little gambling in the company boardroom: The whole operation is carefully planned and well managed. In addition to a hotel in Las Vegas and one in Reno, each of which has an occupancy rate pleasantly close to 100 percent, there are two other smaller casino operations, including one called Slots-A-Fun, and another hotel in Laughlin, Nevada. All Circus Circus locations are due for considerable expansion soon, and there is talk of a move east, possibly to the boardwalk in Atlantic City.

COCA-COLA

The first bottle of Coke was consumed in 1886, and this company is delighted to announce that it would take longer than an average working day for all the Coke ever drunk since then to pour over Niagara Falls. (The people of the state of Georgia, where the company is headquartered, drink about twice as much Coke as any similar-sized group anywhere.) What they won't tell you is what's in the magic syrup that's made them the number one soft drink company in the world. Since 1899, the syrup has been sold to local distributors, who bottle it and get it into the stores. The Coke family includes: Diet Coke, Fanta, Fresca, Hi-C, Mellow Yellow, Ramblin' Root Beer, and Sprite. If you're health conscious you're more likely to drink the company's Minute Maid orange juice, Bright & Early, or Snow Crop Five Alive beverages. About half of Coca-Cola's operating income comes from abroad, and for fun, it owns Columbia Pictures.

COLECO INDUSTRIES

ColecoVision, the company's video game system, was dealt a near-fatal blow when that industry all but keeled over. Their Adam computer — letter-quality printer included — which was supposed to grab a healthy share of the home computer market, has been plagued by quality-control problems and just plain lack of consumer interest. It may even be moribund by the time you read this. The company is also heavy on short-term borrowing. *But*, Cabbage Patch Kids are still a phenomenon, and as long as that continues, Coleco will remain in the black.

CIRCUS CIRCUS ENT. — NYSE

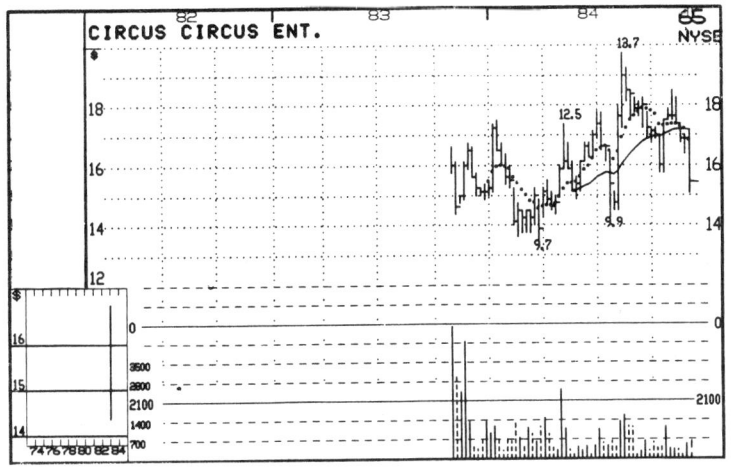

TCKR: CIR
HIGH: 19¾
LOW: 13½
PRICE: 16½
EARN: 1.41
P/E: 12
DEBT: 243
YIELD: —

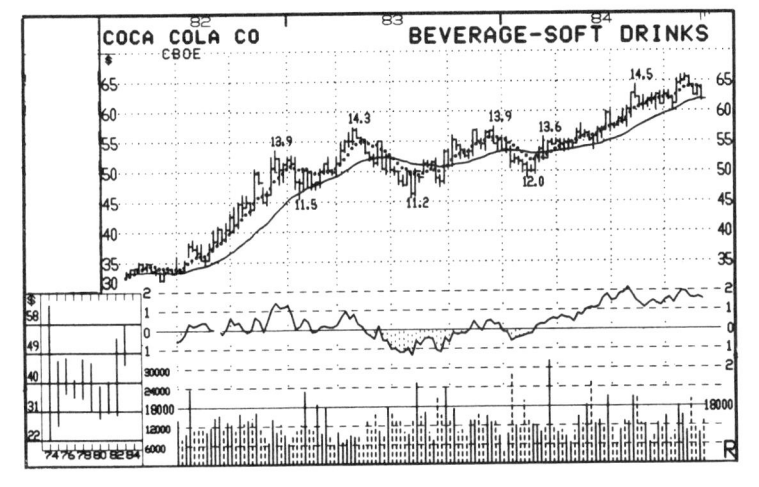

COCA COLA CO — BEVERAGE-SOFT DRINKS — CBOE

TCKR: KO
HIGH: 66
LOW: 49
PRICE: 60⅞
EARN: 4.67
P/E: 13
DEBT: 820
YIELD: 4.5

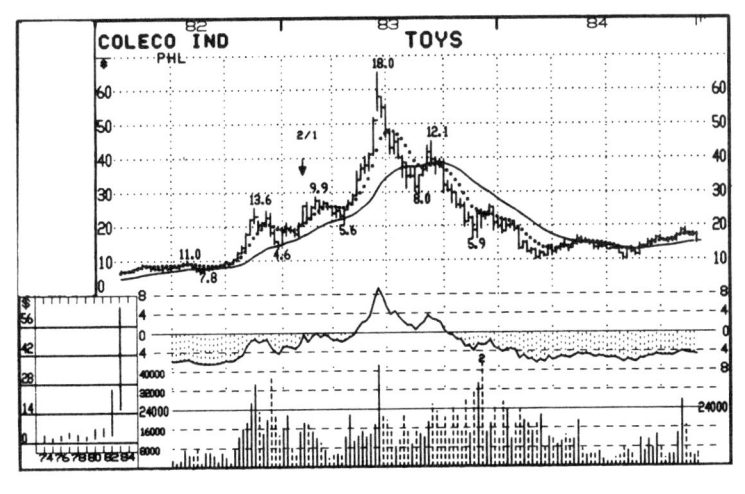

COLECO IND — TOYS — PHL

TCKR: CLO
HIGH: 26¼
LOW: 9⅝
PRICE: 15
EARN: d1.37
P/E: d
DEBT: 129
YIELD: —

COMMODORE INTERNATIONAL

Commodore started as a typewriter manufacturer in 1958, and today it's tops in sales of home computers. In the late 70s its PET line of personal computers was part of the small-machine vanguard, along with Apple and Radio Shack products. Commodore's VIC-20 was the first full-keyboard machine for under $200 (today it's under $100), and its Commodore 64, a 64K machine that got rave reviews and currently sells for about $200, really put the company on top. Commodore has been criticized for relying to much on the model 64, so several new models are in the hopper. There has also been turmoil in the executive suite: CEO Jack Trameiel left last year to try to salvage a badly bruised Atari. Commodore stock has split five times in the last six years.

COMMONWEALTH EDISON

Commonwealth was once part of a shady financial pyramid, in the early days of the Federal Power Commission, when regulation was lax. Today this utility, which serves eight million customers in Chicago and northern Illinois, is very much regulated. No other utility has done as well with nuclear power, or derived more of its power from the atom (70 percent by the end of the decade is its goal). But the Atomic Safety and Licensing Board's delay of a permit for the utility's Byron Unit 1 nuclear plant because of quality control problems has already cost Commonwealth about $100 million.

COMMUNITY PSYCHIATRIC CENTERS

This company may well be in a business whose time — financially — has finally come. Corporate medical plans are increasingly covering hospitalization for mental illness, and it is from that source, rather than Medicare (less than 12 percent of revenues), that growth in Community's business is likely to come. Community owns twenty psychiatric hospitals, seven of them in California. It also owns about forty-five kidney dialysis centers, where the outlook is also sanguine. Community Psychiatric Centers has been constructing new facilities at a steady pace. By the end of this year it will have doubled the amount of beds that were available at their psychiatric facilities in 1982 and will have achieved similar increases at the dialysis centers.

COMMODORE INTL LTD (PHL)

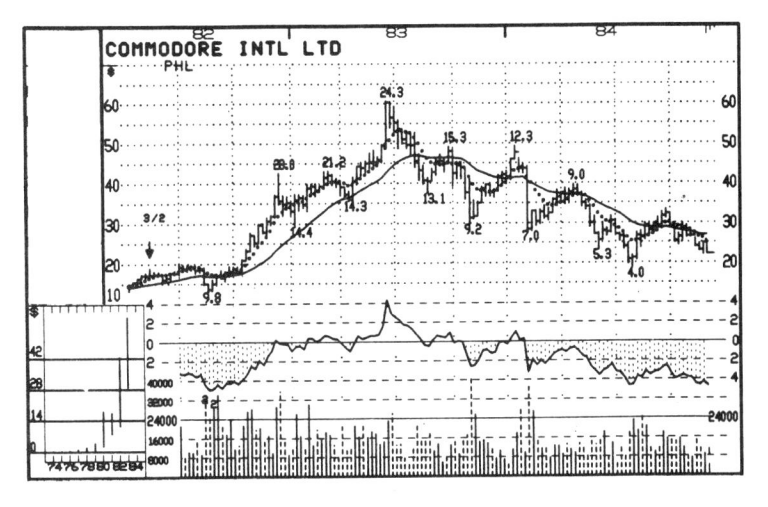

TCKR: CBU
HIGH: 49¾
LOW: 17¾
PRICE: 19¼
EARN: 4.77
P/E: 4
DEBT: 77.3
YIELD: —

COMMONWEALTH ED (CBOE)

TCKR: CWE
HIGH: 28⅞
LOW: 21½
PRICE: 27¾
EARN: 4.26
P/E: 7
DEBT: 5619
YIELD: 11.0

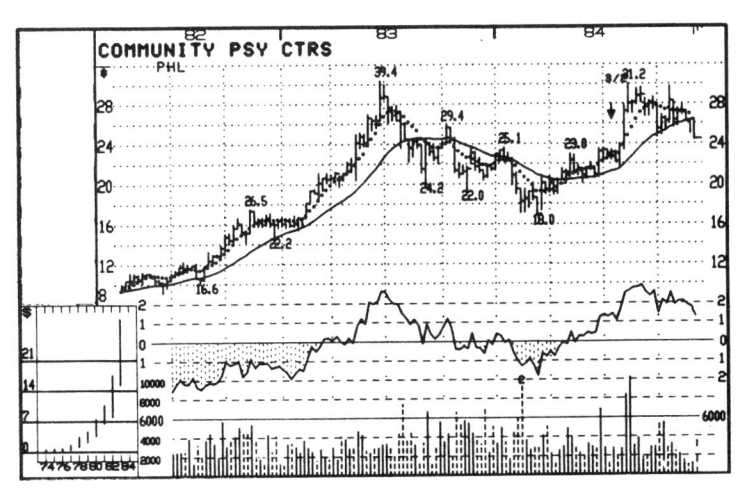

COMMUNITY PSY CTRS (PHL)

TCKR: CMY
HIGH: 30
LOW: 16⅞
PRICE: 24⅜
EARN: 1.14
P/E: 21
DEBT: 21.2
YIELD: 1.0

COMPUTER SCIENCES

This corporation plays middleman between hardware and software manufacturers and customers who need computer systems designed for specific applications. About three-fourths of its revenue is derived from systems sales; two-thirds of total revenue comes from sales to the federal government. Computer Sciences' service division does tax preparation, and it provides management assistance to hospitals through its Infocare system. Infonet, the company's time-sharing network, has not been faring well, because customers have been buying their own mini- and personal computers.

COMPUTERVISION CORP.

The fully automated factory is one in which computers assist humans from drawing board to finished product. Computer-aided design and computer-aided manufacturing, or CAD/CAM as that process is known, is Computervision's product. Its customers range from the aerospace industry to utilities, and the company sells them packages—turnkey systems of hardware and software configured for specific applications. Medusa, one of its more important systems, is the result of Computervision's partnership with Prime Computer and is based on Digital Equipment's VAX machines. Computervision has recently enlarged its sales force and is riding a surge of capital spending in the American economy. And the 32-bit CAD/CAM system it introduced two years ago has done well. But a patent-infringement suit involving a $40 million damage claim against the company has, as of this writing, yet to be resolved.

CONSOLIDATED EDISON

"Dig we must..." Generations of New Yorkers have known that slogan as an indication that Con Ed crews were out and about, making repairs under the Big Apple's street. Cynics have seen it as a reminder that this utility, with its high rates, has always seemed poised for another deep expedition into the consumer's pocket. The fairness of Con Ed's rates is subjective; however, what can't be denied is that Con Ed weathered some tough times in the 70s and has emerged in good shape in this decade. The utility, which serves Westchester County as well as New York City with electricity, gas, and steam, derives 50 percent of its power from oil and 20 percent from its Indian Point nuclear plant. Its power sources should be sufficient into the next decade.

COMPUTER SCIENCES

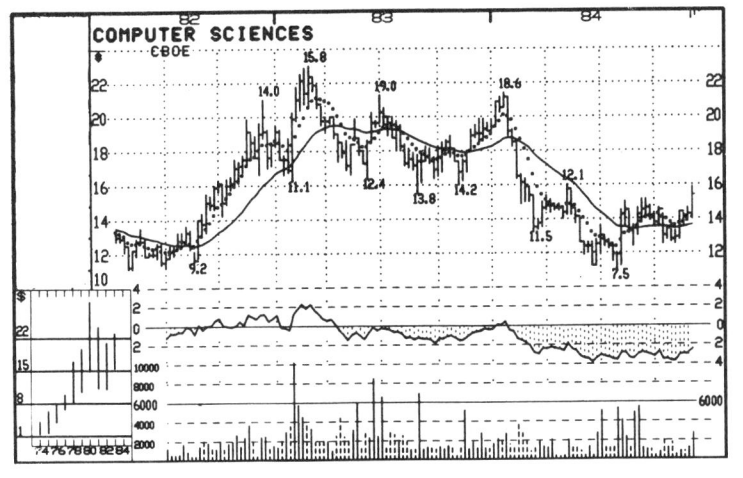

TCKR: CSC
HIGH: 21 3/8
LOW: 11
PRICE: 15 1/2
EARN: 1.40
P/E: 11
DEBT: 39.9
YIELD: —

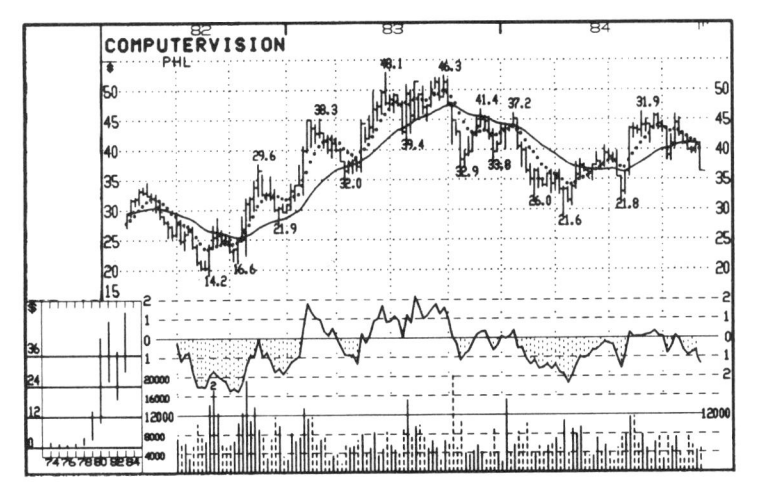

COMPUTERVISION

TCKR: CVN
HIGH: 46 1/4
LOW: 29
PRICE: 36 1/8
EARN: 1.16
P/E: 31
DEBT: 31.7
YIELD: —

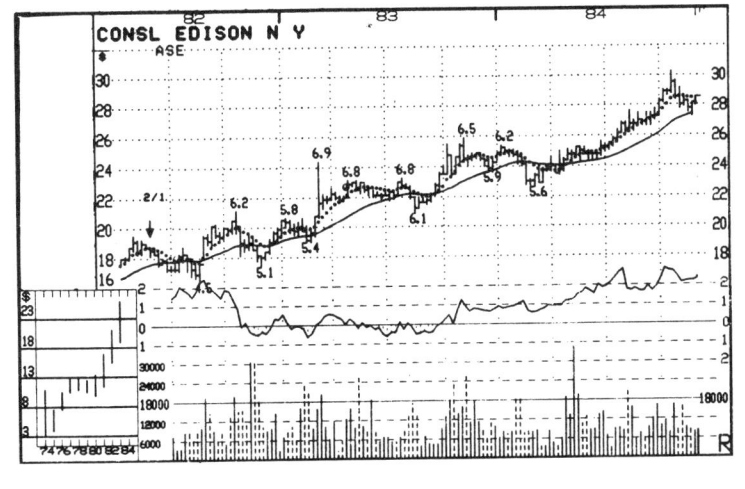

CONSL EDISON N Y

TCKR: ED
HIGH: 30 1/4
LOW: 22 5/8
PRICE: 28 3/4
EARN: 4.40
P/E: 7
DEBT: 2485
YIELD: 7.4

CONSOLIDATED FOODS

There have been times when this company resembled the kitchen sink. In the 70s, in fact, buying and selling companies became such a mania for them that Consolidated made over 140 such transactions. If you can find a Fuller Brush man these days, he works for Consolidated; other products are Electrolux vacuum cleaners, Hanes underwear, and L'Eggs hosiery. Lawson stores and Lyon's restaurants are also Consolidated operations. But processed foods are still the mainstay. Better-known brands include Sara Lee as well as C&C and Shasta soft drinks. Its Foodservice caters to institutions.

CONTROL DATA

This firm's founder, William Norris, was the general manager at Sperry Rand's Univac division, which built and marketed the first commercial computer. Norris carved out a niche for his new company by concentrating on huge machines that even most big institutions couldn't afford to buy, and renting them time on his computers. Control Data still does data processing for a variety of industries, although the time-sharing business isn't what it used to be. They also sell large-scale computer systems, such as the CYBER series, but production of computer disk drives has been stopped. PLATO, a computerized educational system, never really caught fire. Control Data's Commerical Credit Corporation is important in the field of financial services.

CRAY RESEARCH

Cray stands almost alone in an area that is the highest of high-tech: the realm of super-computers. Mass production is out when your product can cost as much as $11 million and there are only sixty-five of them in place throughout the world (about a fifth are rented). At that price, Cray's machines are not used just for any kind of computing — applications most often involve some branch of physical science, such as oil geology or weather prediction. (The company also sells a number of models in lower price ranges.) Cray has installed more than half of all super-computers currently online. That's a good market share in any business, although the American auto industry also dominated *its* field until competition from the East set them back. The same thing could happen here. Is that a rising sun on the horizon?

CONSL FOODS

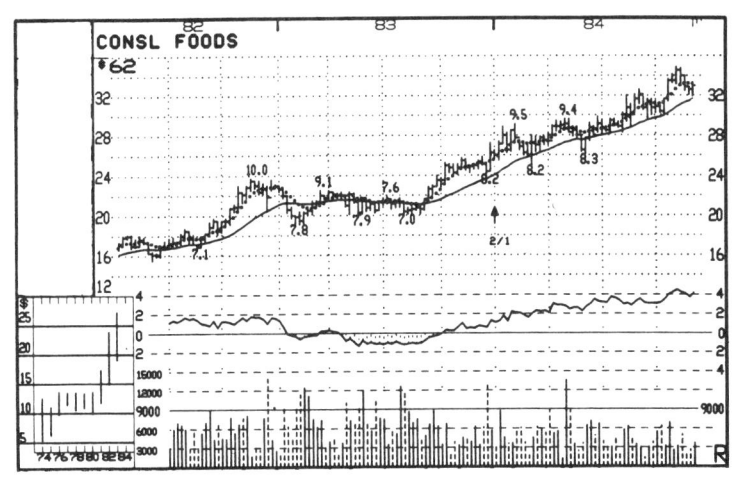

TCKR: CFD
HIGH: 34 7/8
LOW: 24 1/4
PRICE: 31 5/8
EARN: 3.32
P/E: 10
DEBT: 359
YIELD: 4.6

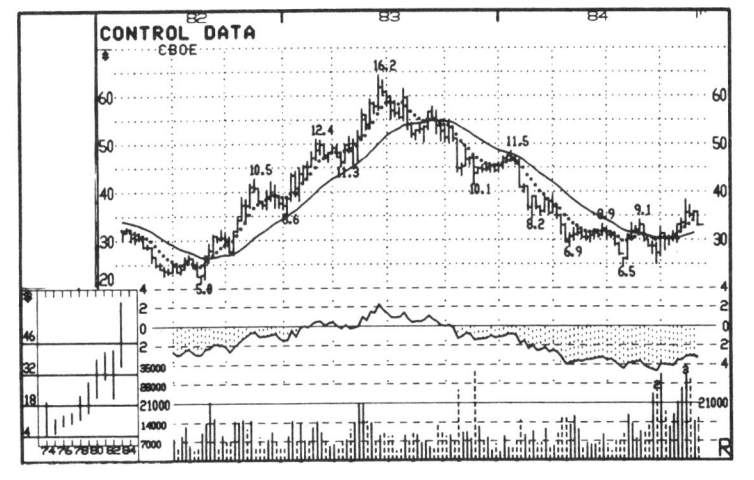

CONTROL DATA CBOE

TCKR: CDA
HIGH: 48 1/2
LOW: 24 3/8
PRICE: 35 1/2
EARN: 2.79
P/E: 13
DEBT: 5722
YIELD: 1.9

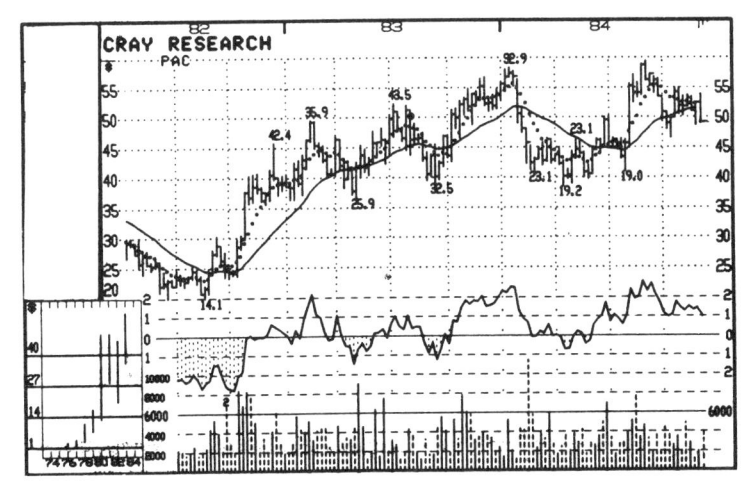

CRAY RESEARCH PAC

TCKR: CYR
HIGH: 59 3/8
LOW: 38 1/2
PRICE: 48 1/2
EARN: 3.29
P/E: 15
DEBT: 32.1
YIELD: . —

DATAPOINT CORP.

This company's products are based on the theory that any business information processing is best done in the place where that information is to be used. In computer terminology this is known as "distributed processing," and one way office employees do this is through the "electronic workstation." Datapoint manufactures many of the computerized components that make up a workstation, *and* the network that enables workstations to communicate with one another and access data centrally stored in a mainframe computer. But there are problems. Datapoint's ARC (Attached Resource Computer) network is installed at 5,000 locations, but customers have insisted that the network be compatible with computer equipment made by other manufacturers. Datapoint has complied, but now must improve the rest of its product mix to insure that some of it ends up being connected to its own network. Datapoint's current automated office software (PRO-VISTA) has been rated fairly easy to learn, an improvement over previous programs.

DEERE & CO.

The biggest farm machinery company in the world was lucky not to have been plowed under by the recent hard times in its industry—management just about moved mountains to keep costs down. Deere also makes machinery that literally *can* move mountains, as well as making garden and lawn equipment. A fifth of the company's sales are abroad, and there are factories in several European countries and South Africa. The John Deere Credit Company finances sales of the parent company's machines.

DETROIT EDISON

Detroit Edison's revenues come almost exclusively from the sale of electricity, and southeastern Michigan is its market — which means that business is highly sensitive to the health of the auto industry. It's a tribute to Detroit Edison's management that the company is in good shape, despite the extended bleak period for automobile sales a few years ago. They've also met adversity in a local regulatory commission that has kept the rate reins tight. Detroit Edison's capital expenditures are easing off as the company ends twenty years of intense construction. Less than 10 percent of its power is derived from nuclear fuel; important in that respect is its Fermi 2 plant, which cost $3.5 billion to bring on line.

DATAPOINT CP.
CBOE

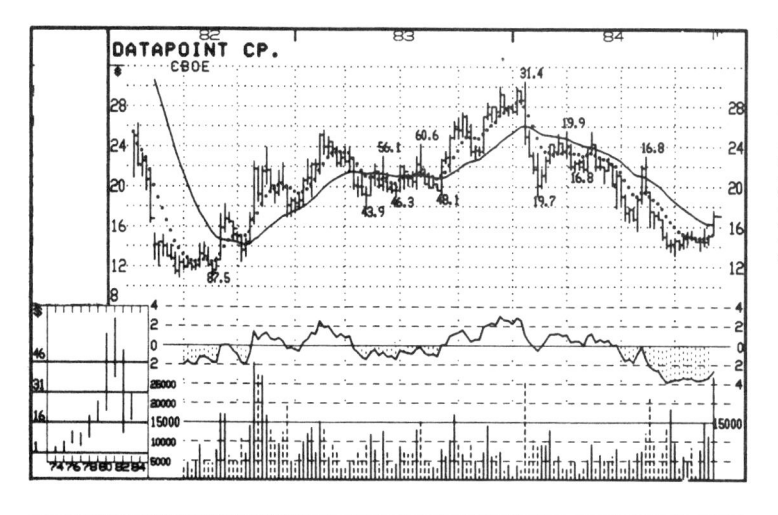

TCKR: DPT
HIGH: 30½
LOW: 13⅛
PRICE: 18
EARN: 1.29
P/E: 14
DEBT: 114
YIELD: —

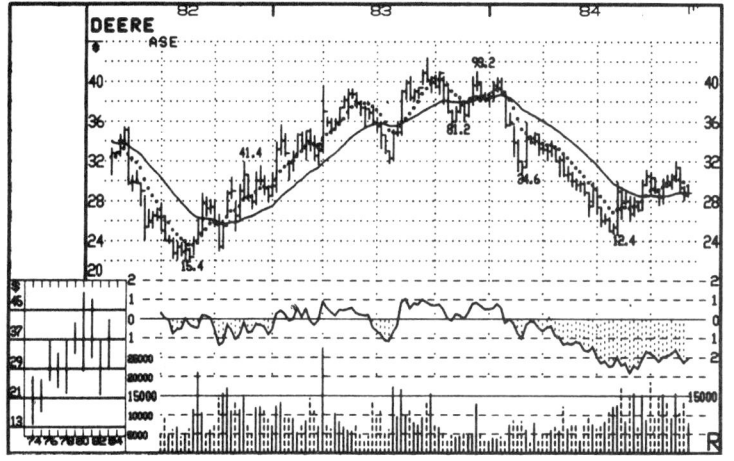

DEERE
ASE

TCKR: DE
HIGH: 40⅜
LOW: 24⅝
PRICE: 29
EARN: 1.47
P/E: 20
DEBT: 1102
YIELD: 3.4

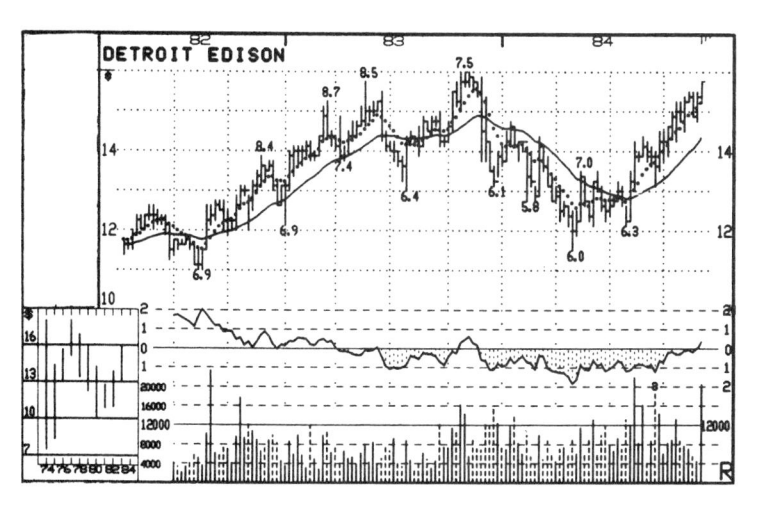

DETROIT EDISON

TCKR: DTE
HIGH: 15¾
LOW: 11½
PRICE: 15
EARN: 2.22
P/E: 7
DEBT: 3560
YIELD: 11.0

DIGITAL EQUIPMENT

This company pioneered the minicomputer, and that is its glory—as well as the source of its present problem. The functions of that venerable little machine are increasingly being performed by personal computers and by minis that are almost small mainframes. Digital's VAX line of minis has traditionally dominated its field, but Venus, the new top of that line, will have to fight for supremacy against similar products from newer firms. The Rainbow, Digital's answer to the IBM PC, has been the victim of some halfhearted and not terribly well-thought-out marketing. Nor has the company grabbed a firm foothold in the office automation field. The authors of *In Search of Excellence* singled out Digital as one corporation where excellence could be found, but present management has yet to show that they can maintain technological innovation *and* sell to customers who are more often general managers than technical personnel.

DOW CHEMICAL

While it struggled to overcome considerable negative publicity in the past decade—it made napalm and Agent Orange—Dow was fighting its way into second place among chemical companies, just behind du Pont. Dow's specialty products are its most profitable; industrial chemicals bring its highest sales. Profits and sales are about evenly divided between foreign and domestic operations. Last year Dow sold one-half of its Dowell energy services company to Schlumberger. Consumer brands include Dow Bathroom Cleaner, Handi-Wrap, Saran Wrap, and Ziploc plastic bags.

DREYFUS CORP.

At Dreyfus corporate headquarters, the feelings are often mutual. In early 1984 about 1.3 million investors thought highly enough of the managers of the various Dreyfus funds to entrust them with billions of their dollars. Dreyfus Liquid Assets, a small investor-oriented fund which has been spurring Dreyfus growth for a decade, began last year with $7.7 billion worth of assets. The Dreyfus Fund, which deals in stocks, is one of the top mutal funds in the country; other Dreyfus funds invest in money markets, tax-exempt bonds, small growth companies, and a variety of private and government debt obligations. The company bought what is now the Dreyfus Consumer Bank in New Jersey in 1982, and last year Dreyfus acquired Hartford Life and Annuity Insurance.

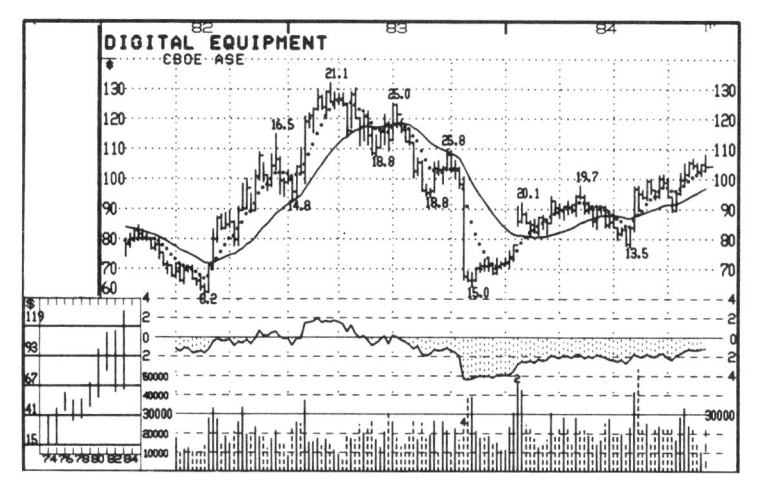

TCKR: DEC
HIGH: 108⅛
LOW: 68¼
PRICE: 103¾
EARN: 7.90
P/E: 13
DEBT: 841
YIELD: —

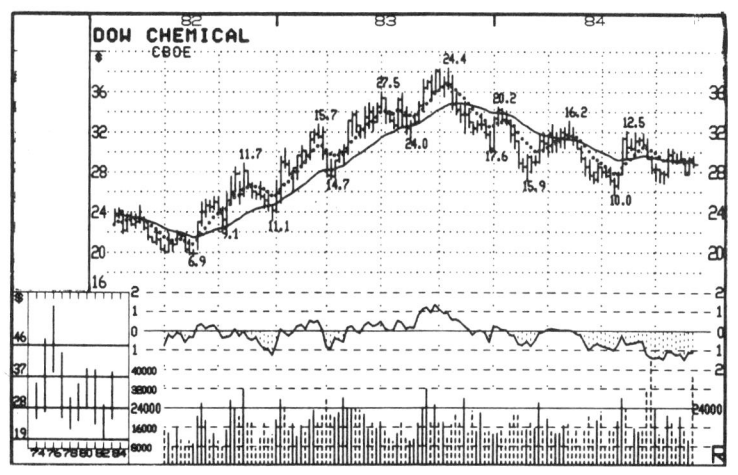

TCKR: DOW
HIGH: 34½
LOW: 25¾
PRICE: 27½
EARN: 2.80
P/E: 10
DEBT: 2529
YIELD: 6.5

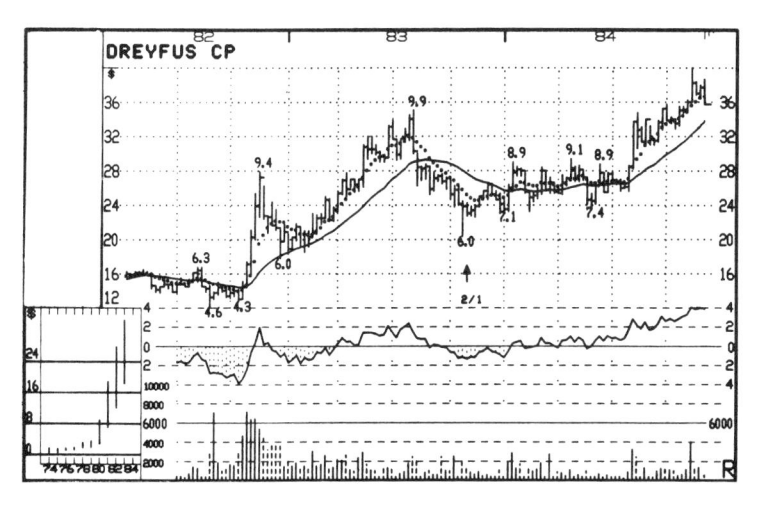

TCKR: DRY
HIGH: 40
LOW: 23¼
PRICE: 37½
EARN: 3.53
P/E: 11
DEBT: 83.6
YIELD: 1.3

DUN & BRADSTREET

This is a company capable of doing well even when times are bad, when credit information becomes a hot commodity. This data is its stock-in-trade, although the stress in recent years has been not only on information but also on how it has been stored and retrieved; that has meant computers and on-line data bases. D & B's information-gathering abilities were enhanced by its 1984 purchase of Nielsen, a market research pioneer and a means by which to further penetrate the European information market. Dun & Bradstreet owns Moody's, Technical Publishing, Technical Data Resources, Reuben H. Donnelley, and National CSS. The sale of six television stations helped finance these purchases, which recently included a British information company and an insurance services company.

DU PONT

In 1981, in the biggest corporate takeover battle the country had seen, du Pont purchased Conoco, then the nation's ninth-largest oil company. Du Pont paid $7.5 billion — $4 billion of which was borrowed — and is still repaying that debt. The company still spends about $1 billion a year on research and development in the laboratories that produced Dacron, Freon, Lycra, Lucite, Mylar, nylon, Orlon, and Teflon (although lately it has been difficult to duplicate such successes). The nation's number one chemical company, du Pont does everything on a big scale. Once they owned 23 percent of General Motors, and they even built their own phone system for the 100,000 calls they handle every day.

EASTERN AIR LINES

Stockholders hope that Eastern's president, former astronaut Frank Borman, has the right stuff. For a while, it looked as though the beleaguered airline was flying on a wing and a prayer. Eastern's debt, still close to 90 percent of its capital, only recently dropped to under $2 a share. The company has reconstituted its schedule to make Kansas City its domestic hub and has induced employees to take substantially reduced wages in exchange for a say in how the company is to be run. Eastern has not paid dividends on common stock for five years.

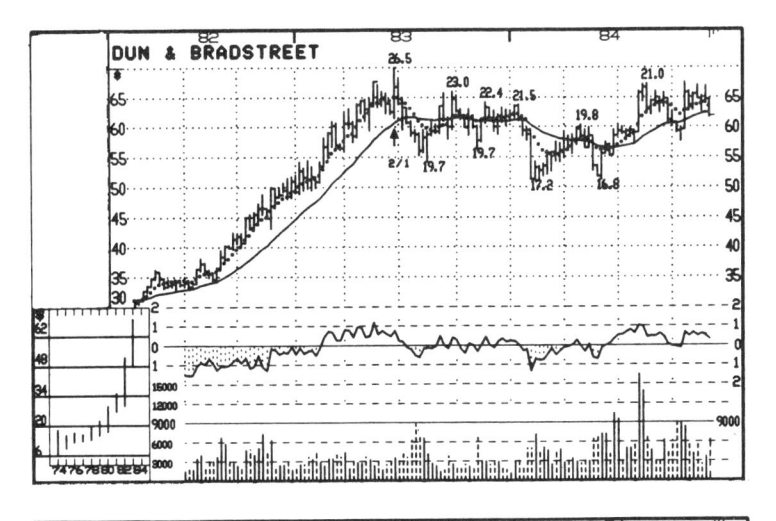

TCKR: DNB
HIGH: 67½
LOW: 51⅛
PRICE: 61½
EARN: 3.26
P/E: 19
DEBT: 22.9
YIELD: 3.1

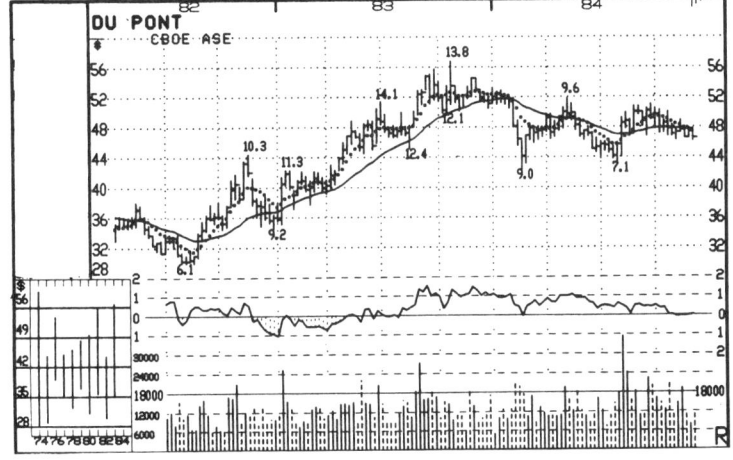

TCKR: DD
HIGH: 53¼
LOW: 42⅜
PRICE: 46¾
EARN: 6.09
P/E: 8
DEBT: 4693
YIELD: 6.4

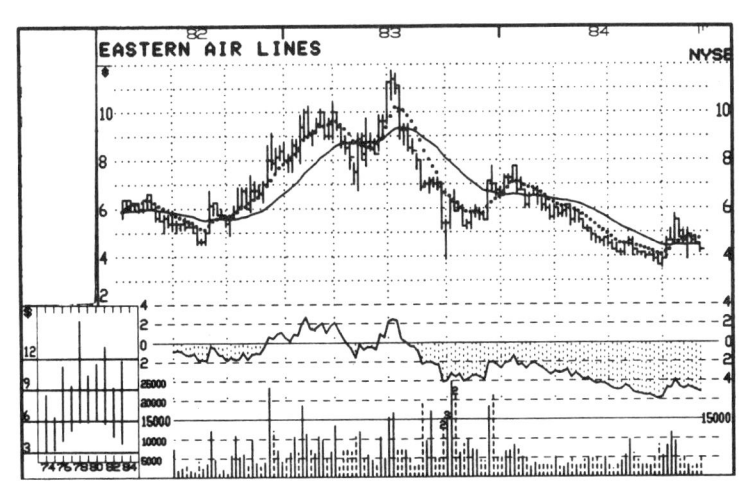

TCKR: EAL
HIGH: 7¾
LOW: 3½
PRICE: 4⅛
EARN: d3.42
P/E: d
DEBT: 2266
YIELD: —

EASTMAN KODAK

They make chemicals, plastics, and synthetics (Kodel) and these constitute a fifth of Kodak's sales. The rest comes from photography. Of that, about half comes from the movie industry, industrial photography, medical film products, copiers, and the like; the other half is derived from getting you to say "cheese." Kodak wants to sell you a camera — cheap — and for good reason: The real money is in supplies and services, film and processing. In that area, Kodak pretty much has its way. When the company said "there shall be disks," behold, there were disks. Everywhere. Nevertheless, decreased consumer spending in the recession of the early 80s, and silver speculation during the rampant inflation of a few years back took their toll. Kodak raised the price of its film and trimmed its work force. Now, the Great Yellow Father has decided to get on the computer bandwagon. Henceforth the company will make disks for mass data storage. This is to be a major division for Kodak.

EDWARDS, A.G. INC.

This holding company has not yet gone the diversification route. Edwards's business is still firmly anchored in the activity in which it first engaged in 1887: selling stocks. About 60 percent of the company's revenues comes from commissions on sales for close to 333,000 customers, approximately 90 percent of whom are individual investors. Investment banking accounts for another 15 percent of revenues. Edwards — operations are concentrated in the Midwest, Southeast and Southwest — has almost doubled its assets in the past six years. Recently the company has put increased emphasis on improving customer service by enhancing its computer facilities.

ENSERCH CORP.

Enserch runs on gas. It's Lone Star Gas Co. transports and sells the stuff in Oklahoma and Texas to more than 1.2 million customers. Enserch Exploration goes out and finds it — and oil, too. They began last year with reserves of 64 million barrels of oil and 550 billion cubic feet of gas. During the year it acquired leases covering about a million acres in the Rockies, substantially increasing the size of their operations. The parent company also sells oil field services through Pool Co.; and its Ebasco Services is an international operation selling construction and engineering services to power plants.

EASTMAN KODAK

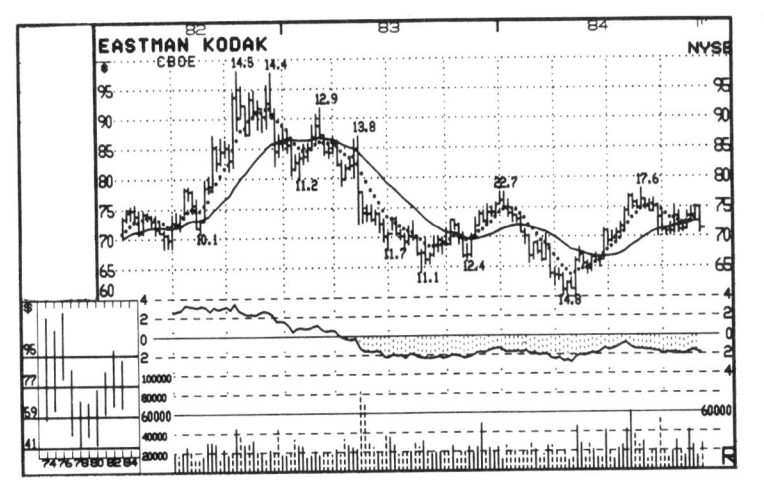

TCKR: EK
HIGH: 78
LOW: 60¼
PRICE: 70
EARN: 4.43
P/E: 16
DEBT: 341
YIELD: 4.6

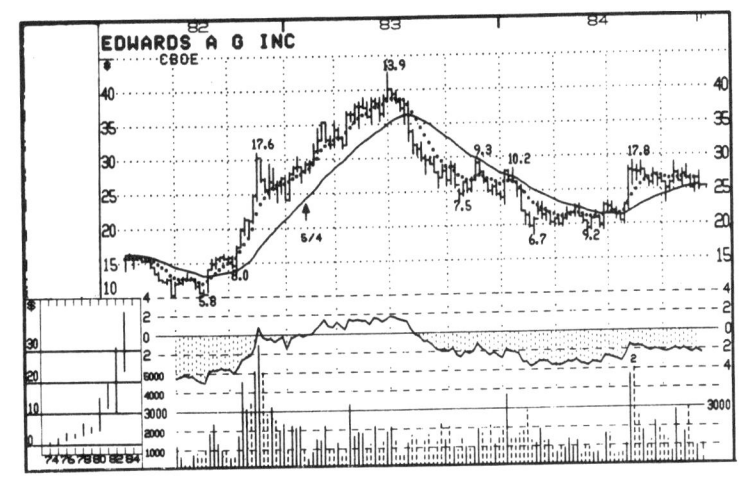

EDWARDS A G INC

TCKR: AGE
HIGH: 29⅛
LOW: 18½
PRICE: 25
EARN: 1.57
P/E: 16
DEBT: —
YIELD: 3.2

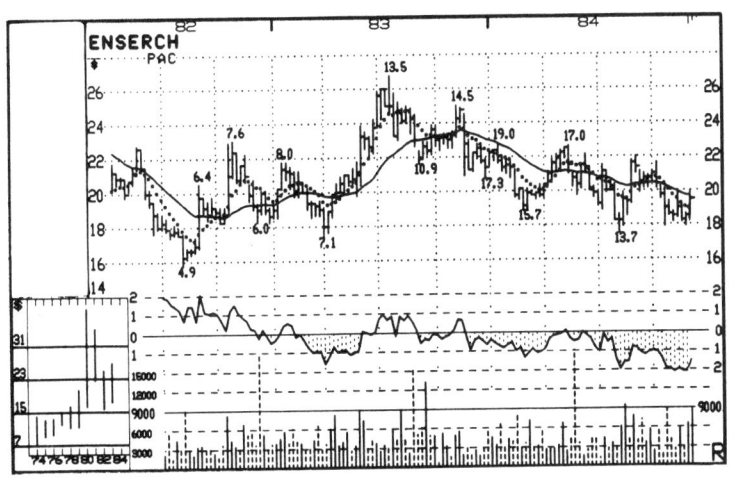

ENSERCH

TCKR: ENS
HIGH: 22¾
LOW: 17½
PRICE: 20½
EARN: 1.16
P/E: 18
DEBT: 866
YIELD: 7.8

EQUIMARK CORP.

This company holds Equibank, which lately has been a little like holding a hot potato. Poor judgment on foreign and real estate loans got this bank, formerly Western Pennsylvania National Bank, into hot water. Now Equimark is putting its wagons in a circle, and concentrating on consumer business in its own region. Equibank, which ranks 75th in the country, is under considerable pressure from Securities and Exchange Commission and the Federal Deposit Insurance Corp. to boost its capital.

EVANS PRODUCTS

This company leases 28,000 railroad freight cars and owns almost 13,000 big trucks, but does it know where it is going? A $332.5 million debt has narrowed Evans's options considerably. In 1984, in order to make a $60 million payment due on that debt, the glass fiber and shelter products divisions, which together accounted for 14 percent of the previous year's profits, were unloaded. Evans also sold the loan portfolio held by its Evans Financial Corp. But that puts the squeeze on current operating income, which must come, to a large extent, from its retail building materials business catering to the do-it-yourself trade. Evans is also in the steel casting and lumber business.

EXXON CORP.

Exxon's annual sales figures are consistently higher than most countries' gross national product. The company produces oil — two and one-half million barrels a day. Nobody produces more. It also has close to fifty billion cubic feet of gas on reserve. In addition to revolutions and terrorism, Exxon executives worry about the weather and the world economy. High temperatures and low economic indices mean "glut," a four-letter word in the corporate boardroom. A strong dollar isn't good because it hurts oil importing countries. But on the whole, fate has been kind to the company that John D. Rockefeller built. Of late, Exxon has been buying back its own stock.

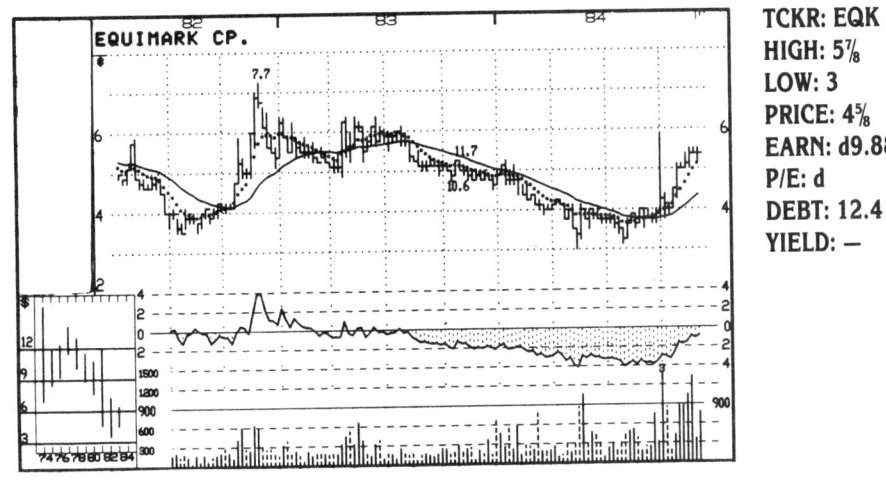

EQUIMARK CP.

TCKR: EQK
HIGH: 5⅞
LOW: 3
PRICE: 4⅝
EARN: d9.88
P/E: d
DEBT: 12.4
YIELD: —

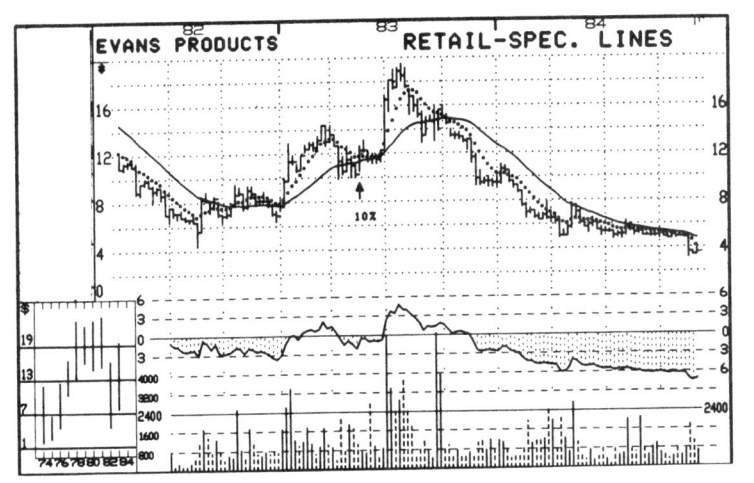

EVANS PRODUCTS — RETAIL-SPEC. LINES

TCKR: EVY
HIGH: 11
LOW: 3
PRICE: 3⅛
EARN: d6.48
P/E: d
DEBT: 44.0
YIELD: —

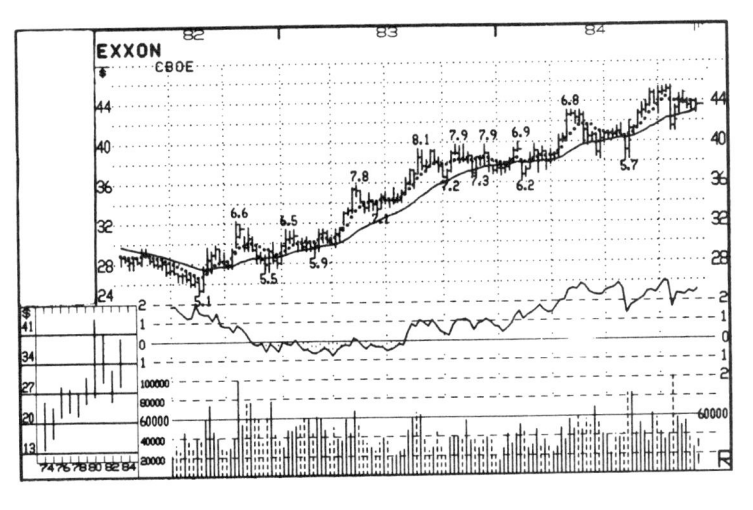

EXXON CBOE

TCKR: XON
HIGH: 45½
LOW: 36⅛
PRICE: 44⅛
EARN: 6.87
P/E: 6
DEBT: 44
YIELD: 7

FAIRFIELD COMMUNITIES

The 1983 purchase of The Florida Companies put Fairfield in the commercial real estate business. But it still has major interests in the area in which it started: building and developing a variety of residential communities. Like much of America, Fairfield has followed the sun, and concentrating on the sunbelt has built homes for those in the mid-career child-bearing years, and for the retired as well. Fairfield has lately smoothed out the peaks and valleys of the cycle endemic to its industry by putting its resources into time-sharing projects (with names like Glade, Plantation, and Sunrise Village), which now account for about one-third of Fairfield's revenues.

FEDERAL EXPRESS

Is American business deep enough into the high-tech 80s to take seriously and make frequent use of a service called Zap Mail? Federal Express executives thought so when they introduced it last year. Zap Mail involves bouncing text and charts off a satellite to produce a two-hour door-to-door delivery time. The company's traditional business, which relies on the familiar airplane and the even more familiar van, now accepts packages weighing up to 150 pounds for overnight delivery. Except for the small percentage that are trucked, all Federal Express packages are funneled to Memphis, Tennessee, where the company's 100 planes and 6,000 vans speed them to their final destinations in 500 cities in the U.S. and Canada. About a quarter of a million packages took that trip last year. Federal Express was founded in 1971 and currently does not pay dividends.

FEDERAL-MOGUL

Its business depends heavily on the fortunes of the automobile, construction equipment, and farm equipment industries. But Federal-Mogul has managed to keep its bearings despite the unpredictable performances of those businesses. In fact, Federal-Mogul not only keeps its bearings, it makes them, too. And it sells them to both OEMs (original equipment manufacturers) and the replacement market. This company also keeps industry running smoothly with its oil seals, pistons, and other diverse products of metal and rubber. Federal-Mogul management measures all its operations against the bottom line—constantly. Anything that doesn't measure up is cut loose.

FAIRFIELD COMMUNITIES

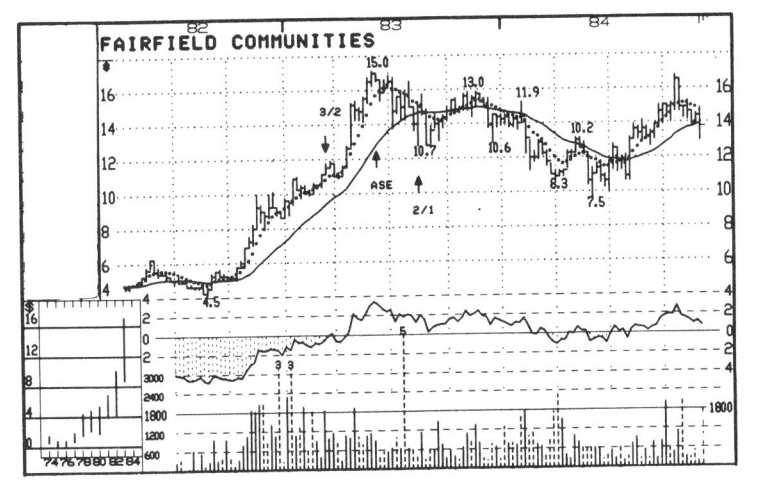

TCKR: FCI
HIGH: 16¾
LOW: 9⅝
PRICE: 13⅛
EARN: 1.64
P/E: 8
DEBT: 201
YIELD: 1.2

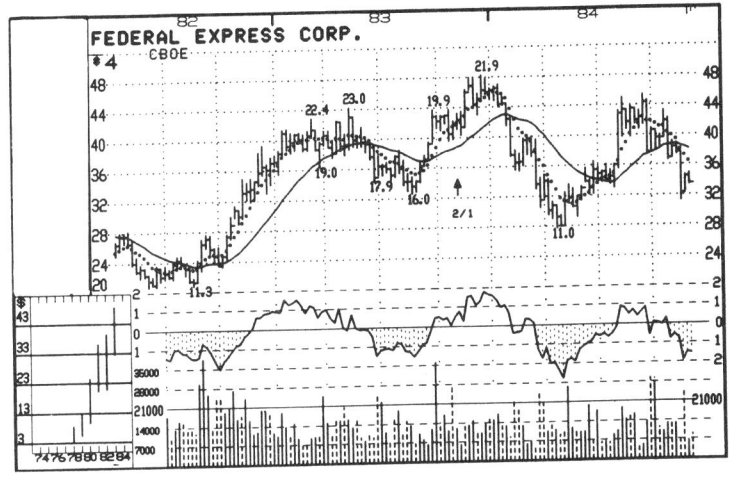

FEDERAL EXPRESS CORP.

TCKR: FDX
HIGH: 48¼
LOW: 27¾
PRICE: 33⅞
EARN: 2.07
P/E: 16
DEBT: 435
YIELD: —

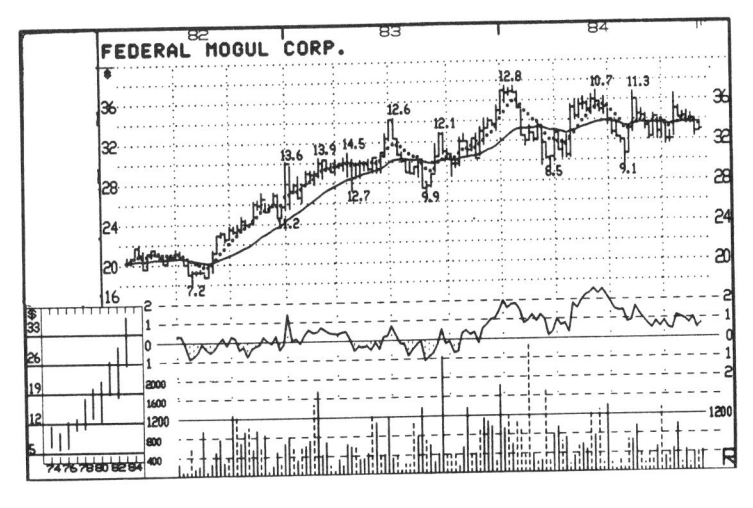

FEDERAL MOGUL CORP.

TCKR: FMO
HIGH: 37½
LOW: 29⅜
PRICE: 31⅝
EARN: 3.49
P/E: 9
DEBT: 127
YIELD: 4.8

133

FINANCIAL CORP. OF AMERICA

FCA is big, and FCA is in big trouble. It is the holding company for American Savings & Loan Association, the country's biggest S & L, which operates out of about 200 locations (150 of them in California). Real estate secured loans are its stock-in-trade, as well as secondary mortgages. SEC scrutiny of American's books, begun three years ago, resulted in a recalculation of the company's earnings last year — and that meant an $80 million loss for the first half of 1984. To increase capital, American is selling some of its more attractive assets, leaving them with a plethora of long-term mortgages, and a vested interest in lower interest rates. Financial Corp. also holds the SCA credit corporation, which deals in commercial finance.

FIRST CITY PROPERTIES

Barring any impending earthquakes in its Southern California bailiwick, First City Properties, formerly State Mutual Investors, is doing fine. First City enlarged its real estate business a few years ago with the purchase of Design-Master Homes, which gave it interests in Phoenix; the company is also active in nevada. it has been edging into the condominium business, and its mortgage loan portfolio is substantial. First City's business philosophy is simple: buy and build — both business and residential projects. The coffers are full, adn First City is always looking to acquire and divest. About two-thirds of the company's stock is owned by the Samuel Belzberg group.

FIRST VIRGINIA BANKS

Drop the last letter from the name and you have the company's biggest holding, a bank that is also the state's seventh largest, with assets of about $1 billion. First Virginia holds twenty banks in all, with total assets of $2.3 billion and over 200 offices, many of them concentrated in the area near Washington D.C. Besides the flagship operation, only one of those banks has as much as $250 million in assets. About half its funds come in as time deposits; more than half go out in the form of installment loans. Subsidiaries provide a wide range of financial services. Last year First Virginia acquired four more banks. Pending legislation in Richmond would permit regional bank mergers, however, and First Virginia would be a prime target.

FINAN CP AMER.

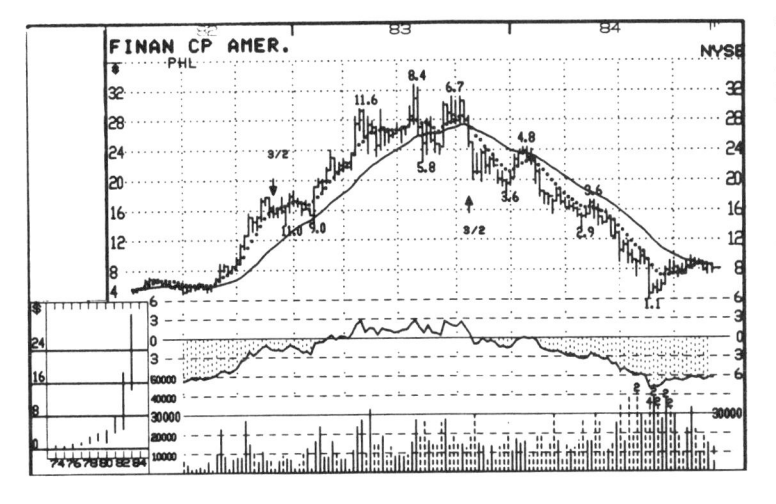

TCKR: FIN
HIGH: 24 3/8
LOW: 4
PRICE: 8
EARN: d1.09
P/E: d
DEBT: 1259
YIELD: 8.5

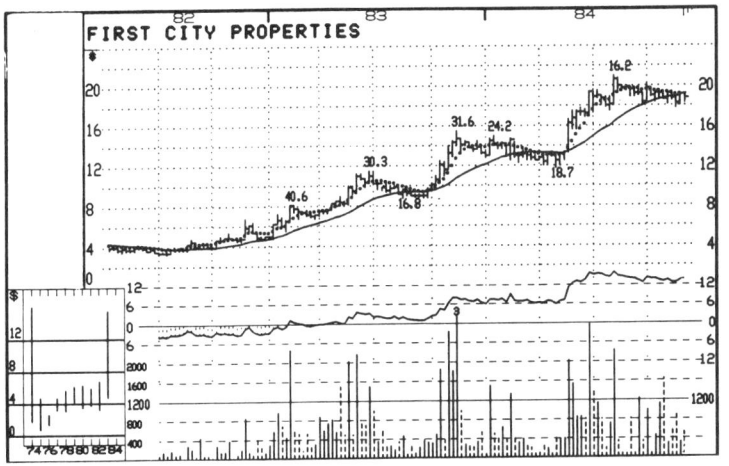

FIRST CITY PROPERTIES

TCKR: FCP
HIGH: 21
LOW: 11 3/4
PRICE: 18 3/8
EARN: 1.21
P/E: 15
DEBT: 202
YIELD: —

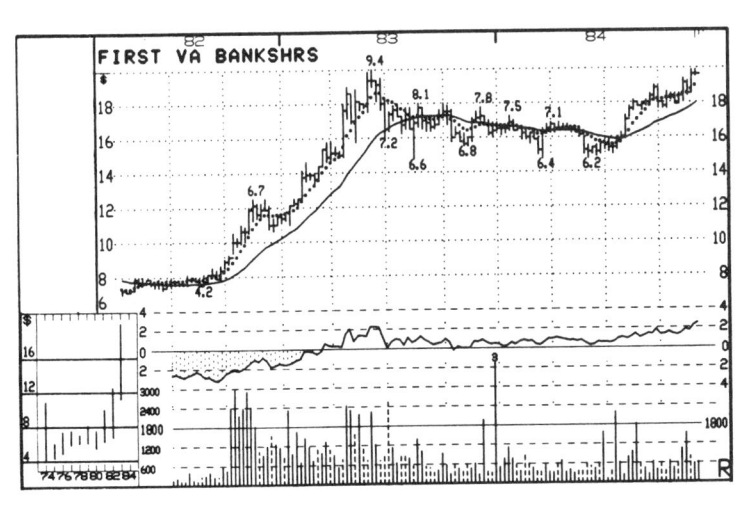

FIRST VA BANKSHRS

TCKR: FVB
HIGH: 19 7/8
LOW: 14 3/4
PRICE: 19 1/4
EARN: 2.43
P/E: 8
DEBT: 45.8
YIELD: 4.4

FLEET FINANCIAL GROUP

About 50 percent of the group's profits comes from financial services, including factoring. The centerpiece of the remainder of Fleet's business is the Fleet National Bank of Rhode Island, the state's biggest bank. Fleet Financial, which already owns 5 percent of the company that controls the Connecticut National Bank, is gearing up to cross state lines and expand banking operations into other parts of New England. Business comes down heavily on the commercial side, although the company's biggest growth opportunities now appear to be in consumer finances, which it provides in many areas outside of New England. Fleet Financial ranks third in the nation for mortgage servicing. By spreading out into a variety of financial fields, Fleet has managed to position itself to benefit from each part of the business cycle. That's what we call covering your assets!

GENERAL ELECTRIC

"It brings good things to life," as the ads say. It hasn't hurt its own stockholders, either. No newcomer to the financial services bandwagon, the company recently melded its GE Credit Corp. into the broader General Electric Financial Services, Inc., and the new group has already purchased Employers Reinsurance Corp. from Texaco for slightly more than $1 billion. The recovery of 1983–84 pulled its consumer appliance division out of the doldrums, and rising defense spending fattened company coffers. Management recently shed GE's natural resource operations and its housewares unit.

GENERAL FOODS

As American as prepackaged apple pie, General Foods has recently been reshuffling its product mix to boost sluggish earnings. On the supermarket shelf you find them in packages marked Birds Eye, Cool Whip, D-Zerta, Entenmann's, Jell-O, Log Cabin, Minute Rice, Shake 'n Bake, and Stove Top. About one-fourth of sales comes from coffee (the flagship brand, Maxwell House, purports to be good to the very last drop). General Foods sells prepackaged meat under the name Oscar Mayer. It also provides food services to institutions. But the company will no longer provision your dog, since the Gaines pet food line was sold.

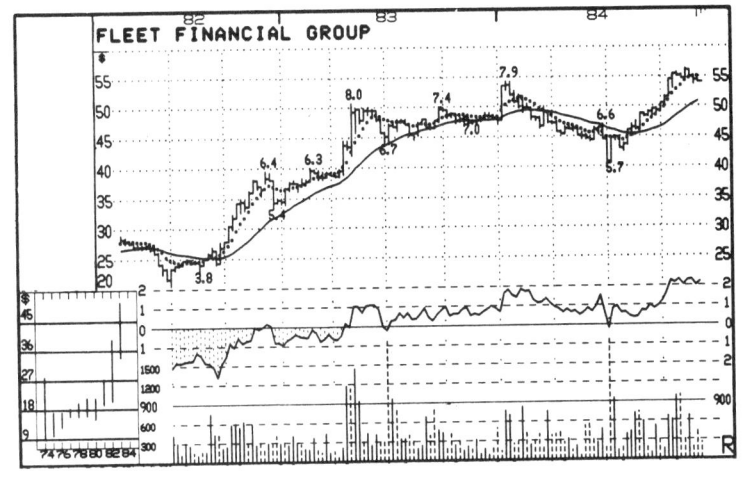

TCKR: FLT
HIGH: 56¼
LOW: 40½
PRICE: 53⅝
EARN: 7.41
P/E: 7
DEBT: 436
YIELD: 4.5

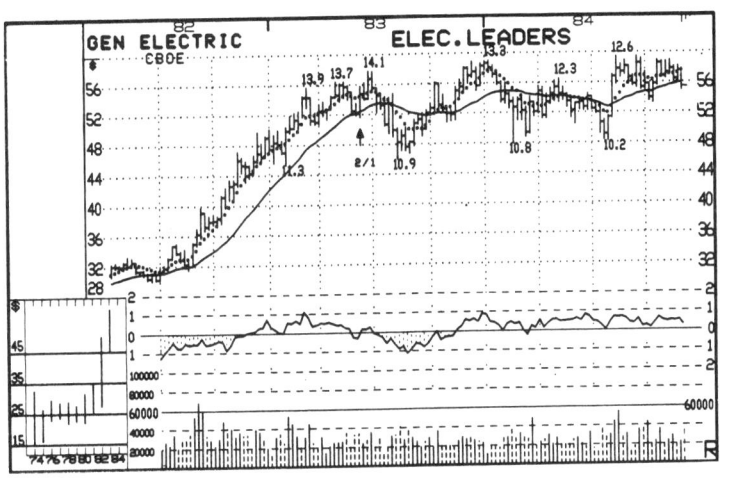

TCKR: GE
HIGH: 59⅜
LOW: 48¼
PRICE: 55
EARN: 4.86
P/E: 11
DEBT: 939
YIELD: 4.0

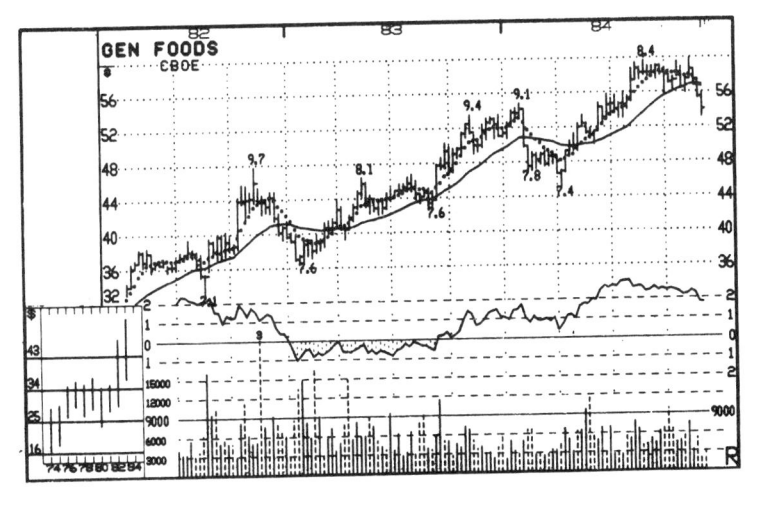

TCKR: GF
HIGH: 59⅞
LOW: 45⅛
PRICE: 55⅝
EARN: 6.91
P/E: 8
DEBT: 723
YIELD: 4.5

GENERAL INSTRUMENT

This is an electronics company whose operations are a gamble, with the final results often in doubt as the competition races down to the wire. But no matter what the outcome, the company stays on the track. General Instruments makes betting equipment, much of it found at major racetracks around the country. The company goes to the post in a few other fields as well: cable television equipment (converters are their specialty), television antennas, and semiconductors are also product lines. Last year it bought TOCOM, a manufacturer of cable television and security equipment. Lotteries are also a burgeoning growth area for General Instrument equipment.

GENERAL MILLS

It started with Wheaties and Betty Crocker. Now it includes Foot Joy, Fundimensions, Izod Lacoste, Kenner, Monet, and Ship'n Shore. Other subsidiaries include York Steak Houses and Red Lobster Inns, the latter's decor and menus recently overhauled to improve business. General Mills is still on top of the packaged food business; present brands include Bisquick, Hamburger Helper, Nature Valley, Gold Medal, Gorton's, Potato Buds, and Yoplait. Then there's Parker Brothers, which licenses the characters in *Star Wars* and Strawberry Shortcake — making General Mills the biggest *toy* manufacturer in the world.

GENERAL MOTORS

As in "as big as..." More than half of all U.S.-made cars roll off its production lines. But the American romance with the American car has been shaky for some time. "Restraint" on Japanese imports works both ways for GM, since the company itself imports some of its cars from the East (as does Chrysler). GM has countered Japanese competition with plans for joint ventures (with Toyota, for one), a diversified product line, and an almost single-minded concern with efficiency. Robots may yet be the answer, although the UAW will have something to say about that. In the meantime, GM, the biggest auto maker in the world, still has the competitive edge over Japan in the manufacture of big cars for upscale consumers.

GEN INSTR PHL

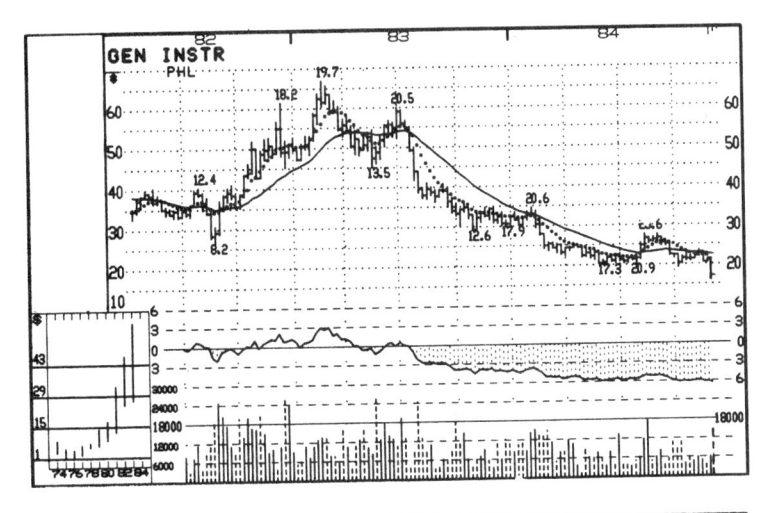

TCKR: GRL
HIGH: 34⅝
LOW: 15½
PRICE: 16¼
EARN: 1.07
P/E: 15
DEBT: 31.1
YIELD: 3.1

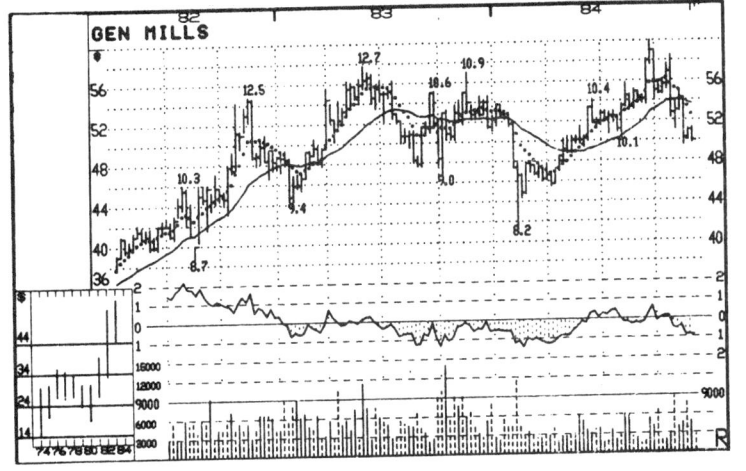

GEN MILLS

TCKR: GIS
HIGH: 60
LOW: 41⅝
PRICE: 49
EARN: 4.66
P/E: 11
DEBT: 423
YIELD: 4.6

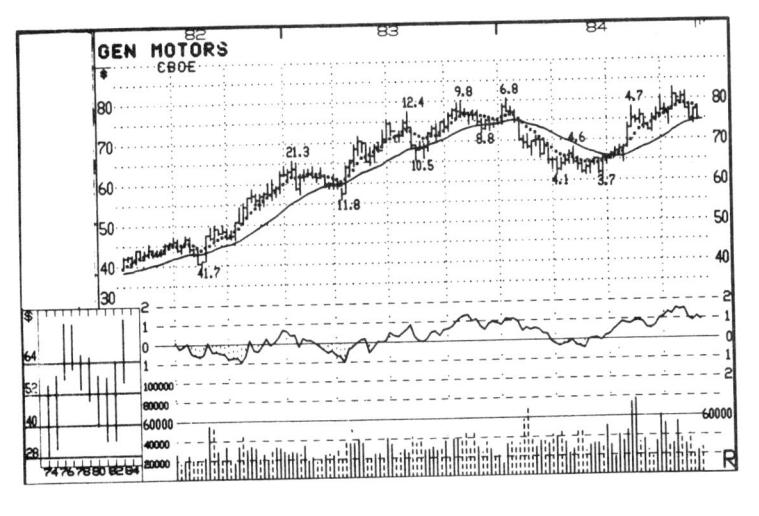

GEN MOTORS CBOE

TCKR: GM
HIGH: 82¾
LOW: 61
PRICE: 74⅝
EARN: 15.62
P/E: 5
DEBT: 2583
YIELD: 6.4

GENERAL SIGNAL

If it moves through pipes or wires, General Signal will measure and control it. This company began to shed its consumer appliance holdings a few years ago and has since concentrated its operations in some of the hottest fields around: automation, energy, semiconductors, and telecommunications (microwave and fiber optics). Its work on air traffic control systems has garnered defense contracts. General Signal has recently become rather heavily involved in the production of air brakes, which has brought in large orders but also made it dependent on continued demand for new railroad and subway cars.

GENESCO, INC.

About 75 percent of this company's sales are generated by some part of the shoe industry. The rest comes from a variety of apparel lines. Genesco sells men's and women's hosiery and shoes (through more than 1,000 of their stores) under a variety of names in addition to its own, the upscale Johnston & Murphy among them. From the knees up, Genesco clothes only men; name brands include Aquascutum, Donald Brooks, Hardy Amies, Lanvin, and Valentino, as well as several of the Ralph Lauren lines. Between 1977 and 1983 the company sold off much of what it considered to be dead wood, and it's currently shopping around for a going concern in the consumer products area. *Caveat*: Long-term debt is still more than 50 percent of total capital, and a steep recession could bring quite a crunch.

GEO INTERNATIONAL

GEO began life in 1981 as a spin-off of Peabody International. Those were gushingly good times for any business connected with oil exploration; and GEO, which specializes in oil field equipment, services, and refinery quality control (as well as quality control services at other kinds of plants), partook of the feast. But the sobering mid-80s caught GEO with excess plant and equipment, so it's resolutely cutting back there and on personnel. Oil equipment and services and quality control operations each account for about a third of their sales, and with that balance, its outlook should be no worse than that for other similar companies in the field.

GEN SIGNAL

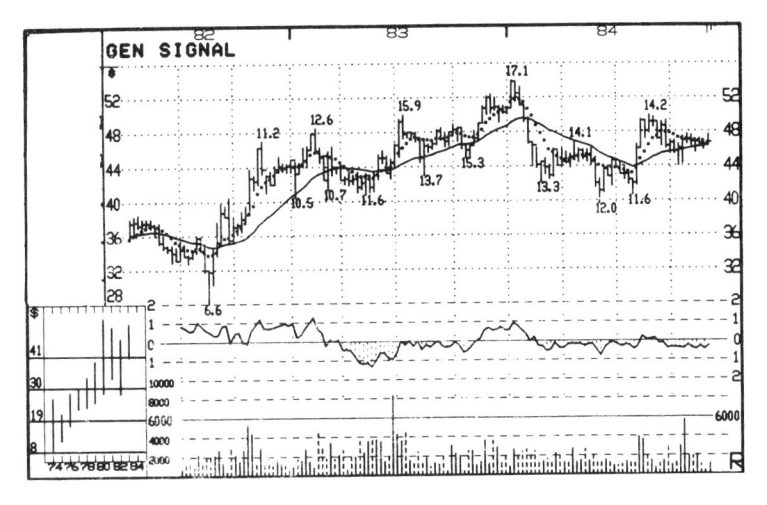

TCKR: GSX
HIGH: 54
LOW: 39⅝
PRICE: 45½
EARN: 3.72
P/E: 12
DEBT: 85.0
YIELD: 4.0

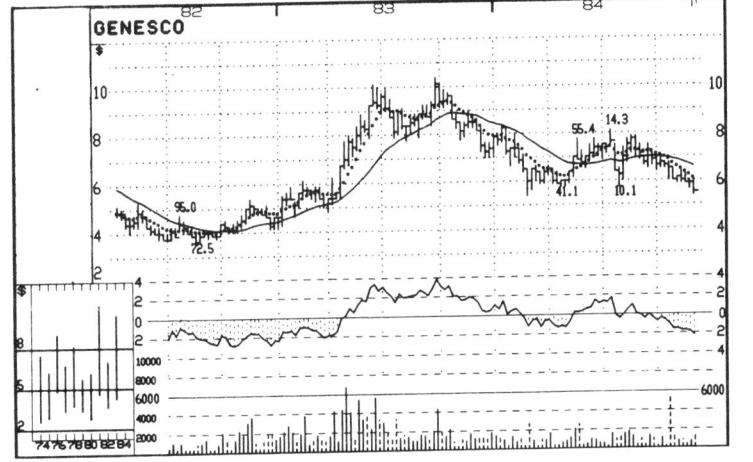

GENESCO

TCKR: GCO
HIGH: 8⅜
LOW: 5¼
PRICE: 5¾
EARN: 0.57
P/E: 10
DEBT: 134
YIELD: —

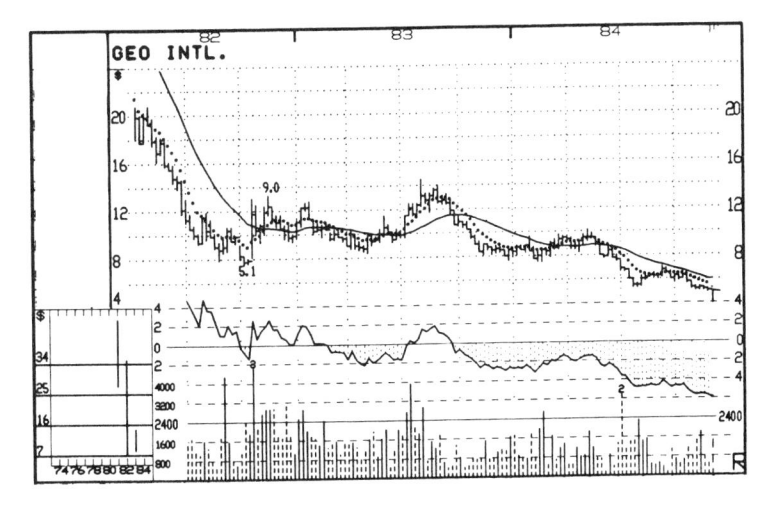

GEO INTL.

TCKR: GX
HIGH: 10⅛
LOW: 4
PRICE: 4½
EARN: d1.13
P/E: d
DEBT: 68.6
YIELD: —

141

GERBER SCIENTIFIC

Gerber is another firm capitalizing on the computer's ability to translate an idea for an industrial design into a finished product with hardly the touch of a human hand. Its systems handle metals, and a variety of other materials as well: The Gerbercutter, for example, is a computer-guided machine that does precision cutting of materials such as leather, plastics, and textiles. Gerber's sales of CAD/CAM factory automation systems increased by more than 50 percent last year over sales for the previous year, although stiffer competition in the field will make it difficult to duplicate that often. In 1984, Gerber bought R.P.N. Systems, which specializes in computerized operations in the garment industry. It also purchased EOCOM, a reprographics company.

GIBRALTAR FINANCIAL

Its flagship, Gibraltar Savings, a California savings and loan association with over eighty branches, ranks in the top twenty of banks of its type in the country. It started in 1984 with $6 billion in assets and about $400,000 in savings accounts, and during the year added six branches to its collection via acquisitions. Gibraltar Financial also bought the Queen City Savings and Loan Association of Seattle last year, an institution that had fallen on hard times. The corporations's expansion into financial services in the past three years has brightened Gibraltar's revenue picture, but it has also upped its administrative overhead.

GLOBAL MARINE

Global has shared the ups and downs of the contract oil drilling business with a host of other companies. There has been a glut of mobile oil rigs as well as of oil itself lately, and day rates for the use of those rigs have been depressed. But operations starting up in the Gulf of Mexico and the North Sea loom as good future sources of drilling contracts for Global Marine. In the meantime, the company began work in 1984 on a three-year, $100-million contract with Exxon to drill offshore in Alaska. Global also supplies drilling services to the oil industry through Applied Drilling Technology, and, through Challenger Minerals, Inc., hunts down black gold.

GERBER SCIENTIFIC

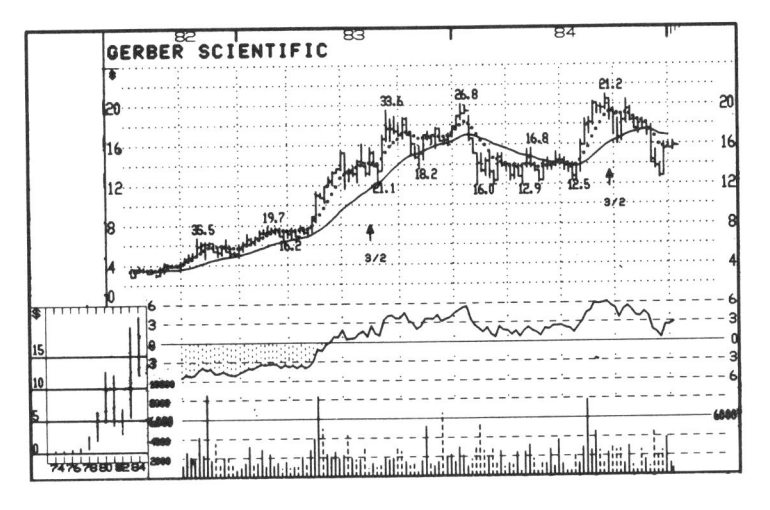

TCKR: GRB
HIGH: 21
LOW: 12
PRICE: 13⅝
EARN: 1.13
P/E: 12
DEBT: 24.2
YIELD: 0.9

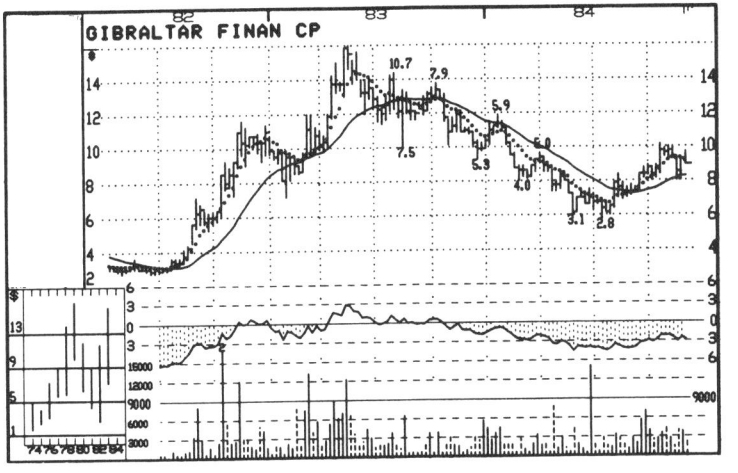

GIBRALTAR FINAN CP

TCKR: GFC
HIGH: 11⅞
LOW: 5¾
PRICE: 8¾
EARN: 2.03
P/E: 4
DEBT: 890
YIELD: —

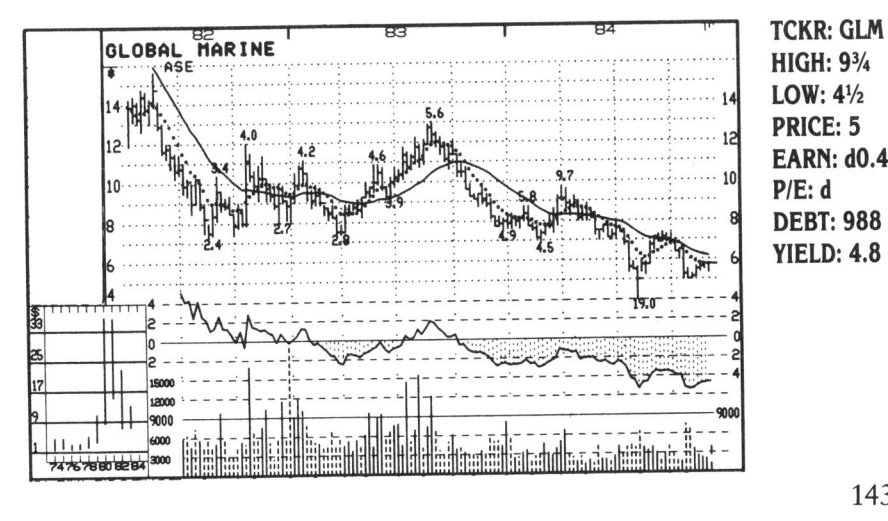

GLOBAL MARINE

TCKR: GLM
HIGH: 9¾
LOW: 4½
PRICE: 5
EARN: d0.45
P/E: d
DEBT: 988
YIELD: 4.8

GOODYEAR TIRE AND RUBBER

As the auto industry goes, so goes Goodyear. So, how did Goodyear go when Detroit recovered from the disaster of the early part of the decade? Only so-so. The wheel of fortune spun better for several other auto-related enterprises, but Goodyear management is not sitting around waiting to see where the next auto sales downturn drives them. They purchased Celeron, an oil and gas transmission firm which currently garners about 10 percent of Goodyear's profits. Consequently, a California-Texas pipeline looms as large in the future as, well, a blimp approaching a football stadium. But Goodyear will not be able to go to the well for profits from this pipeline until the end of the decade, so extensive borrowing and a boost in the company's debt-to-equity ratio are in order.

GREAT NORTHERN NEKOOSA

Its gains (which have been good lately) are mostly paper profits, and it wouldn't have it any other way. Paper is this company's business. Your letterhead may be its stationery, your daily paper could be printed on its newsprint (particularly if you live in the Northeast), and you may recently have purchased something packed in its container board. This company also makes grocery bags and produces the material used for the covers of paperback books. Most of Great Northern's wood comes from its own forests in Maine, and timberland and a mill in Mississippi were recently added. Already strong profits are bolstered since the company provides much of its own energy requirements.

GREATWEST HOSPITALS

Greatwest, which has only been in existence since 1981, operates in the hotly competitive Southern California health care market. The company owns seven actute-care institutions with 650 beds and manages five others with 243 beds — and another facility has just been finished. About half the accounts receivable in this part of the operations are collected from Medicare. Greatwest Hospital's occupancy rate is only about 40 percent, which is probably why its health maintenance operations are getting more attention now. Last year Greatwest added a second HMO with the purchase of a controlling interest in the Independence Health Plan, Inc.; the two organizations together serve a total of 170,000 patients.

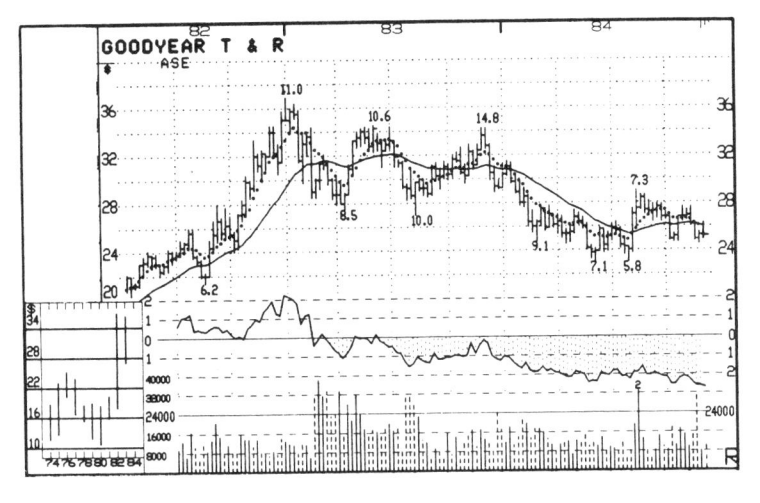

TCKR: GT
HIGH: 31½
LOW: 23
PRICE: 24⅞
EARN: 3.94
P/E: 6
DEBT: 616
YIELD: 6.4

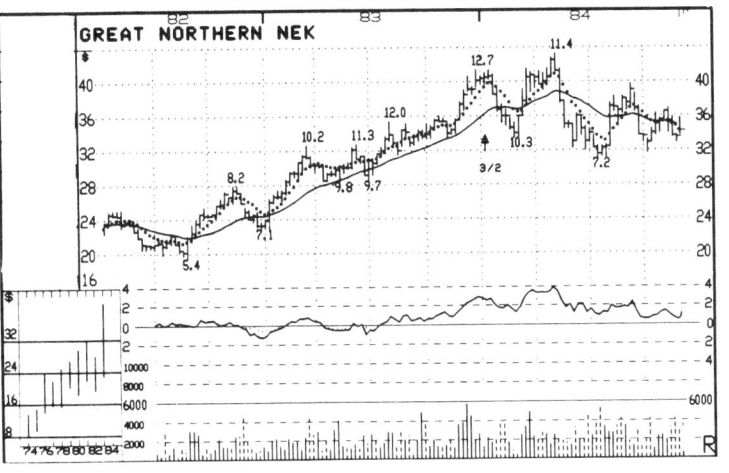

TCKR: GNN
HIGH: 43¼
LOW: 31
PRICE: 34
EARN: 4.84
P/E: 7
DEBT: 501
YIELD: 4.5

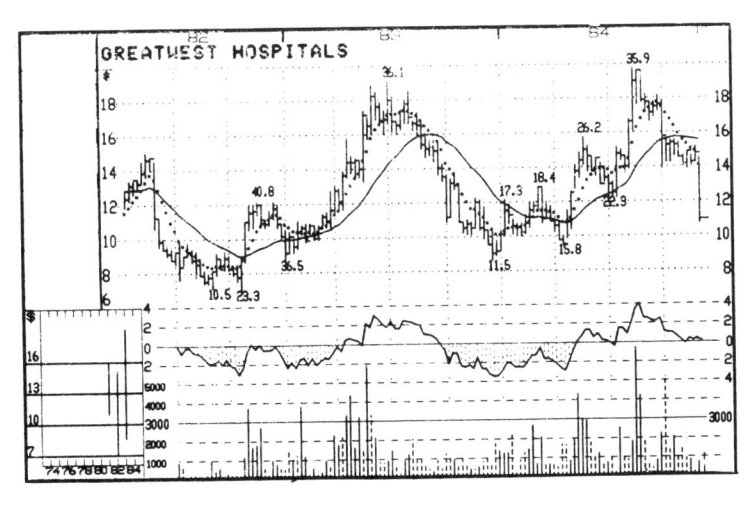

TCKR: GHI
HIGH: 19¾
LOW: 8⅝
PRICE: 11¼
EARN: 0.55
P/E: 20
DEBT: 74.1
YIELD: —

HEINZ, H.J.

Heinz had more than "57 Varieties" when its slogan was created in 1892 by Henry Heinz, the company's founder (he settled on that number because he liked the way it sounded). You might say Heinz is the IBM of the ketchup world — more than half of the stuff poured in the U.S. comes out of its bottles. Heinz is number one in the British canned soup market (about one-third of the company's revenue come from abroad); it also sells half the frozen potatoes consumed in this country. Aside from food packaged under its own name, Heinz also sells to consumers under the names Star-Kist, 9-Lives, Ore-Ida, Alba, and Weight Watchers, which is also a Heinz company.

HERCULES, INC.

Hercules was showing strength in its aerospace and explosives products division last year, thanks largely to the acquisition of Simmond's which brought with it high operating margins in that field. Hercules makes electronic equipment, graphite fibers, and rocket motors for NASA and the Defense Department. Plastics account for about 25 percent of its sales, as do organic chemicals. Profits have been greatest in specialty chemicals, and the company has been doing especially well with its polypropylene operation, which it shares with Montedison. Hercules's earnings suffered somewhat last year, however, from its role in the settlement of the Agent Orange lawsuit.

HONEYWELL, INC.

Honeywell specializes in instruments that control — thermostats, for example. This division constitutes about one-third of their operations, and it did especially well a few years ago when energy conservation was on everyone's agenda. Honeywell devices are also found in automated manufacturing processes and in the complex systems that control the environment inside commercial buildings. Micro Switch makes control devices used in cars and home appliances. Synertek, which makes semiconductors, suffered from the video game collapse but is doing well lately, thanks partly to space and defense orders. Its 1970 purchase of General Electric's computer division made Honeywell a major force in that field; minicomputers start at about $30,000 and run into the millions for mainframes.

HEINZ, H. J.

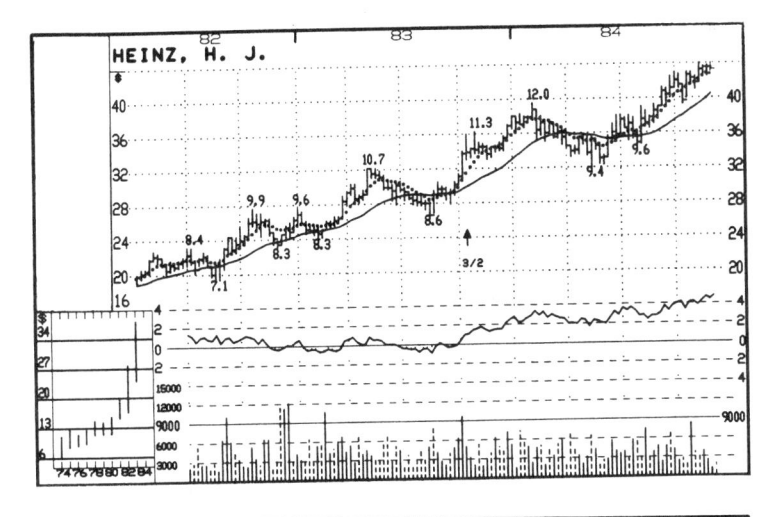

TCKR: HNZ
HIGH: 45
LOW: 32
PRICE: 43¾
EARN: 3.59
P/E: 12
DEBT: 291
YIELD: 3.7

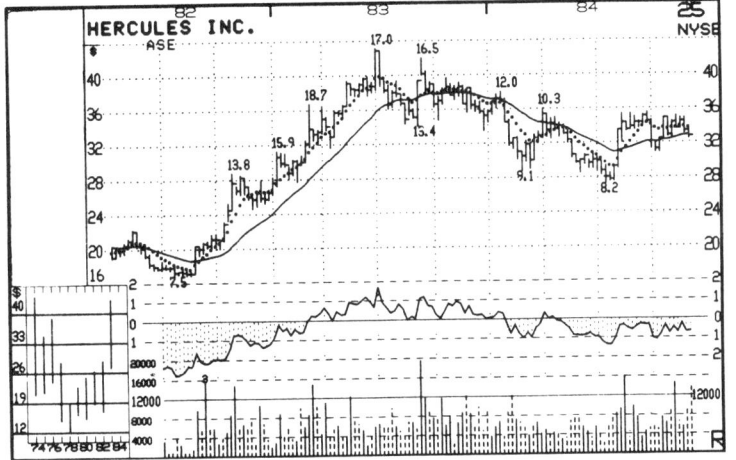

HERCULES INC.

TCKR: HPC
HIGH: 38
LOW: 27¼
PRICE: 32¾
EARN: 3.65
P/E: 9
DEBT: 369
YIELD: 4.9

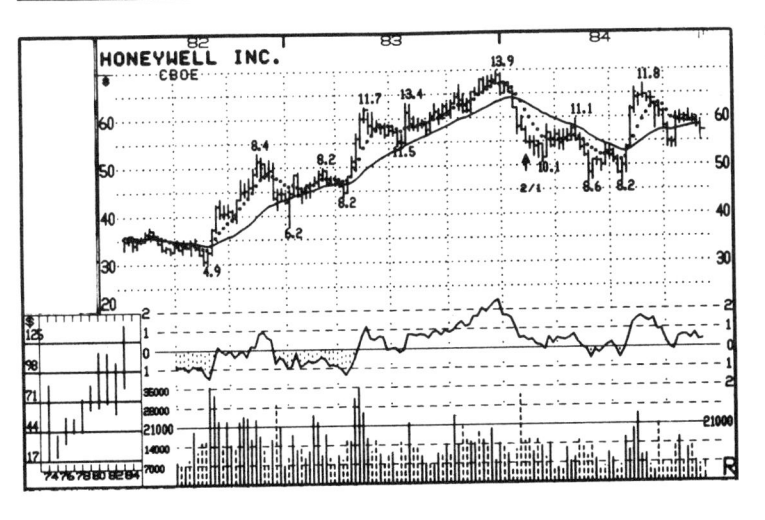

HONEYWELL INC.

TCKR: HON
HIGH: 69¾
LOW: 46⅜
PRICE: 59¼
EARN: 6.40
P/E: 9
DEBT: 670
YIELD: 3.2

HOUSTON NATURAL GAS

This company ships and sells gas in Texas, primarily in the Houston and Galveston areas. Natural gas operations, at last count, accounted for about 80 percent of profits. By mid-1984, it had bought back five million of a projected eight million shares of its stock. Management is tightening their operations by concentrating more on the company's strong gas division. Toward that end, coal interests and marine services, which had constituted about 10 percent of sales, have been divested. Last year Houston Natural Gas fought off a takeover attempt by Coastal Corp.

HUGHES TOOL

Anyone who wants to sink a hole — be it for a building foundation, mine, or oil well — is likely to use a Hughes product. Unfortunately for Hughes, the company is also in a hole: At one time the employment of this firm's assets was subject to the whims of its reclusive founder, Howard Hughes, and although he's gone the company has yet to recover. Its specialty remains equipment for the oil and gas industry, with primacy in the manufacture of drilling bits. If all the furious consolidating and trimming they have been engaged in works, it may yet resurface as a prosperous enterprise. One thing that would signal good times ahead would be an increase in deep well drilling.

IBM

Does this company dominate the worldwide market for mainframe computers? Was King Kong a big monkey? IBM's mainframe market share is currently about 70 percent, and should stay that way. Within two years of the introduction of their PC, IBM executives had the pleasure of watching the rest of the industry fall all over themselves in a contest to see which other personal computers were *truly* "IBM-compatible." Continued strong sales of the PC in its several variations indicate that IBM has thoroughly ensconced itself as the industry standard, although with its amateurish keyboard the original PC Jr. was not necessarily a chip off the old block. It was redesigned, resulting in a relatively minor setback for a company of IBM's size. Their recent purchase of Rolm will pit them directly against AT&T in office automation and telecommunications, and their penetration of the personal computer software market is already making big waves. And — they still make those great electric typewriters.

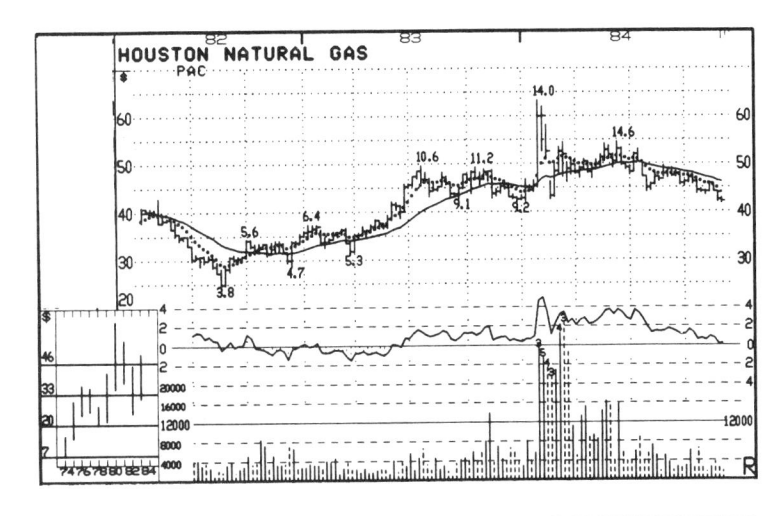

TCKR: HNG
HIGH: 63¼
LOW: 41½
PRICE: 44¼
EARN: 4.43
P/E: 10
DEBT: 488
YIELD: 4.5

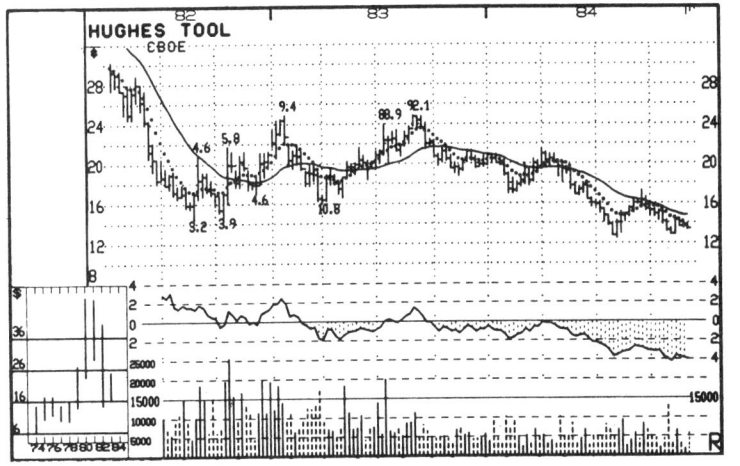

TCKR: HT
HIGH: 21⅜
LOW: 12½
PRICE: 13⅛
EARN: d3.79
P/E: d
DEBT: 401
YIELD: 3.7

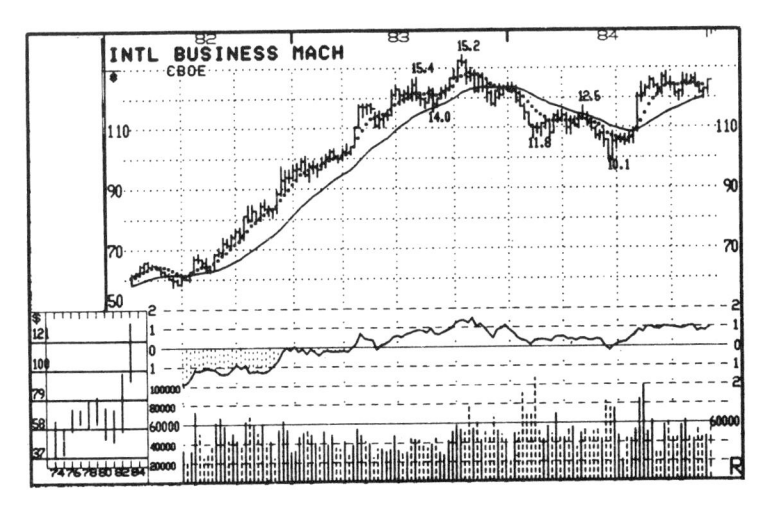

TCKR: IBM
HIGH: 128½
LOW: 99
PRICE: 119⅛
EARN: 10.28
P/E: 12
DEBT: 3646
YIELD: 3.7

149

ICN PHARMACEUTICALS

Drugs, vitamins, and the like account for about 75 percent of ICN's sales and profits. Half of the profits are generated abroad in a large operation that includes companies such as SPI and Viratek. Recently ICN, which spends heavily on research and development, introduced two new promising anti-viral drugs. One is Virazole, said to be effective against herpes and currently undergoing testing. The other is Ribavirin, an anti-viral agent. ICN is involved in nucleic acid research and also has a life sciences division, which produces isotopes and a variety of reagents for research. Last year Eastman Kodak bought into ICN to the tune of more than $8 million, with the aim of developing joint operations in several of ICN's specialties.

ILLINOIS POWER

For another year or so, it will be coal that will almost exclusively be stoking the fires of Illinois Power. But then about 25 percent of their fuel will be atom generated, as the $2.5 billion Clinton nuclear plant — 80 percent of it company owned — comes on line. There was to have been a second Clinton unit, but that was scrubbed in 1983 at a cost of $20 million to Illinois Power and, possibly, its 900,000 customers. Electricity, 50 percent of which is sold to businesses, accounts for 80 percent of Illinois Power's profits; gas, the remaining amount. Illinois Power Co.'s capital budget will contain between $300 and $400 million in each of the next four years.

INEXCO OIL

Inexco does contract oil drilling through Wilson Brothers Drilling Co. and Wilson Brothers Corp. It also exploits its own deposits and at the beginning of the last year had reserves of 12.5 million barrels of oil and 340 billion cubic feet of gas. More than half the revenues from oil and gas sales last year came from the sale of gas, which continues to be a highly volatile business. Most of Inexco's drilling is onshore, but that does not necessarily mean the company is on solid ground — its debt still adds up to $400 million, making its profits very interest rate-sensitive.

ICN PHARMACEUTICAL

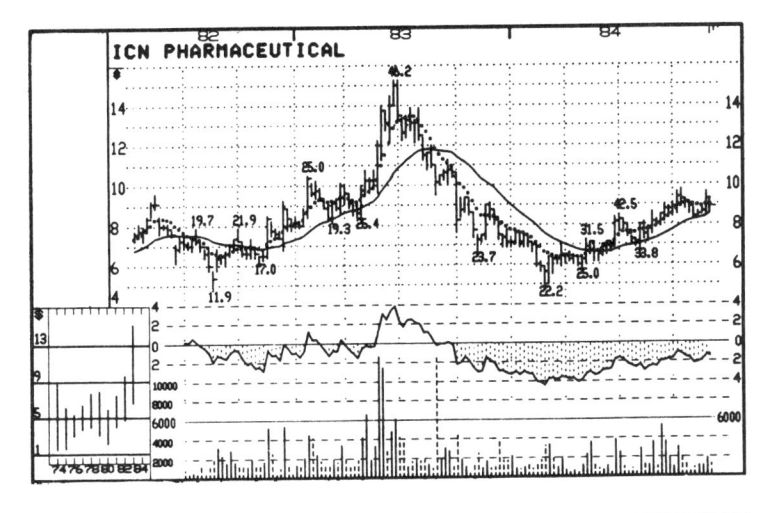

TCKR: ICN
HIGH: 9¾
LOW: 4⅞
PRICE: 8⅝
EARN: 0.14
P/E: 62
DEBT: 25.1
YIELD: —

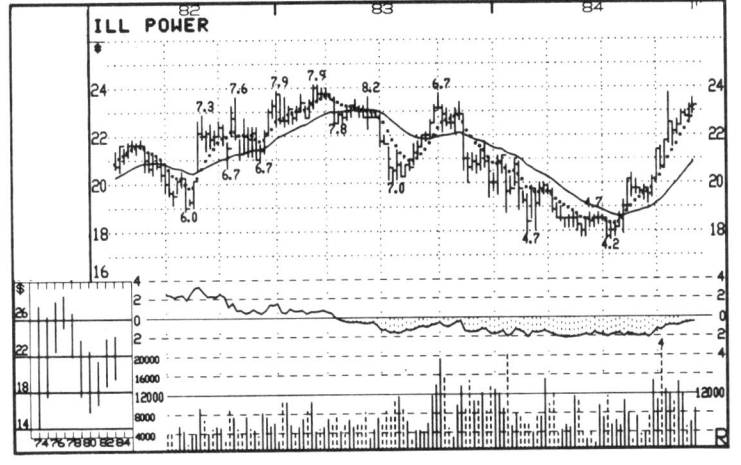

ILL POWER

TCKR: IPC
HIGH: 23¾
LOW: 17⅝
PRICE: 22⅜
EARN: 3.99
P/E: 6
DEBT: 1500
YIELD: 12.0

INEXCO OIL

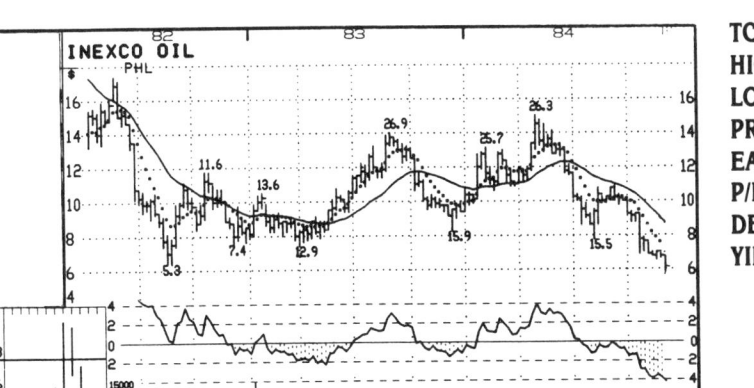

TCKR: INX
HIGH: 15
LOW: 5½
PRICE: 6⅜
EARN: 0.42
P/E: 15
DEBT: 401
YIELD: 2.2

151

INFORMATICS GENERAL

Informatics, a computer software systems firm, was at one time a subsidiary of Equitable Life. Informatics still caters to the insurance industry (about 15 percent of its software sales are in that area), although lately that has not been a terribly lucrative field. The company is now completely out of the time-sharing business and devotes all its resources to serviing a broad spectrum of industries and professions with customized and off-the-shelf software. Informatics has made a bid to get into an important sector of the personal computer software business by jointly marketing with Ashton-Tate dBASE/Answer, a program designed to enable microcomputer users to access mainframe data bases.

INSILCO CORP.

Half of its profits come from the sale of computer-related equipment; the other half are brought in by consumer and office products. Insilco's Times Fiber Communications makes fiber optics equipment and more conventional coaxial cable for cable television. Its Miles Homes Co. sells raw materials to individuals who are out to beat the high cost of housing by putting up their own; Miles also helps them with their financing. Nationwide Homes produces manufactured housing; Taylor Publishing puts out high school and college yearbooks; Enterprise, Red Devil, and Sinclair are paints. Stewart makes precision metal parts, while Rolodex is one of the most famous brands in office equipment. Last year Insilco bought into the heat transfer–components field with the purchase of Thermal Components. It also owns Signal Transformer.

INTERCO, INC.

Interco is the top shoe manufacturer in the United States, its large retail network including 800 shoe stores and about 50 shoe departments in department stores. You buy its products under the names Duane's, Florsheim, Florsheim Thayer McNeil, and Miller Taylor. Interco also has extensive apparel and furniture divisions, which sell through more than 550 retail outlets. Furniture brands include the popular Broyhill and Ethan Allen. Last year Abe Schrader Corp., a manufacturer of women's clothing, was added to their apparel line, which lately has been Interco's weak link.

INFORMATICS GENERAL

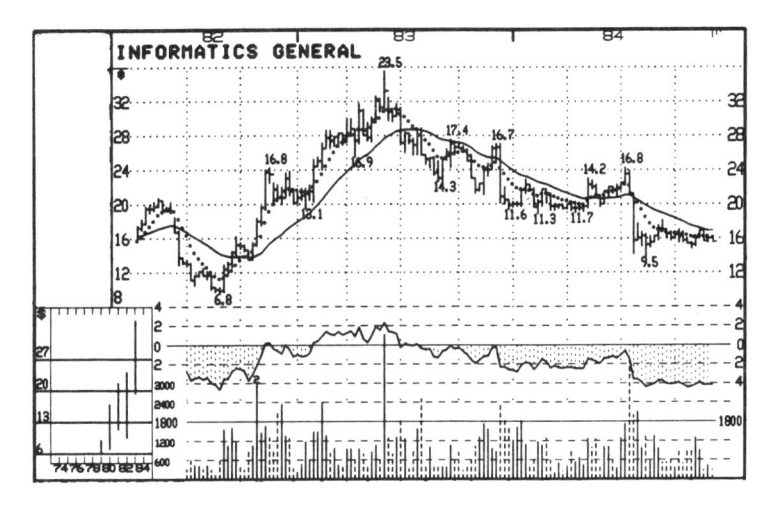

TCKR: IG
HIGH: 24¼
LOW: 13¾
PRICE: 15½
EARN: 1.13
P/E: 14
DEBT: —
YIELD: —

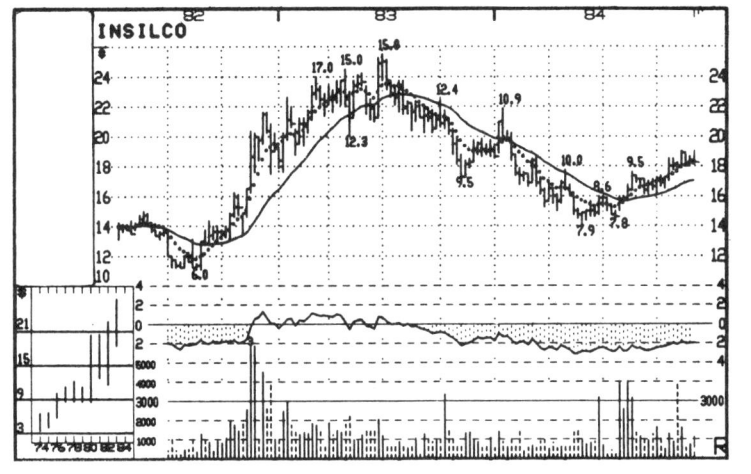

INSILCO

TCKR: INR
HIGH: 21⅞
LOW: 14
PRICE: 18⅝
EARN: 1.89
P/E: 10
DEBT: 120
YIELD: 5.4

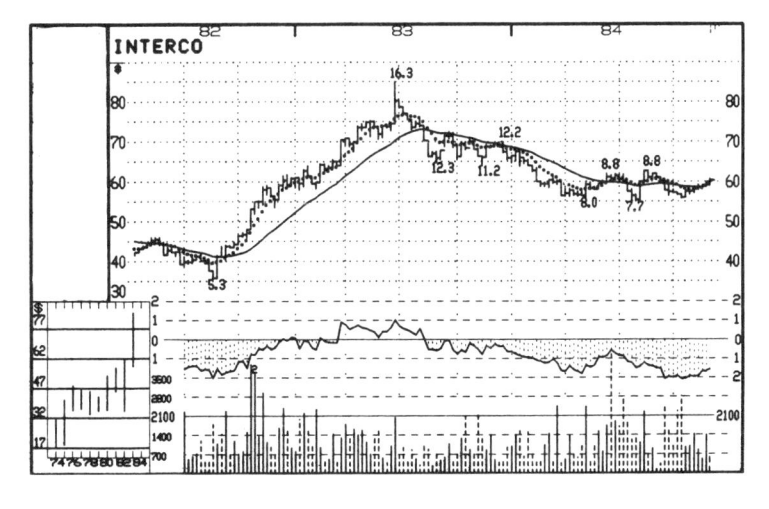

INTERCO

TCKR: ISS
HIGH: 70
LOW: 55
PRICE: 58¾
EARN: 6.96
P/E: 8
DEBT: 175
YIELD: 5.2

153

INTERFIRST CORP.

The biggest bank holding company in Texas (and in the Southwest) has seen big trouble of late. In keeping with the nature of its market, the company was heavily exposed in energy-related loans — about 25 percent of its total. The performance of those loans has not exactly been strengthened by the oil glut. In fact, Interfirst's nonperforming loans constitute about 5 percent of its portfolio. The company owns sixty-five banks in all, the biggest being Interfirst Bank Dallas, the state's third largest. But per Texas law, each bank may have only one branch. Interfirst also owns a merchant bank in London. Lately the company has been converting its real estate holdings to liquid assets. The Bass family has bought into Interstate to the tune of about 5 percent of outstanding shares.

INTERNATIONAL HARVESTER

The company that began with Cyrus McCormick's reaper seemed to be facing the Grim Reaper a few years ago — along with Chrysler, it appeared to be on the verge of going under. Facing a sluggish farming economy and continued competition from Caterpillar and John Deere, International Harvester finally realized that the market for farm equipment wasn't likely to improve in the near future, and in a recent giant divestiture sold off its farm-equipment producing assets to Tenneco, Inc. A strong economy, however (and, International Harvester hopes, its 3,000 dealers on the North American continent), will boost its truck sales, which constituted a bigger part of the company's operations than plows and tractors. Currently there are no dividends paid on International Harvester stock.

INTERNORTH, INC.

Cold weather warms its profit climate. About 50 percent of Internorth's operations involve natural gas, and another 25 percent deal with liquid fuels. Internorth retails natural gas, supplies gas to seventy-five utilities in mid-America through a 25,000-mile pipeline, and produces petrochemicals. Currently it has a small oil and gas exploration and production division, although Belco Petroleum, acquired two years ago, may improve its position in that field. In the offing for Internorth is a $500 million gas transmission line from Ohio to Pennsylvania, which will be built in partnership with ANR Pipeline. A coal slurry pipeline venture, in which Internorth was to have a 25 percent interest, did not pan out and has been dropped.

INTERFIRST CORP

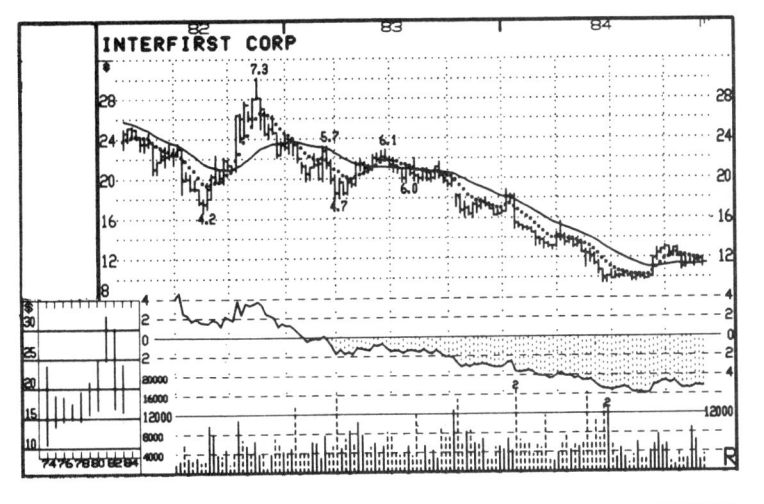

TCKR: IFC
HIGH: 17⅞
LOW: 9½
PRICE: 10¾
EARN: 1.79
P/E: 6
DEBT: 560
YIELD: 5.6

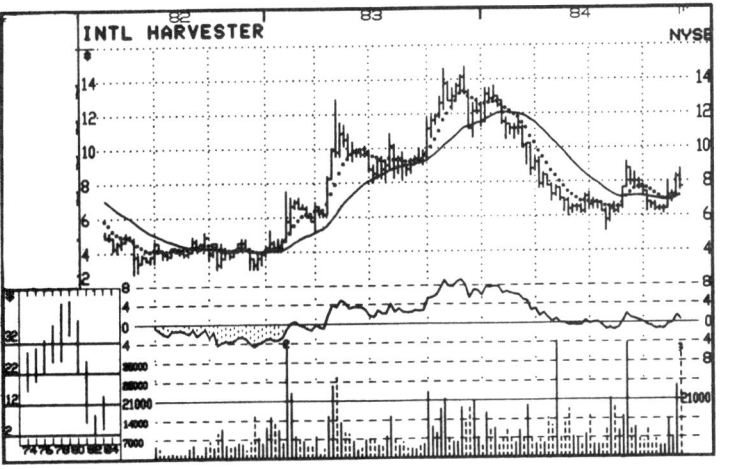

INTL HARVESTER

TCKR: HR
HIGH: 13⅝
LOW: 5⅛
PRICE: 7¼
EARN: d4.02
P/E: d
DEBT: 1413
YIELD: —

INTERNORTH

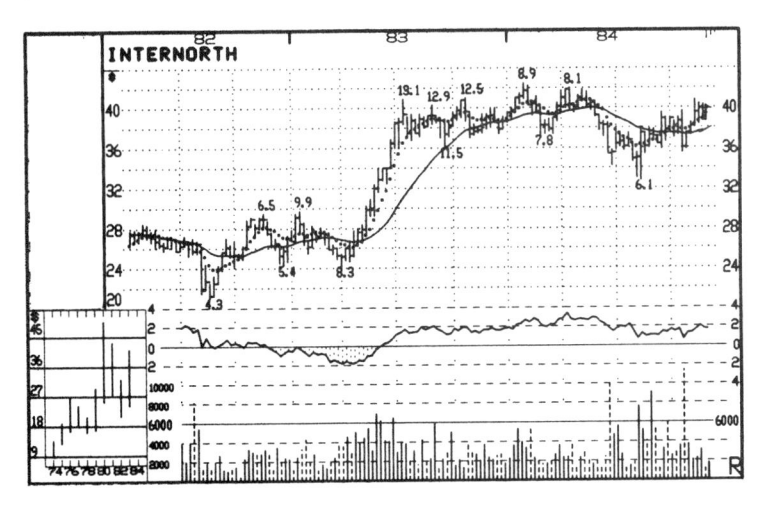

TCKR: INI
HIGH: 42½
LOW: 32¾
PRICE: 40⅜
EARN: 5.39
P/E: 7
DEBT: 1087
YIELD: 6.1

INTERSTATE BAKERIES

This company recently got out of the computer-leasing business—but not out of millions of dollars of debt relating to that operation. So although there's plenty of bread being made, a good slice of it goes toward retiring that debt. In its current form the company is the number three wholesale baker in the country, with products packaged under names like Blue Ribbon, Blue Seal, Buttermaid, Butternut, Dolly Madison, Eddy's, Holsum, Millbrook, Mrs. Karl's Four-S, Sap's, Sweetheart, and Weber's. It's got 30 plants and 5,000 trucks and sells to food-service operations as well as to retail stores. Interstate is in a highly competitive industry, where prices are cut almost as much as cookies.

INTERSTATE POWER

Its revenue comes chiefly from the sale of electricity, 95 percent of which is generated by burning coal. About 80 percent of that power is transmitted to customers in rural areas and small cities and towns in Iowa, the rest to Illinois and Minnesota. About a third of its customers are residential. Under Iowa regulatory legislation, the building of excess generating capacity is discouraged, and the state regulatory commission has the option of denying a return on such capacity. Hence Interstate Power's conservative capital budget of $40 million for 1984, and the fact that the company purchases some of its power elsewhere.

IOWA ELECTRIC LIGHT & POWER

This company sells electric power exclusively in Iowa and gas in that state and in Colorado, Minnesota, and Nebraska. Its power business is divided almost equally among commercial, industrial, and residential customers. About a third of that power is atomic, derived from the Duane Arnold nuclear plant, of which Iowa EL&P owns 70 percent. That plant went on line in 1974, before building cost-overruns set off a chain reaction in the rising price of nuclear power. Coal supplies another third of its power; the rest is purchased. Rate increases do not come easily in Iowa, the company's home state; Iowa EL&P's response is to run a tight operation. Currently a wage freeze and an early retirement plan are in effect.

INTERSTATE BAKERIES

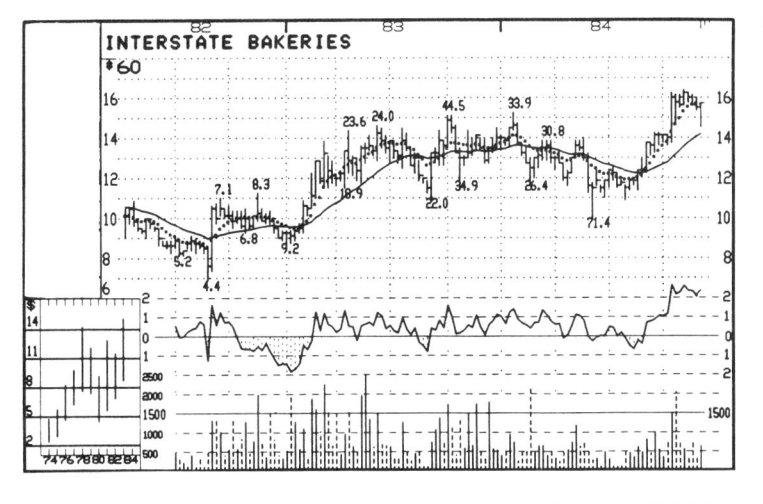

TCKR: IBC
HIGH: 16 3/8
LOW: 10
PRICE: 15 3/8
EARN: d2.75
P/E: d
DEBT: 41.7
YIELD: —

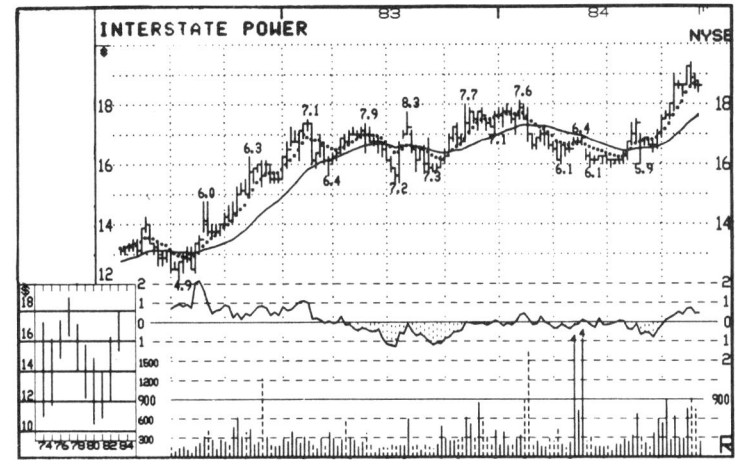

INTERSTATE POWER — NYSE

TCKR: IPW
HIGH: 19 3/8
LOW: 15 7/8
PRICE: 18 5/8
EARN: 2.69
P/E: 7
DEBT: 219
YIELD: 10.1

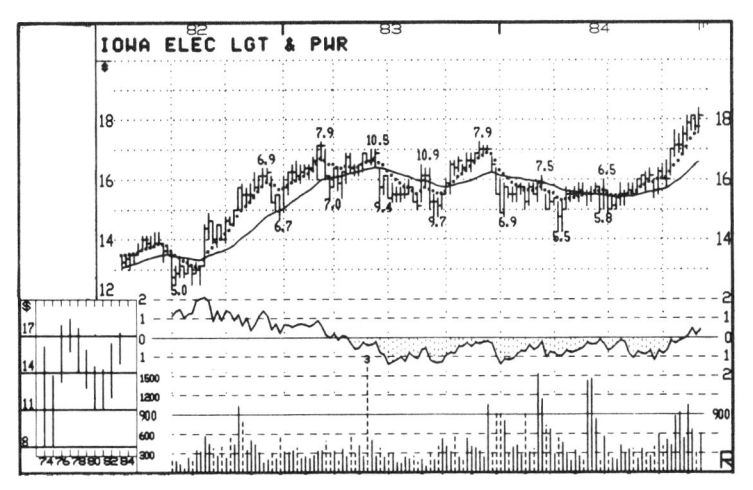

IOWA ELEC LGT & PWR

TCKR: IEL
HIGH: 18 3/8
LOW: 14 1/4
PRICE: 17 1/2
EARN: 2.21
P/E: 8
DEBT: 225
YIELD: 10.9

JAMESWAY CORP.

This discount chain, whose stores are found mainly in New York, New Jersey, and Pennsylvania, has eighty outlets, up from sixty five years ago. Jamesway is strong in rural areas. Previously hard goods got the lion's share of space in these discount emporiums, which average about 60,000 square feet each. But Jamesway is remodeling and will now put a greater emphasis on clothing, to the tune of about 60 percent of available space. Advertising, budgeting, and merchandising are controlled from the company's New Jersey base, but the stores are independently operated. Jamesway's present plans are to discount even more than they do now. Seven new stores were opened last year, and ten are on tap for 1985.

JOHNSON & JOHNSON

The 1982 poison scare involving this company's Tylenol product caused a wound that no Band-Aid could cover up. But Johnson & Johnson's vaunted marketing division — which had taken Tylenol, a product of the McNeil Laboratories, and made a consumer staple of it in the first place — managed to heal the scar. In less than two years, the nonaspirin pain remedy, which had become the object of consumer suspicion, had regained most of its original market, and there's no reason to believe that the marketing hotshots won't be able to cope creatively with the challenge of ibuprofen, a new nonaspirin pain reliever, as well. Stiff competition may be on the horizon for the company's various birth control products (especially the Ortho-Novum pill) if the contraceptive sponge catches on; and J & J's expensive diagnostic scanners have been facing price resistance in the hospitals. Its big baby product line, of course, is always affected by a change in the birth rate.

JOY MANUFACTURING

There may or may not be joy in their boardroom, but there is at least a degree of contentment. This company, which makes digging equipment for the coal mining business and machinery for industries that use compressed air, is doing well. Joy provides the petroleum industry with various kinds of tools and devices used to build and maintain pipe systems. It also produces dry scrubbers to keep smokestacks from polluting the air. Last year it acquired — mostly with cash — several companies that serve the oil and gas business; one of them cost $234 million alone.

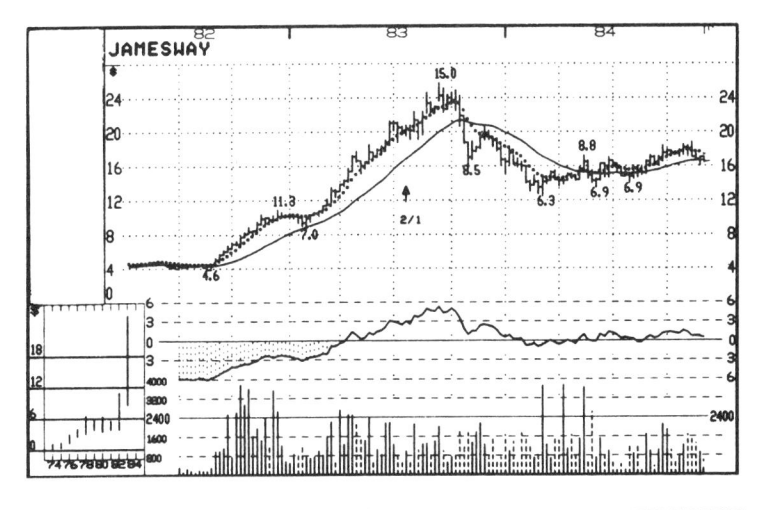

TCKR: JMY
HIGH: 19¼
LOW: 12½
PRICE: 16⅝
EARN: 2.04
P/E: 8
DEBT: 47.2
YIELD: 0.6

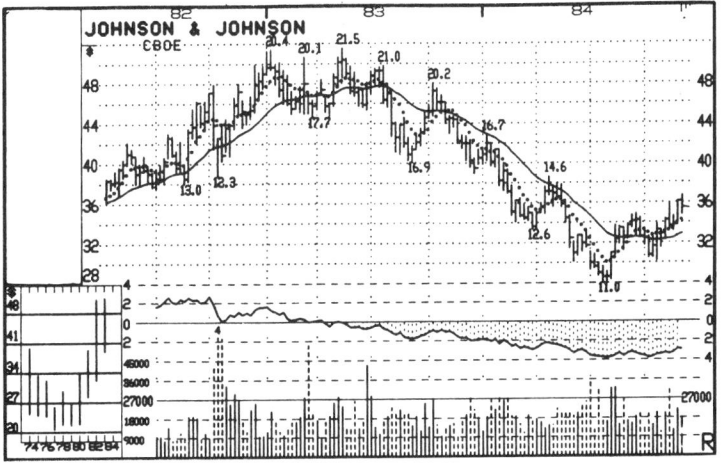

TCKR: JNJ
HIGH: 42⅞
LOW: 28
PRICE: 35⅝
EARN: 2.50
P/E: 14
DEBT: 281
YIELD: 3.4

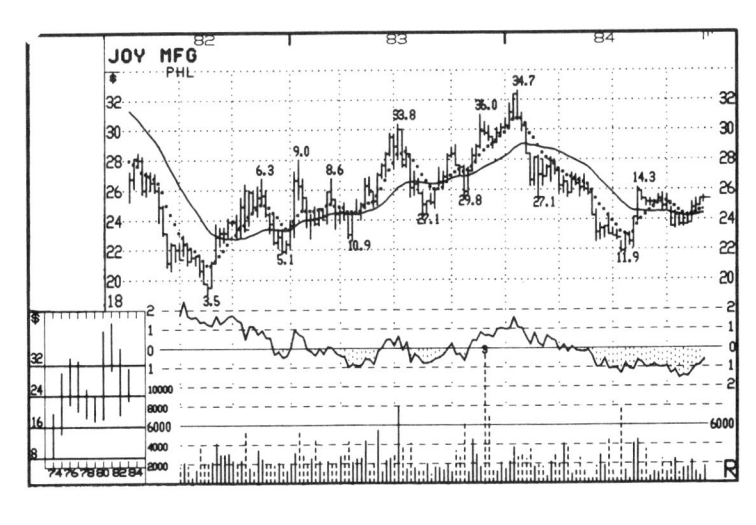

TCKR: JOY
HIGH: 32⅝
LOW: 21¾
PRICE: 25⅛
EARN: 1.52
P/E: 17
DEBT: 68.1
YIELD: 5.6

KERR-McGEE

This company has not lacked for publicity in the past few years: Karen Silkwood's death — the subject of articles, a book, and a movie — still haunts its image. Actually, Kerr-McGee's uranium operations are not a major activity at this time. In fact, the chemical division has not done well lately, although things are looking up. Kerr-McGee has been actively drilling for oil, currently the source of about two-thirds of company profits. Coal accounts for another third. The company also does some contract drilling, an area in which it hopes to improve profit margins.

KN ENERGY

Gas is still its main product, although the former Kansas-Nebraska Natural Gas now deals also in coal, oil, and uranium. This company sells natural gas in Colorado, East Texas, Kansas, Nebraska, and Wyoming. Its Western Oil Co. explores for and produces gas and oil. Wyoming Fuels mines coal and uranium and is just now beginning to exploit coal desposits in Colorado's Raton Basin. Plains Production Co., an oil production operation, may soon be spun off. KN no longer builds pipelines, and last year it got out of the alfalfa dehydration business as well. A one-fifth interest in a coal slurry pipeline never got off the drawing board. But in 1983, Mesa Petroleum was unsuccessful in an attempt to take over KN.

LA QUINTA MOTOR INNS

La Quinta, whose operations have been confined to the Midwest, Southeast, and Southwest (with Texas as a focal point), is growing: 20 inns were to put out the hospitality mat last year, and 18 opened their doors for the first time the year before. The company currently runs about 125 units, licenses approximately 15 to others, and is itself a licensee in 6 operations. The inns, 15,000 or so modestly priced rooms, are occupied mainly by businesspeople. They are located near major roadways, feature swimming pools and restaurants, and have a recent occupancy rate of about 75 percent. Profits have been somewhat circumscribed by write-offs and high interest rates on capital used for expansion. Management keeps a close watch on unit performance, and there has been divestiture activity in each of the past ten years.

KERR MCGEE (CBOE)

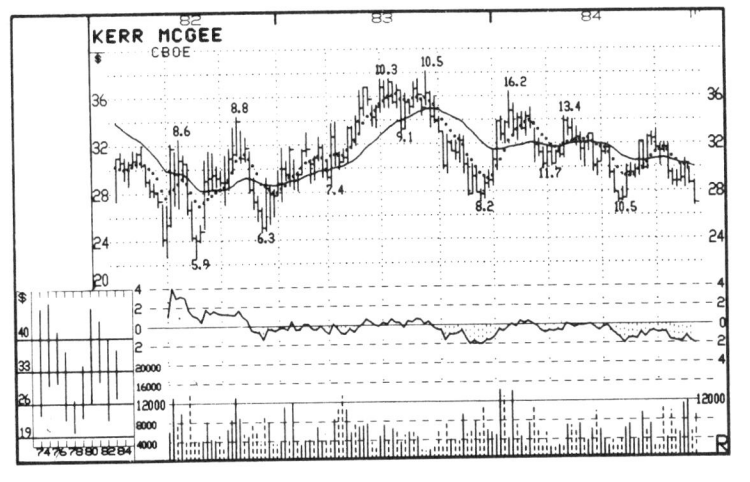

TCKR: KMG
HIGH: 36 3/8
LOW: 26 1/2
PRICE: 27 1/2
EARN: 2.22
P/E: 12
DEBT: 616
YIELD: 4.0

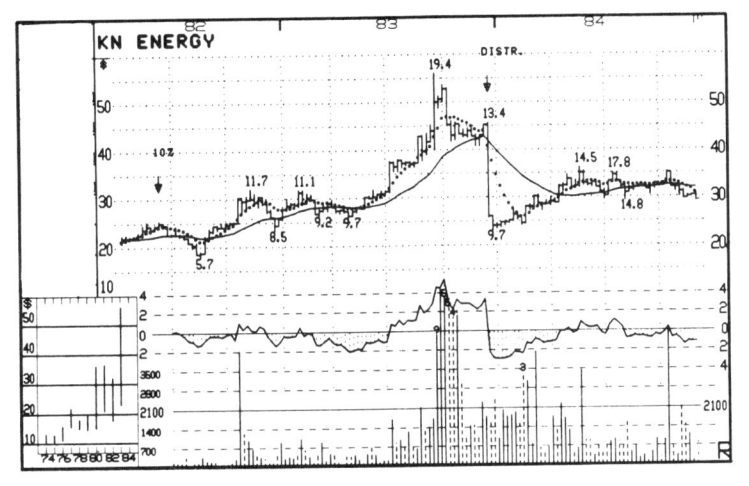

KN ENERGY

TCKR: KNE
HIGH: 36 1/8
LOW: 23
PRICE: 29 5/8
EARN: 2.31
P/E: 13
DEBT: 119
YIELD: —

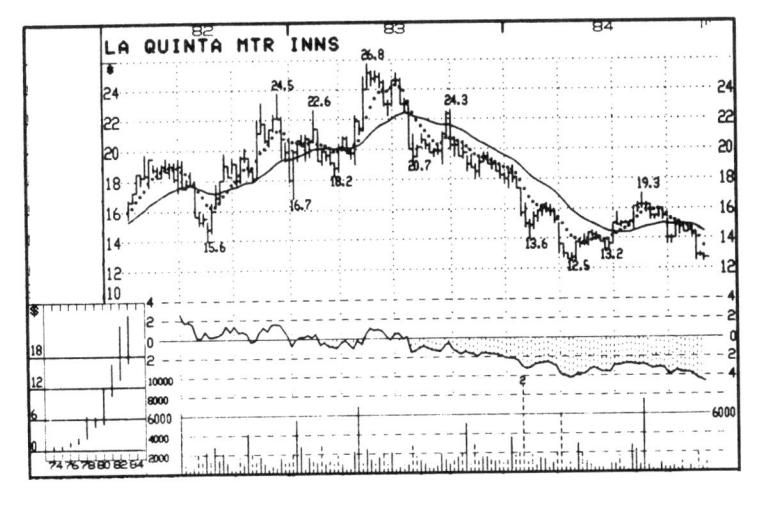

LA QUINTA MTR INNS

TCKR: LQM
HIGH: 19
LOW: 12 1/2
PRICE: 12 3/4
EARN: 0.88
P/E: 14
DEBT: 294
YIELD: —

LEAR PETROLEUM

Lear is a major gas transmission company. Their lines in Kansas, Louisiana, Oklahoma, and Texas increased their throughput in 1983 (the most recently available figures) by 50 percent over the previous year. Lear also explores for and produces oil and gas. At the end of 1983, it completed the purchase of McRae Consolidated Oil and Gas, Inc., adding about three-quarters of a billion barrels to their reserves. But McRae's profit margins have needed bolstering to bring them up to the level of their parent company.

LOWENSTEIN, M.

It might be useful if somehow Kevlar, the bulletproof fabric produced by Lowenstein's Clark-Schwebel division, could be used to protect the parent company's apparel fabrics operation, which has lately seen its market penetrated in force by imports. In fact, Clark-Schwebel's fiberglass fabric business, which sells to industry, is doing quite well, while the apparel division has something of a bleached-out look. Management has tightened that operation but the foreign goods still present a problem. Two of this fabric and textile company's major consumer brands are Pacific and Wamsutta. Recently Lowenstein's stock was split and the dividend upped.

MANOR CARE

This company cares for all manner of guests. Aside from being number four in the U.S. nursing home industry, it also operates Quality Inns. Manor Healthcare Corp. accounts for three-quarters of the revenues of this holding company, and an even higher proportion of its profits. Manor Care is represented in half the states with a total of about 150 facilities containing 20,000 beds. Its ratio of private to Medicare patients is considerably more favorable than that which prevails in the rest of the industry. Demand for places in its homes is therefore high, and new Medicare regulations stipulating earlier discharge of patients from hospitals will increase that part of its clientele. Manor's Quality Inns operate on four continents and have over 650 units with 75,000 rooms; wholly owned units are not doing as well as franchises. Profit margins are highest in the nursing homes, which is where the money from the sale of hotels is now going.

LEAR PETRO.

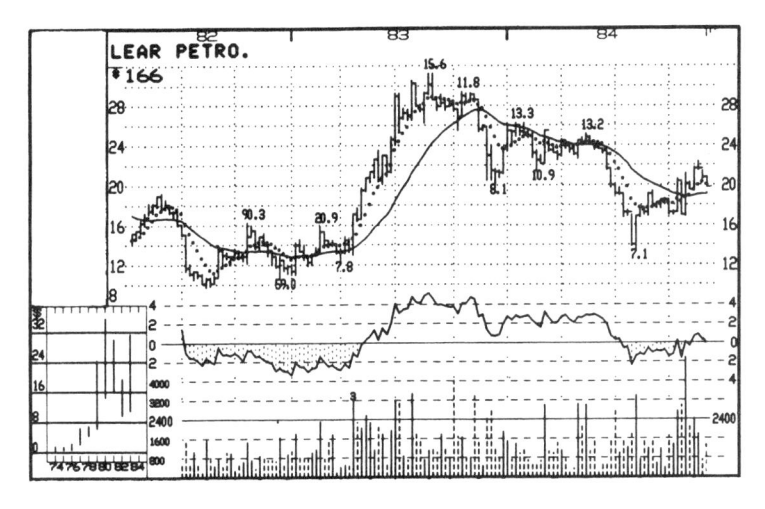

TCKR: LPT
HIGH: 26¼
LOW: 13½
PRICE: 19½
EARN: 1.90
P/E: 10
DEBT: 333
YIELD: 1.0

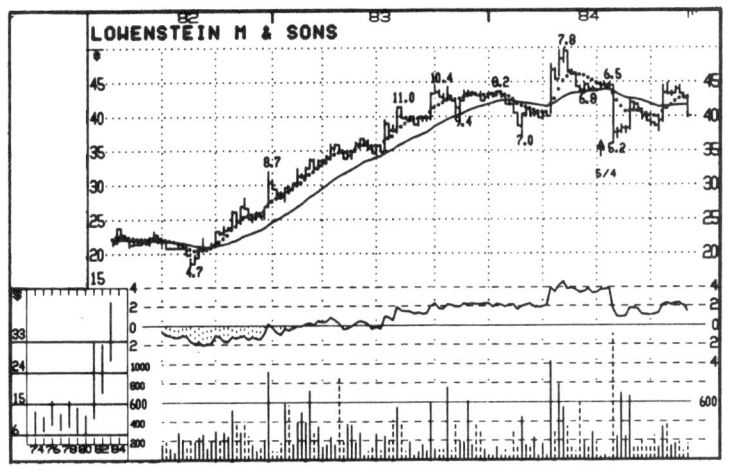

LOWENSTEIN M & SONS

TCKR: LST
HIGH: 49¾
LOW: 36
PRICE: 39
EARN: 7.29
P/E: 5
DEBT: 63.4
YIELD: 5.1

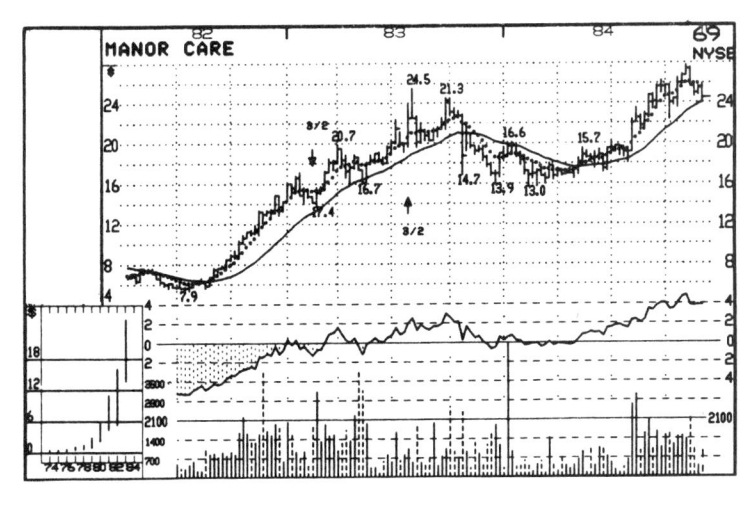

MANOR CARE

TCKR: MNR
HIGH: 18½
LOW: 10½
PRICE: 17⅝
EARN: 1.39
P/E: 13
DEBT: 331
YIELD: —

163

MERCK & CO.

The patent for Aldomet, Merck's lucrative high-blood-pressure drug, expired last year, and the race is on for the lion's share of that market. But the company spent $400 million on research and development in 1984, and it's always introducing new drugs. The anti-inflamation drugs Indocin and Clinoril continue to do well, as does Elavil, a much-prescribed anti-depressant. About one-fifth of Merck's sales (but only about 10 percent of its profits) comes from chemical and environmental products such as Calgon. Merck owns more than one-half of Torii and Banyu, two Japanese pharmaceutical houses, and about half the company's sales are overseas.

MERRILL LYNCH

The largest brokerage firm in the country and in the world is "bullish on America," although the loss of $1.00/share/quarter at the beginning of 1984 sorely tested company optimism. Merrill, Lynch, Pierce, Fenner & Smith has over 500 offices and a tradition of promoting the sale of stocks to even the smallest investor; in fact, it pioneered the marketing of stocks to the general public after World War II when other firms still catered only to the well-to-do. Lately Merrill Lynch has been trying to unbuckle itself from the stock market roller coaster and branch out into a broader line of financial services. Toward that goal, Merrill Lynch Individual Services will help you figure out how to multiply your capital. Merrill Lynch Capital Markets serve industry and government. Merrill Lynch Realty serves the general real estate market, while its subsidiary, Merrill Lynch Hubbard, deals exclusively with institutions. Merrill Lynch recently started operating a special, limited-service "non-bank" bank in New Jersey, the Merrill Lynch Bank & Trust Co.

MESA PETROLEUM

Two years ago, Mesa's T. Boone Pickens, Jr., managed to keep his name in the financial news for several weeks running in an ultimately unsuccessful attempt to grab control of Gulf Oil. Mesa had bought into Gulf to the tune of 13 percent of its shares before Gulf management managed to thwart Pickens' plan to turn Gulf into a royalty trust. With oil and gas earnings sluggish, Mesa has nonetheless done quite well with its financial wheelings and dealings, the Gulf episode notwithstanding. Buying stock in other companies, pressing them to improve operations that would be reflected in higher prices, and then selling out, has been a profitable method of doing business for Mesa. Last year, in a deal closer to home, the company bought back Mesa Royalty Trust, which had been spun off five years previously.

MERCK & CO
CBOE

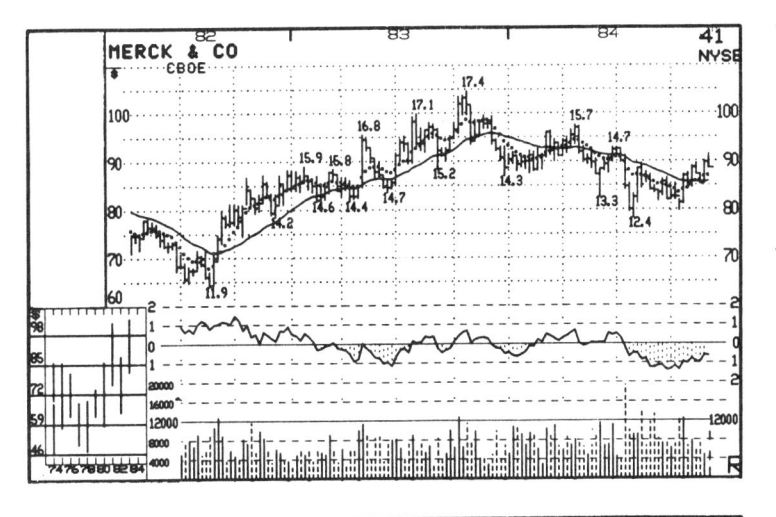

TCKR: MRK
HIGH: 97½
LOW: 78¼
PRICE: 88½
EARN: 6.54
P/E: 14
DEBT: 159
YIELD: 3.6

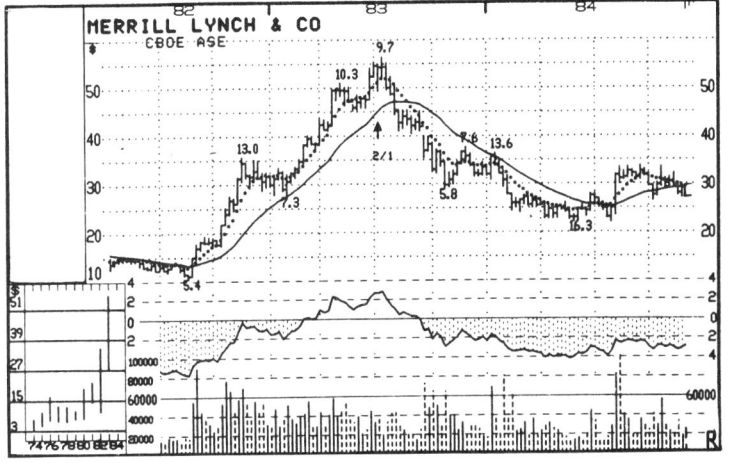

MERRILL LYNCH & CO
CBOE ASE

TCKR: MER
HIGH: 36⅜
LOW: 22
PRICE: 27⅛
EARN: 0.20
P/E: 136
DEBT: 2598
YIELD: 2.9

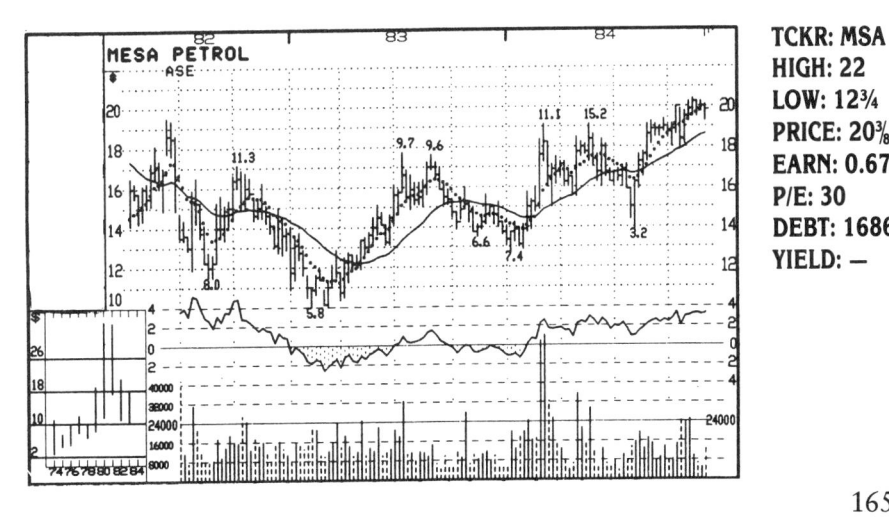

MESA PETROL
ASE

TCKR: MSA
HIGH: 22
LOW: 12¾
PRICE: 20⅜
EARN: 0.67
P/E: 30
DEBT: 1686
YIELD: —

MISSION INSURANCE GROUP

American Financial Corp. owns just under 50 percent of this company, three-fourths of whose premium revenues come from workers' compensation (most of it originating in California). The Mission Insurance Co. and the Holland-American Insurance Co. are in the casualty and property line; reinsurance is handled by Mission Re Management and Pacific Reinsurance Management Co.; Sayre & Toso is Mission's brokerage insurance firm. Mission also owns Carillion Manager's International, George S. Kausler Ltd., and SFO, Inc. Last year saw cuts and delays in the compay's dividends, which reflected the unfavorable spread between premium rates and benefit payouts.

MITEL CORP.

About 90 percent of this Canadian company's profits come from the sale of PBX (private branch exchange) systems, the increasingly complex telephone switchboards that are becoming a vital part of office automation and a prime area of growth in the telecommunications industry. Even so, Mital now has on the drawing boards a system that will be able to switch up to 10,000 lines. Mitel also produces PBX-associated telephone equipment. About half of Mitel's revenues are from U.S. sales, some of which come through RCA distribution. Mitel's research and development are substantial, and its newer products — including digital switching equipment — figure to brighten their profit picture.

MOHAWK DATA SCIENCES

MDS Systems, the company's main division, specializes in data entry systems, distributed processing, and electronic mail. Quantel makes hardware and writes software for various manufacturing and retail operations and sells Sports Pac, software designed to help manage athletic teams. MDS Storms produces computer supplies. And about three-quarters of the photo-ID driver's licenses in the U.S. are produced by MDS Dek Identification Systems. But last year Mohawk lost $53 million. Quantel's profits were drained by a lawsuit, and Mohawk wrote off the costs of folding its MDS Trivex company, which made computer terminals.

MISSION INS GROUP

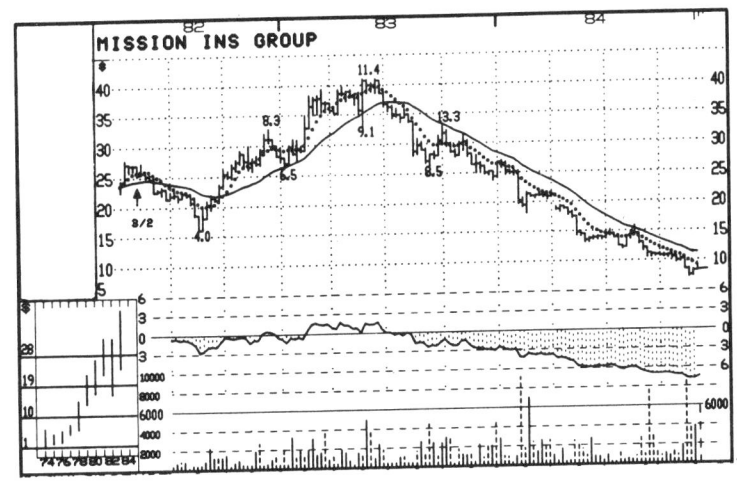

TCKR: MEQ
HIGH: 27
LOW: 7¼
PRICE: 8⅝
EARN: d7.29
P/E: d
DEBT: 71.0
YIELD: —

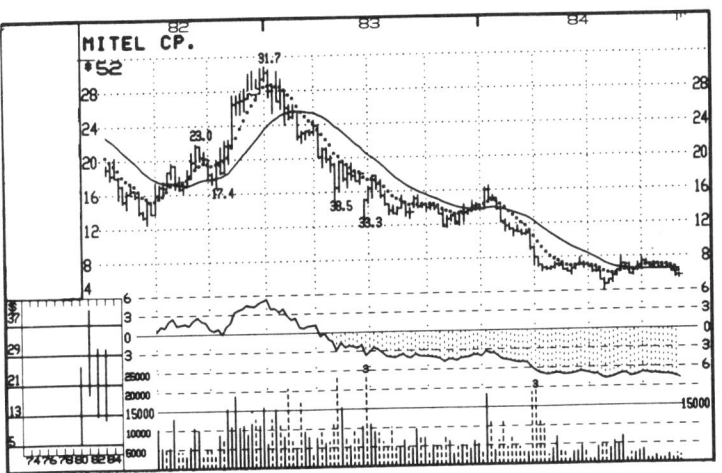

MITEL CP.

TCKR: MLT
HIGH: 16½
LOW: 4
PRICE: 5
EARN: d1.13
P/E: d
DEBT: 199
YIELD: —

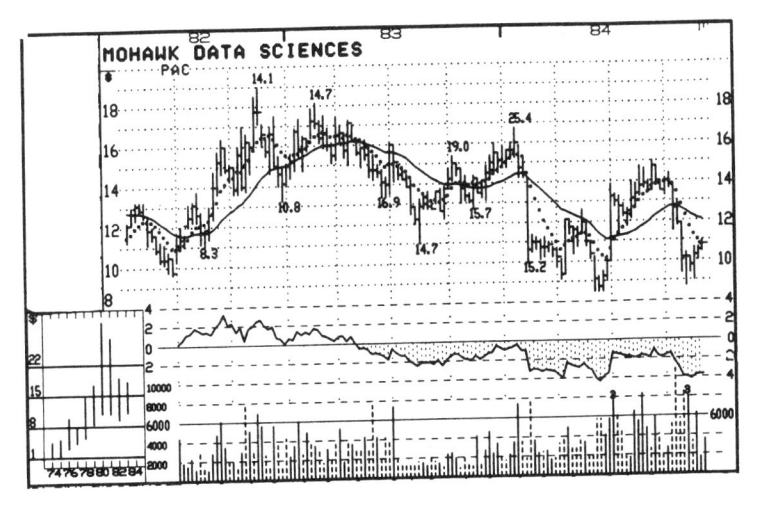

MOHAWK DATA SCIENCES

TCKR: MDS
HIGH: 16¾
LOW: 8½
PRICE: 10¾
EARN: d3.85
P/E: d
DEBT: 143
YIELD: —

MONTANA-DAKOTA UTILITIES

It really ought to be "Dakota-Montana," because North Dakota, where M-D sells nearly 50 percent of its electric power, is by far its biggest market. The company also serves Minnesota, Montana, South Dakota, and Wyoming with electricity and gas. Montana-Dakota's electricity is produced almost exclusively from coal — about 6 million tons a year comes from its own mines. The company transmits gas through their Williston Basin Interstate Pipeline. Montana-Dakota has not gotten the gas rate increases that it felt it needed to make a fair profit, but that situation may change soon.

NATIONAL EDUCATION

Because in recent years Americans have put a high value on vocational education, National Education's main thrust, this company began 1984 with a streak of nine consecutive years of improved earnings. And their product mix makes it a business for all economic seasons: When the economy is healthy, National Education's industry-contracted training programs flourish; during economic downturns, individual enrollment in vocational courses increases as workers seek to provide themselves with skills that will help them in a tight job market. Operations in National's ICS-Intext division include North American Correspondence Schools and International Correspondence Schools. Steck-Vaughn is its educational publishing company. Last year National Education flirted with the possibility of buying Bell & Howell, but finally pulled back.

NATIONAL MEDICAL ENTERPRISES

Sometime ago management in this company took a temperature reading and found it a bit off. Their prescription was an efficiency program — aimed at improving profit margins. National now presides over about 20,000 beds in acute-care hospitals. Half the revenues from those units come from Medicare. It also operates approximately 30 psychiatric hospitals, a few drugstores, and close to 300 nursing homes. Abroad, National provides health care services in Saudi Arabia. A year ago the company bought a Florida health maintenance organization called AV-MED and started HealthPace, a health insurance plan.

MONTANA DAKOTA UTIL

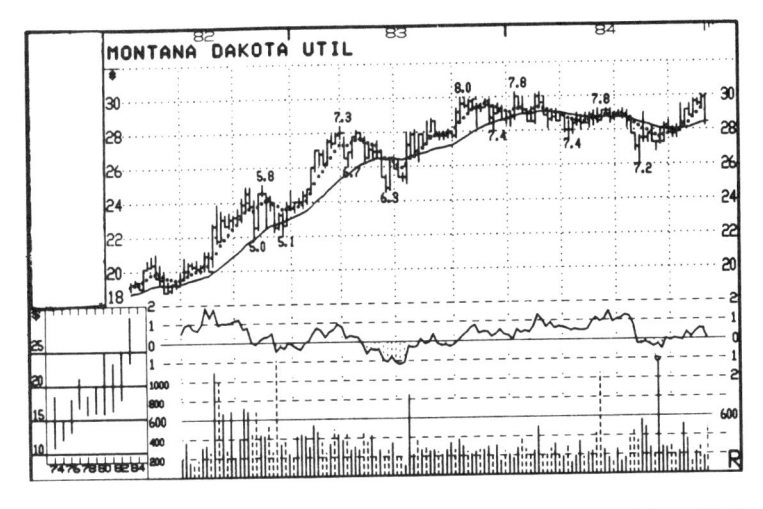

TCKR: MDU
HIGH: 30¼
LOW: 26
PRICE: 28¾
EARN: 3.90
P/E: 7
DEBT: 206
YIELD: 8.9

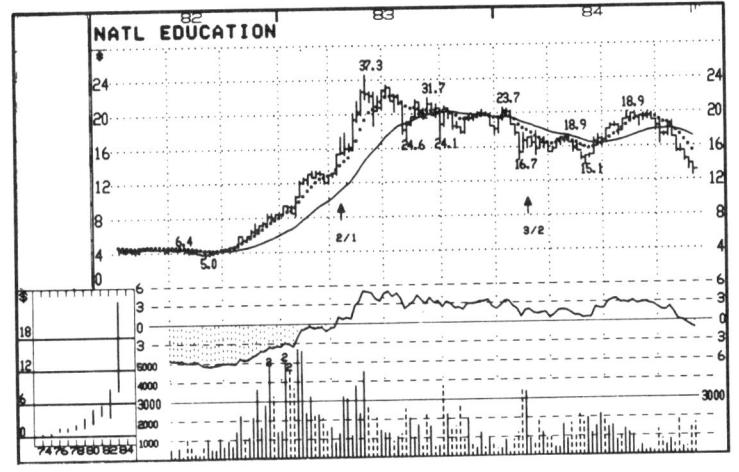

NATL EDUCATION

TCKR: NEC
HIGH: 20⅝
LOW: 12½
PRICE: 14
EARN: 1.13
P/E: 12
DEBT: 8.10
YIELD: —

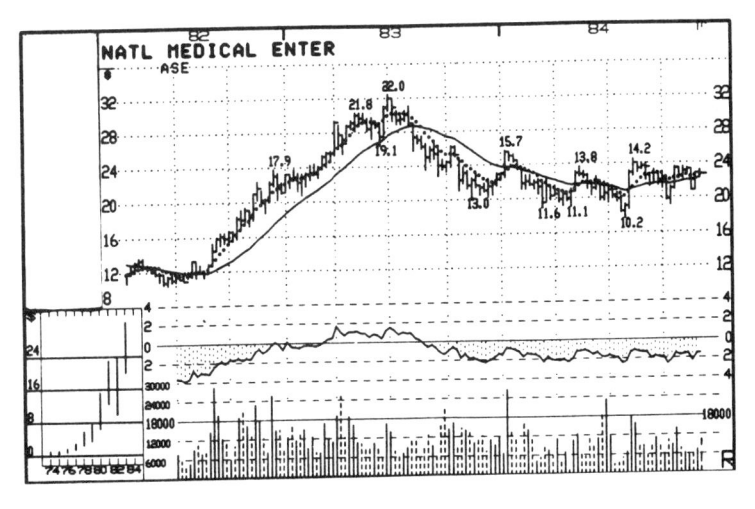

NATL MEDICAL ENTER

TCKR: NME
HIGH: 25⅝
LOW: 17⅞
PRICE: 22¼
EARN: 1.82
P/E: 12
DEBT: 1029
YIELD: 2.3

NATIONAL SEMICONDUCTOR

The company makes IBM-compatible computers — and so do a lot of other companies. In addition to manufacturing complete computers it also supplies the electronics industry with the vital integrated circuits and microprocessors that are at the heart of computerization. In that area National is well positioned to take advantage of the large demand for metal-oxide semiconductors projected for the next few years. National Semiconductor also makes speech synthesizers and the logic circuits used in calculators. Production of the company's thirty-two-bit microprocessor, in demand for engineering applications, has been partially farmed out to Texas Instruments to ensure a sufficient supply. National's Datachecker/Dts makes point-of-sale devices for supermarkets, while National Advanced Systems sells and services mainframe computers.

NCNB CORP.

North Carolina National Bank, the biggest bank in the Southeast, heads the list of this company's bank holdings. Its NCNB National Bank of Florida is one of that state's largest. Last year's acquisition of the Ellis Banking Corp., also in Florida, made NCNB's Florida-based assets — which are often employed by the construction industry — 30 percent of the company's total. Commercial loans and leases constitute about one-third of NCNB's assets, with savings accounts and CD's their prime source of funds. Nonperforming loans have recently been under 1 percent. NCNB has upward of 500 branch offices in the United States, and 6 abroad.

NCR CORP.

National Cash Register's name just doesn't do it justice: This corporation has long since gone beyond cash registers to become a big force in high-tech office machinery of many types. The company stresses office automation and data processing and sells a full line of computer peripherals. NCR derives approximately half its revenues from foreign operations, which caused the price of its stock to dip in 1984, in part because of pressure from a strong dollar on overseas profits.

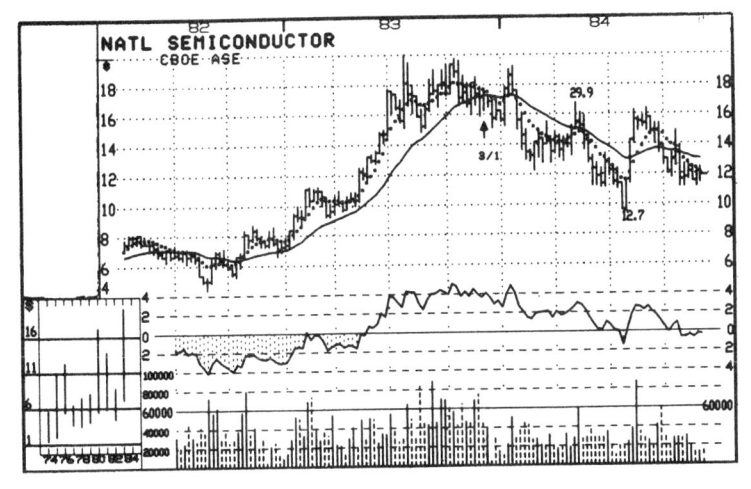

TCKR: NSM
HIGH: 19¼
LOW: 9½
PRICE: 12
EARN: 0.88
P/E: 14
DEBT: 87.4
YIELD: —

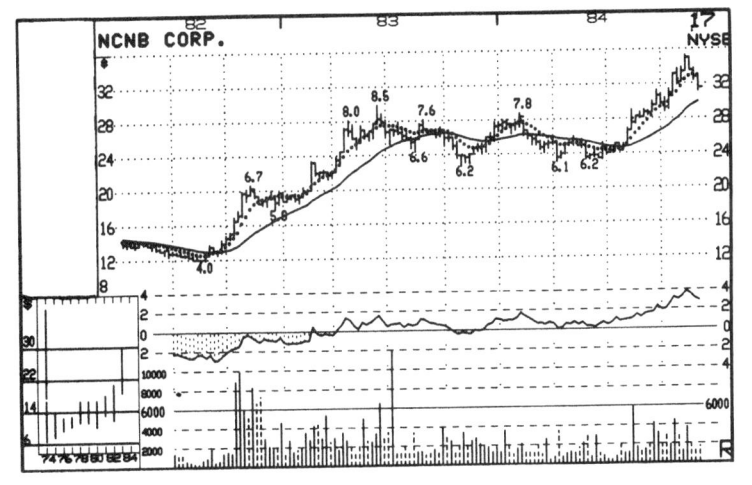

TCKR: NCB
HIGH: 35¼
LOW: 23
PRICE: 32⅝
EARN: 3.98
P/E: 8
DEBT: 326
YIELD: 4.0

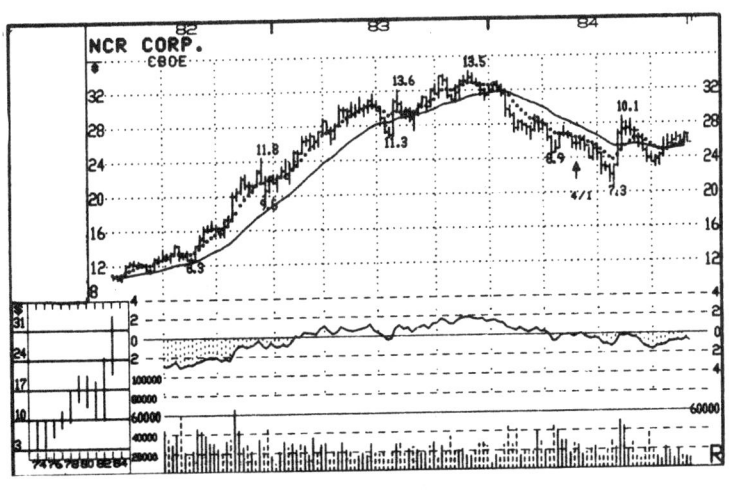

TCKR: NCR
HIGH: 33
LOW: 20⅝
PRICE: 26⅛
EARN: 3.15
P/E: 8
DEBT: 248
YIELD: 3.1

171

NL INDUSTRIES

This company has purposefully gone off the deep end. NL, which is in the top five in the petroleum services industry, has been concentrating much of its activity in deep drilling operations, with the focus on gas production. But the market for that gas has been weak, leaving NL in somewhat of a hole; and Baroid, NL's drilling-fluid company, has been stuck in the mud of competition and price cutting. The demand for general drilling services is very important to NL's profit picture, and lately the demand has been picking up. NL shares ownership of Titanium Metals Corp. with Allegheny International, where titanium dioxide pigments have been doing well, although future prospects are not clear. Last year NL acquired Digicon, an oil exploration service company.

NORTH AMERICAN PHILIPS

North American Philips has close ties to N.V. Philips, the Dutch company that developed the audio cassette in the 60s. The American firm draws on the Dutch for new consumer electronics technology, much of it sold through its Magnavox, Norelco, Philco, and Sylvania divisions. Magnavox and Sylvania, for example, are now featuring versions of the compact disk player, the machine that is on the frontier of stereo sound reproduction. Philips is also in the lighting business: Two years ago it substantially boosted its interest in that area with the purchase of Westinghouse Electric's lamp division and Corning Glass's Kentucky glass bulb plant. Philips sells electronic equipment to the cable television and health-care industries, and electronic components to the Defense Department. The company also manufactures furniture and musical instruments.

NORWEST CORP.

This Minneapolis-headquartered holding company, which used to be called Northwest Bancorp., controls eighty-six banks in Minnesota, Iowa, Nebraska, Montana, South Dakota, and Wisconsin. About 40 percent of its business is in commercial loans. Bad times on the farm in 1982 and 1983 mean nonperforming loans; and as of this writing, farm profits are still problematic. One key to the future success of this area of Norwest's business would be a decline in the value of the dollar, which would boost agricultural exports. Norwest Financial Services represents the company's growing interest in that consumer-oriented business.

NL IND.
PAC PHL

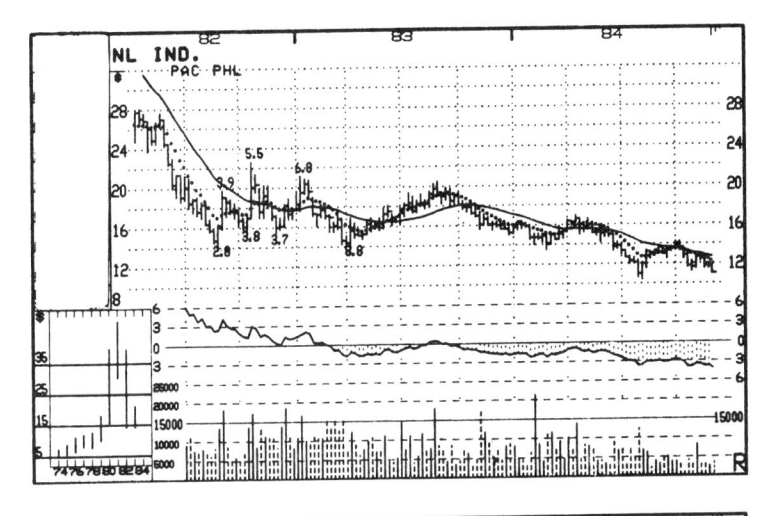

TCKR: NL
HIGH: 17
LOW: 10 3/8
PRICE: 11
EARN: 0.68
P/E: 16
DEBT: 268
YIELD: 1.8

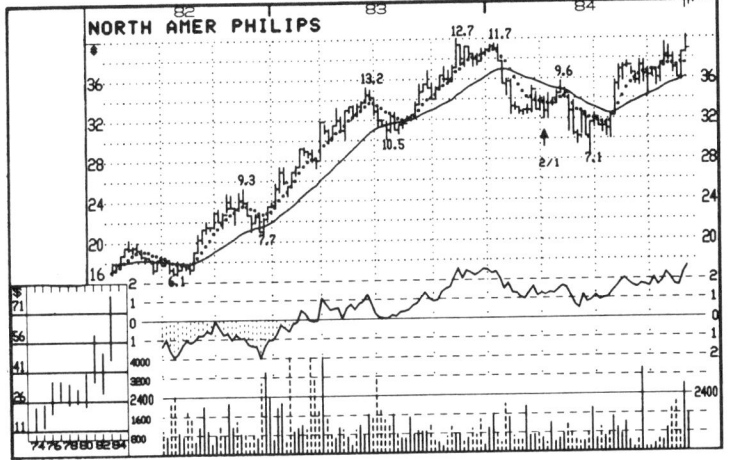

NORTH AMER PHILIPS

TCKR: NPH
HIGH: 40 1/2
LOW: 28 1/2
PRICE: 38
EARN: 4.39
P/E: 9
DEBT: 454
YIELD: 2.6

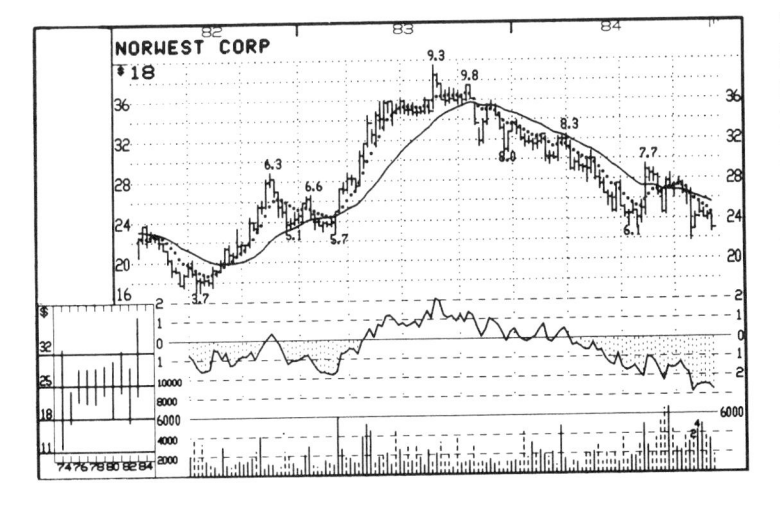

NORWEST CORP

TCKR: NOB
HIGH: 33 7/8
LOW: 21 1/2
PRICE: 22 3/8
EARN: 1.81
P/E: 12
DEBT: 1722
YIELD: 8.0

OAK INDUSTRIES

Oak has carved out a niche for itself in noncable pay television, but how desirable is that niche? Customer base has dropped to 350,000, with Los Angeles and Chicago its strongholds; Oak's Miami system has been all but beaten into the ground by competing cable services. The company also produces equipment used by similar over-the-air services and, hedging their bets, makes devices used by cable television systems. Oak/Adek, the electronics controls systems division, depends partly on military contracts, which have not been garnered in big numbers. Oak does have high hopes for its Sigma System, a cable television signal anti-pirating device.

OCEAN DRILLING AND EXPLORATION

A plus for Ocean Drilling and Exploration is that offshore drilling is not likely to be greatly affected by anything OPEC might do in the next few years. That's a pleasant prospect for a company that happens to have one of the largest fleets of deep water-oriented offshore rigs (43 at last count) in the world. Its once tepid Gulf operations are picking up, as are operations in the North Sea. Current reserves total about 70 billion barrels of oil and slightly more than 350 billion cubic feet of gas. Almost two-thirds of its profits come from overseas operations. They own Sub Sea International (a diving service) and Mentor Insurance (property/casualty).

ORION PICTURES

Low budgets, the banking of television rights before anybody cries "action," and coproduction are some of the ways that the former Filmways has sought to make it in the competitive atmosphere of Hollywood. Its method is to contract with independent producers, finance their works, and then take title to the completed film. Orion, which will release about fifteen films this year, sells to all parts of the television market, from the networks to home video. HBO is an important investor in Orion, as well as an important customer. Orion management, part of which used to be with United Artists, had little to give thanks for last year, when several of the company's releases turned out to be turkeys. Orion apparently believes in product mix: Recent films include *Amadeus* and *Return of the Living Dead*. Orion also owns $15 million worth of *The Cotton Club*.

OAK IND

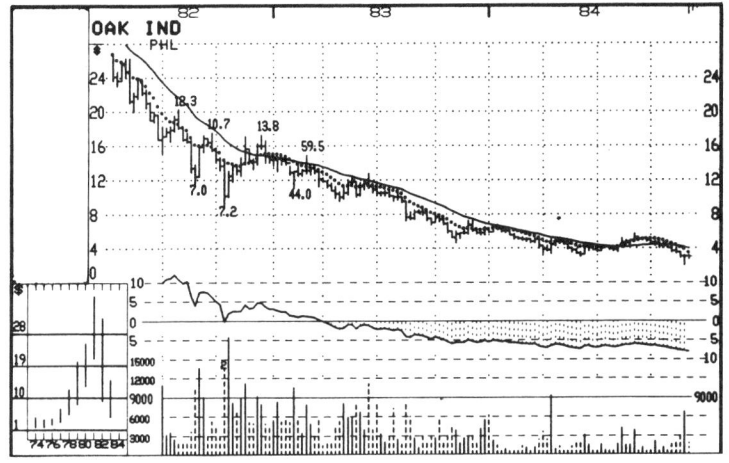

TCKR: OAK
HIGH: 6¾
LOW: 2
PRICE: 2⅝
EARN: d5.65
P/E: d
DEBT: 226
YIELD: —

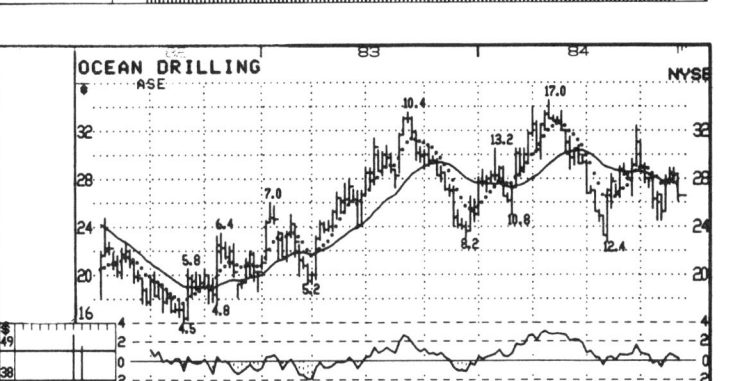

OCEAN DRILLING

TCKR: ODR
HIGH: 34½
LOW: 22¾
PRICE: 25⅛
EARN: 1.65
P/E: 15
DEBT: 189
YIELD: 4.0

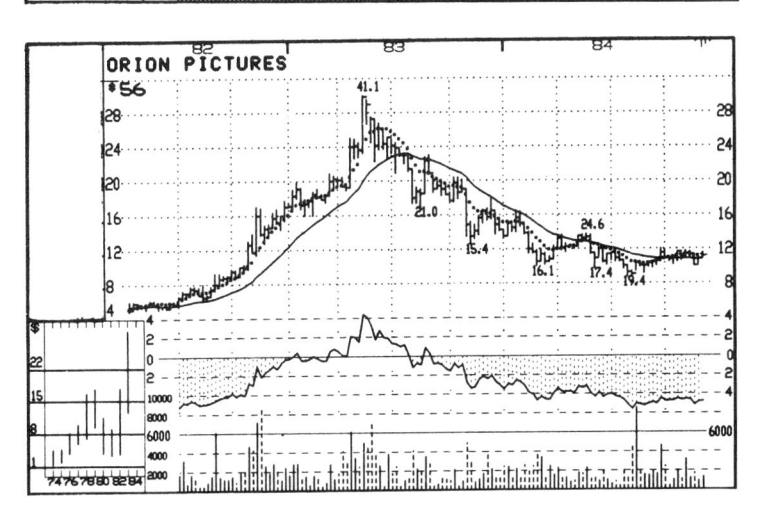

ORION PICTURES

TCKR: OPC
HIGH: 16½
LOW: 8¾
PRICE: 9½
EARN: 0.33
P/E: 29
DEBT: 95.5
YIELD: —

OWENS-ILLINOIS

If it's a glass container and it's found in a supermarket or drugstore, there's a good chance that it's made by Owens. The company also makes containers out of metals, plastics, and wood-based fibers. It is also known for container board, which is homegrown: Owens owns about a million acres of trees. Last year the company bought Prudent Supply, Inc., a health-care products distributor, and was in the process of purchasing Dougherty Brothers Co., which manufactures plastic health-care products. Other recent acquisitions include U.S. Cap & Closure and Brockway's tube operations. Owens's glass product growth prospects are less than crystal clear, and management has been considering expansion into other areas, including financial services. Unresolved lawsuits involving past Owens asbestos operations cast a small shadow over the balance sheet.

PACIFIC GAS AND ELECTRIC

This company's area is in northern California. About a quarter of its power comes from dams, a third from the burning of oil and gas, and some is geothermally produced. But the 10,000,000 customer base is growing quickly, and some time ago PG&E decided that they would need to go atomic. Unfortunately, the Diablo Canyon nuclear plant was built — at a cost of $5 billion — on top of an earthquake fault, and that has led to some devilish problems. Full testing of Diablo's unit 1 has been held up while its safety is debated.

PACIFIC SCIENTIFIC

This company makes snubbers, inertia reel lap belts, and other exotic-sounding products. Snubbers cushion sensitive facilities, such as nuclear plants, against earthquake shock (sales are off because of the dearth of activity in the nuclear plant construction industry); the belts are used by airplane pilots. In fact, more than 90 percent of Pacific Scientific's profits come from products which restrain something. Pac-Sci also makes instruments that monitor quality control in various industries; one division produces bellows and seals. Last year the company bought Honeywell's Motor Products operations. Those motors are used in computer peripherals and robotics products and may offer some growth opportunities.

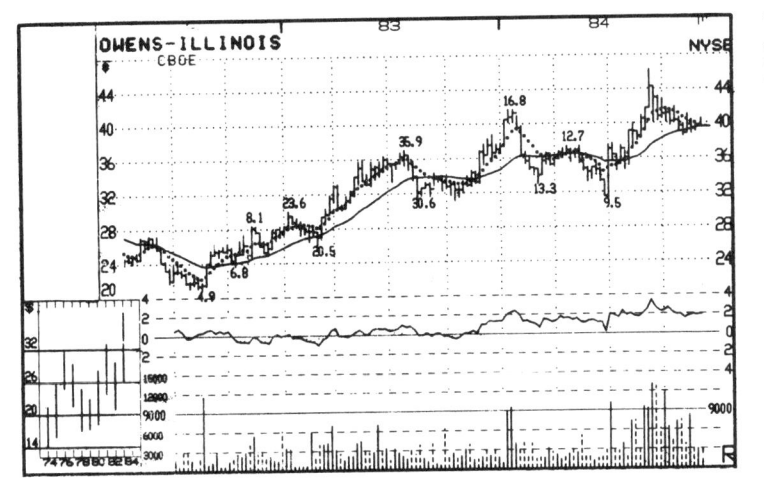

TCKR: OI
HIGH: 46¼
LOW: 31¼
PRICE: 38⅞
EARN: 4.83
P/E: 8
DEBT: 512
YIELD: 4.3

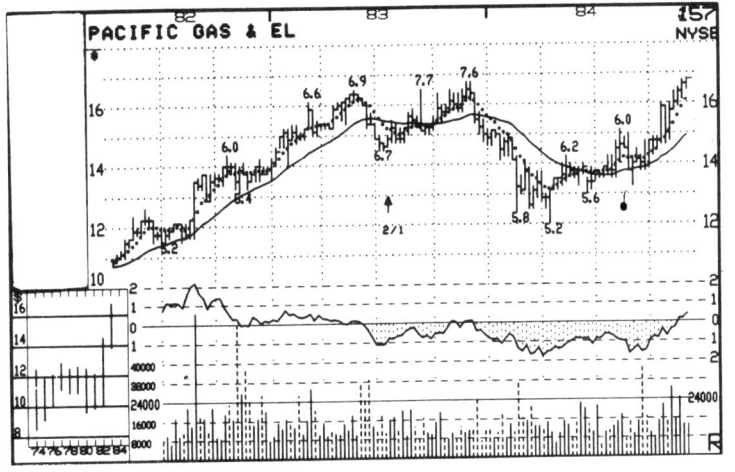

TCKR: PCG
HIGH: 16¾
LOW: 12⅜
PRICE: 16
EARN: 2.40
P/E: 7
DEBT: 6074
YIELD: 10.9

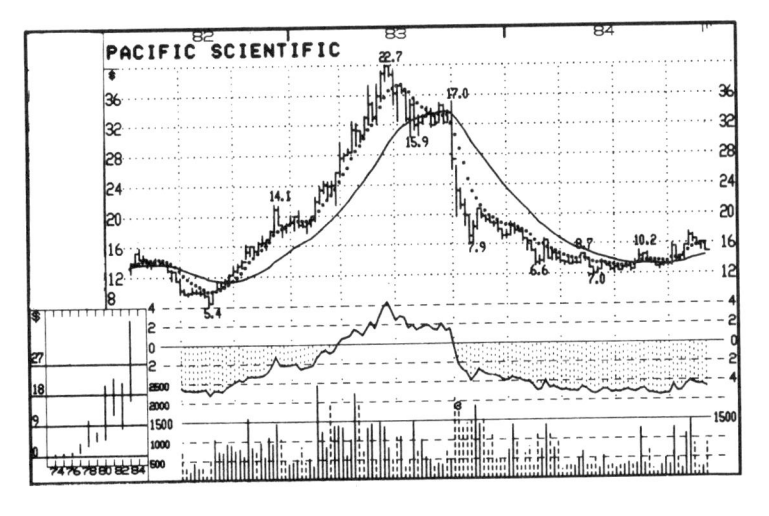

TCKR: PSX
HIGH: 19
LOW: 11⅞
PRICE: 14¼
EARN: 1.25
P/E: 11
DEBT: 30.8
YIELD: 2.8

177

PAINE WEBBER GROUP

The flagship of this holding company is Paine, Webber, Jackson & Curtis, with over 250 branch offices (double the number in the late 70s) and upwards of 4,000 brokers. Institutional research is conducted by Paine Webber Mitchell Hutchins, and investment banking by Blyth Eastman Paine Webber. Paine Webber Real Estate Securities markets government-guaranteed issues. Two years ago the company acquired two regional securities firms: First Mid America, Inc., and Rotan Mosle Financial Corp. Last year the firm was in the process of acquiring Rouse Co.'s mortgage banking operations, making mortgages a more important part of the Paine Webber product mix.

PARKER-HANNIFIN

This company's assets may vary in liquidity, but the material Parker works with rarely does. Its equipment pumps, pushes, cools, and contains a variety of liquids. Aerospace companies, the U.S. Defense Department, and the automobile industry use Parker-Hannifin devices to control and manipulate fluid systems. Last year, Parker's cylinders, seals, pumps, and valves brought the company a 20 percent increase in sales over the previous year, with aerospace products a leading factor. Parker-Hannifin's small biomedical division is only four years old and may yet produce big things. Parker-Hannifin continues its tradition of substantial research and development expenditures.

POGO PRODUCING

This onetime Pennzoil affiliate explores for oil and gas. Drilling locations include Oklahoma, New Mexico, Texas, and widespread areas in the Rockies. Pogo is also bouncing around the Texas Gulf, looking for offshore deposits there. As of the middle of last year, Pogo was selling more gas but enjoying it less: Canadian competition and the generally depressed gas price level put a crimp on gas profits. The company has reserves of about 20 million barrels of oil and 268 billion cubic feet of gas. Its biggest gas customer is United Energy Pipeline. Two years ago, Pogo management met the enemy, who turned out to be Northwest Industries, Inc., and SEDCO, Inc., which tried unsuccessfully for an unfriendly joint takeover.

PAINE WEBBER GROUP INC

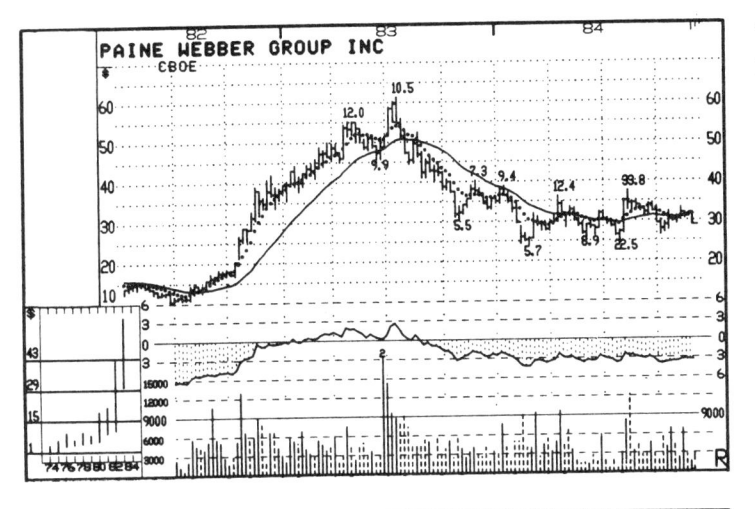

TCKR: PWJ
HIGH: 38 7/8
LOW: 23 5/8
PRICE: 28
EARN: 0.77
P/E: 36
DEBT: 245
YIELD: 2.1

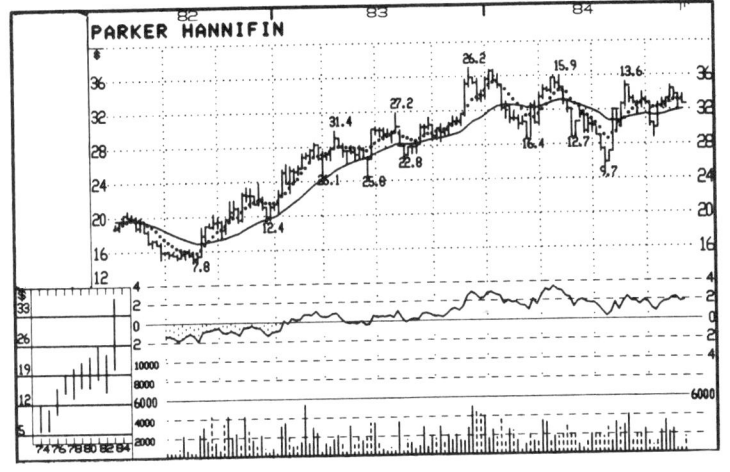

PARKER HANNIFIN

TCKR: PH
HIGH: 36 3/4
LOW: 25 1/4
PRICE: 32
EARN: 3.02
P/E: 11
DEBT: 146
YIELD: 3.5

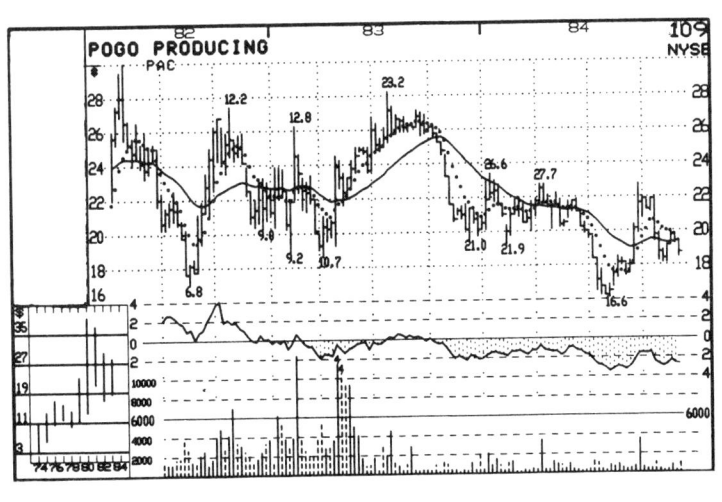

POGO PRODUCING

TCKR: PPP
HIGH: 23 3/8
LOW: 16 1/8
PRICE: 17 3/8
EARN: 0.93
P/E: 19
DEBT: 390
YIELD: 3.5

PRIME COMPUTER

The company may very well be *in* its prime, with capital budget and product introduction up, an increased sales force, and substantial sums allocated for marketing. The main target of all this activity is Prime's traditional customer base — the Fortune 500, to whom Prime sells both hardware and software. Although this company makes just about every part of its computer systems (except peripherals) itself, the focus is on thirty-two-bit minicomputers. Current emphasis is on CAD/CAM systems (sales of which are approaching $100 million a year) and office and factory workstations. The company also sells a variety of software, including programs enabling Prime machines to link up with any other computer, regardless of manufacturer.

PRIME MOTOR INNS

The motel sign may say Days Inns, Howard Johnson, Ramada, or Sheraton, but if it's in New Jersey, Florida, or New York, there's a good chance your host is really Prime Motor Inns. Prime is a franchisee for those chains, with about 50 units and 6,000 rooms to clean — that is, until the company added 7,000 more from Holiday, which came with Prime's purchase of American Motor Inns. Business travelers are this company's prime customers. In 1984 Prime's occupancy rate was 60 percent, and management is aiming for an annual growth rate of 25 percent in available rooms. PMI hopes to achieve that through purchases — 11 Cindy's Budget Inns last year — and building more of its own units. Prime has been carefully raising room rates in locations that will bear it.

PROCTER & GAMBLE

Its products clean your wash, body, breath, teeth, hair, and sink. They will also help you bake a cake and eat it, too — with coffee or tea. They are: Bold, Bounce, Bounty, Camay, Cascade, Charmin, Cheer, Coast, Comet, Crest, Crisco, Dawn, Downy, Duncan Hines, Era, Folger's, Head and Shoulders, Hires, Ivory, Jif, Joy, Luvs, Mr. Clean, Oxydol, Pampers, Pepto-Bismol, Pringle's, Safeguard, Scope, Secret, Spic and Span, Tenderleaf, and Tide. In 1983, Proctor & Gamble, with Citrus Hill, went head-to-head with Tropicana and Minute Maid into the big orange juice market. P&G fights competition on a wide front along its product line battlements, but its brands are always backed with big research and development and marketing muscle.

PRIME COMPUTER

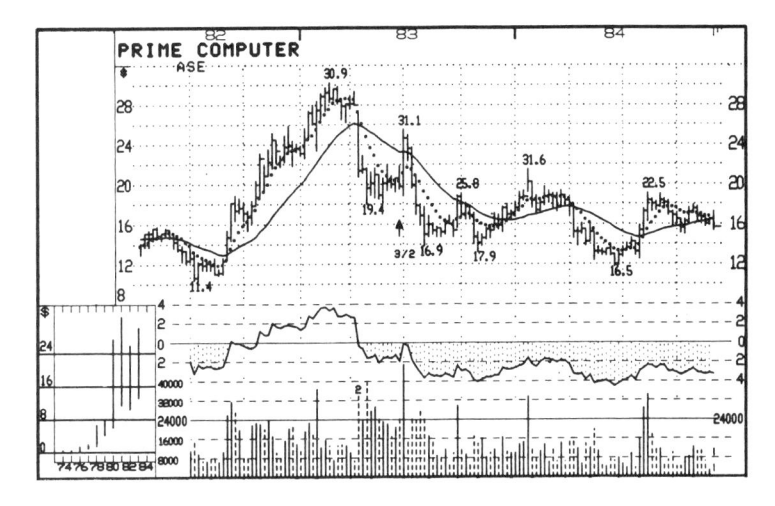

TCKR: PRM
HIGH: 21½
LOW: 11¾
PRICE: 15¾
EARN: 1.15
P/E: 14
DEBT: 18.4
YIELD: —

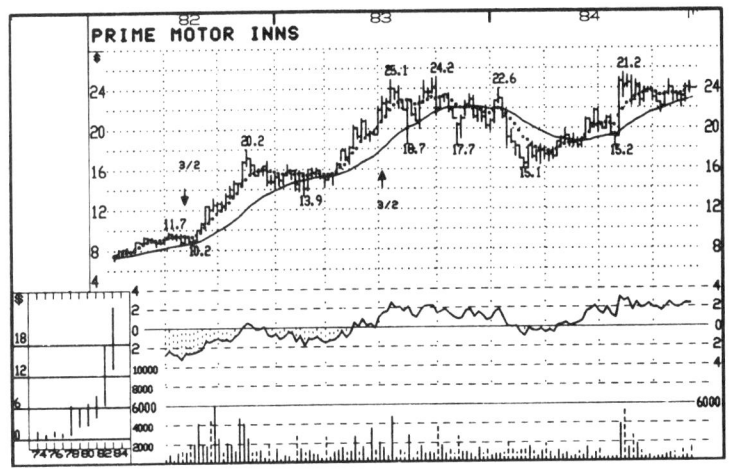

PRIME MOTOR INNS

TCKR: PDQ
HIGH: 25½
LOW: 16
PRICE: 23⅛
EARN: 1.20
P/E: 19
DEBT: 88.9
YIELD: 0.5

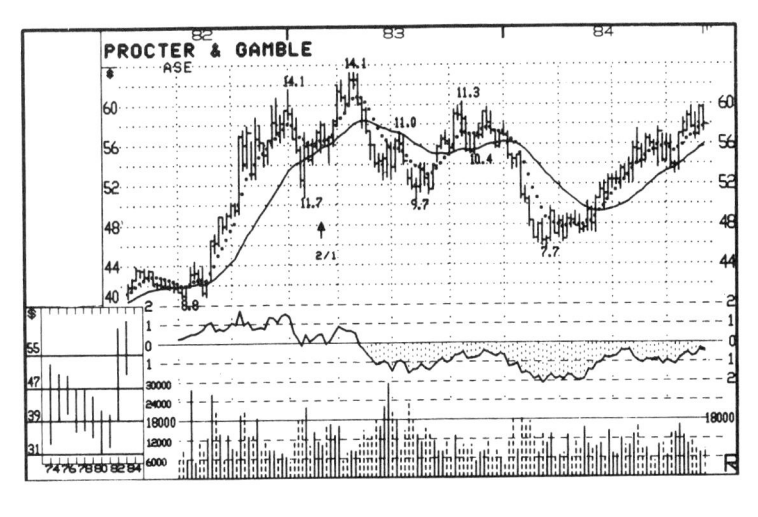

PROCTER & GAMBLE

TCKR: PG
HIGH: 59⅞
LOW: 45⅝
PRICE: 58⅝
EARN: 5.05
P/E: 12
DEBT 628
YIELD: 4.4

PUBLIC SERVICE OF COLORADO

Sales of gas and electricity each account for about 50 percent of Public Service's profits. Coal generates 90 percent of its power, which is sold primarily in the Cheyenne and Denver areas. Less than 5 percent is produced by PSC's one nuclear plant. The company also buys power from other sources. Fuelco is Public Service of Colorado's oil and gas exploration and production company; Bannock Center Corp. is its real estate division. Public Service's four-year construction plan currently calls for the expenditure of a billion dollars.

QUAKER OATS

Investors older than thirty-five may recall from the early days of television the cowboy star Gabby Hayes shooting Quaker Oats cereal from a cannon. Were he around today, the white-bearded cowpoke might use a shotgun, because Quaker Oats has begun to scatter its efforts in a number of directions. To be sure, Quaker Oats still makes cereal. But, they also sell other food brands, including Aunt Jemima, Celeste, Flako, Gatorade, Stokely-Van Camp and Wolf — not to mention Ken-L-Ration and Puss 'n Boots for the furry four-legged set. The company also owns Fisher-Price, the top company in the manufacturing of toys for younger children. Quaker is also in direct mail sales, marketing a variety of merchandise through Brookstone, Herrschners, and Joseph A. Bank Clothiers. A cash flow surplus makes an addition to Quaker's diverse activities more than likely.

RAMADA INNS

Ramada has found security and steadiness — and substantial profits — in gambling. This prominent American innkeeper has hotels and casinos in Las Vegas and Atlantic City — one such establishment in each location, each named The Tropicana. (And it's not orange juice they're pouring out.) Ramada depends on these casinos for more than 50 percent of its revenues and, understandably, dotes on them — especially the one in Atlantic City. It will get a big new showroom this year; an adjacent amusement park, new parking garage, and enlarged gambling area are also in the works. Then there are the rest of the ubiquitous (but aging) Ramada Inns. About 70 units — with approximately 14,000 rooms — are owned directly, but the company is moving away from sole ownership. Another 80,000 or so rooms in about 525 units are licensed out; Ramada also manages a few units for other companies.

PUBLIC SV CO COLO

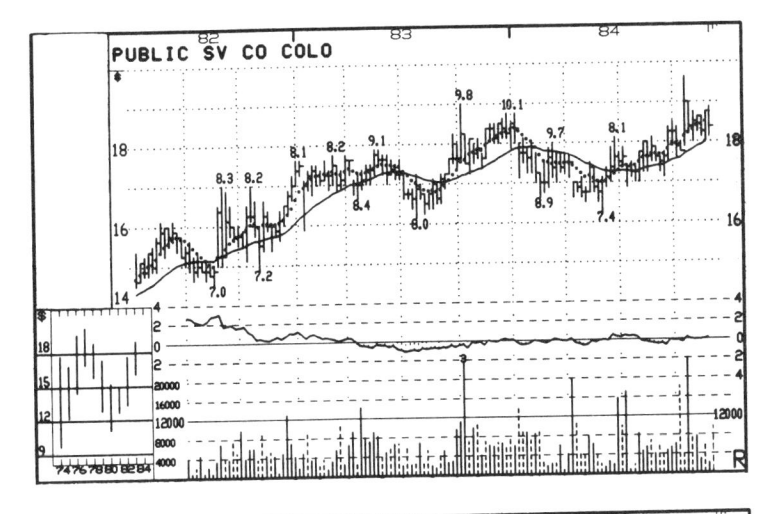

TCKR: PSR
HIGH: 19⅝
LOW: 16¼
PRICE: 18¾
EARN: 2.33
P/E: 8
DEBT: 893
YIELD: 10.2

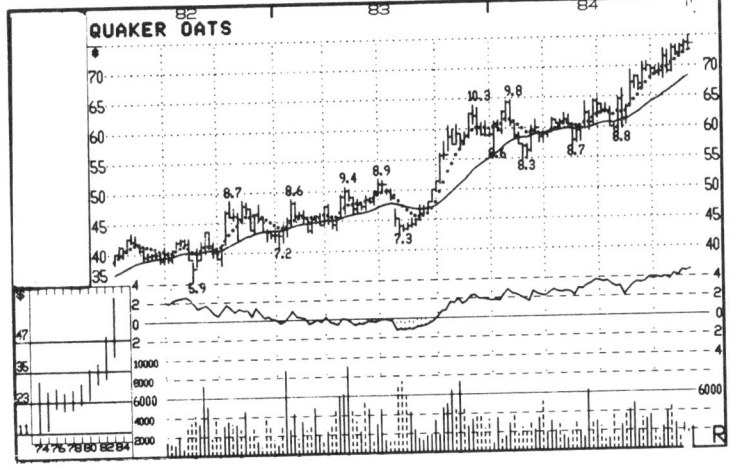

QUAKER OATS

TCKR: OAT
HIGH: 37¾
LOW: 27¼
PRICE: 36½
EARN: 6.58
P/E: 6
DEBT: 200
YIELD: 3.5

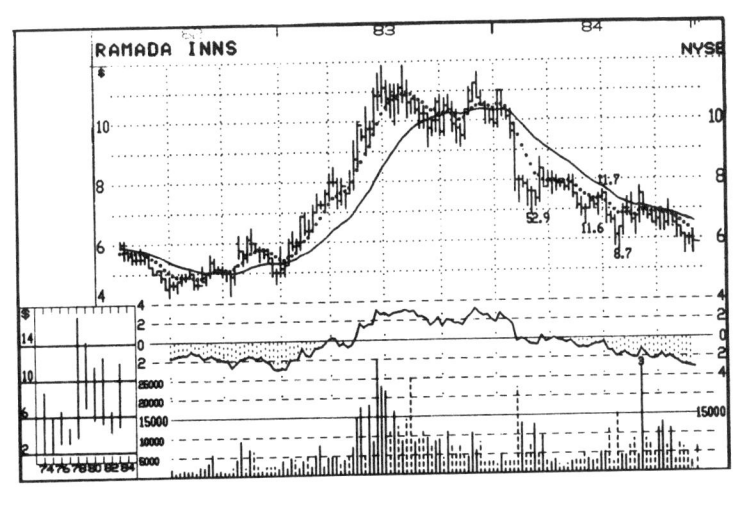

RAMADA INNS

TCKR: RAM
HIGH: 11
LOW: 5⅛
PRICE: 5¾
EARN: 0.18
P/E: 32
DEBT: 417
YIELD: —

RANGER OIL LTD.

This Canadian firm brings up a good deal of gas in its own country, and next year it will be part of a consortium that will test the waters off China as oil drilling spreads to a previously fallow area. But Ranger's main area of concern, in more ways than one, lies in the North Sea. Last year it drew up only slightly more than half the oil produced there the previous year—partly the result of turning off the spigot to perform maintenance operations. But the prospects for future Ranger success at this location, according to industry analysts, are by no means clear. What is certain is that Ranger has just about run out of the tax credits that have been so handy in recent years.

RECOGNITION EQUIPMENT

Its number one customer is the Internal Revenue Service. And the IRS could be using one of this company's products to put the finger on *you*—that is, if your tax return is atypical enough to be singled out by one of Recognition Equipment's optical scanners. These devices—the sensors through which printed information may be assimilated directly by the computer without it having to be typed out on a keyboard—are used to provide input from standard forms and other documents into central computers. Through optical character recognition, the machines process checks for banks, and their bar code scanners serve as point-of-sale devices in retail stores. The credit card industry also uses Recognition products. About 40 percent of Recognition profits are derived from overseas business, so continuing strength in the dollar will pose a problem.

REDMAN INDUSTRIES

This company used to make mobile homes and deal in real estate. Now it concentrates on manufacturing complete houses, an industry in which output is measured in so many "floors" per month or year. In the past few years, however, Redman has had to worry less about floors and more about the possibility of mortgage rates going through the roof. When rates are reasonable and the market is good, Redman's eighteen factories sell basic homes to a steady flow of average Americans who are looking in the $9,000 to $40,000 range. The company's building products line (doors, windows, etc.) accounts for about one-third of its sales.

RANGER OIL LIMITED

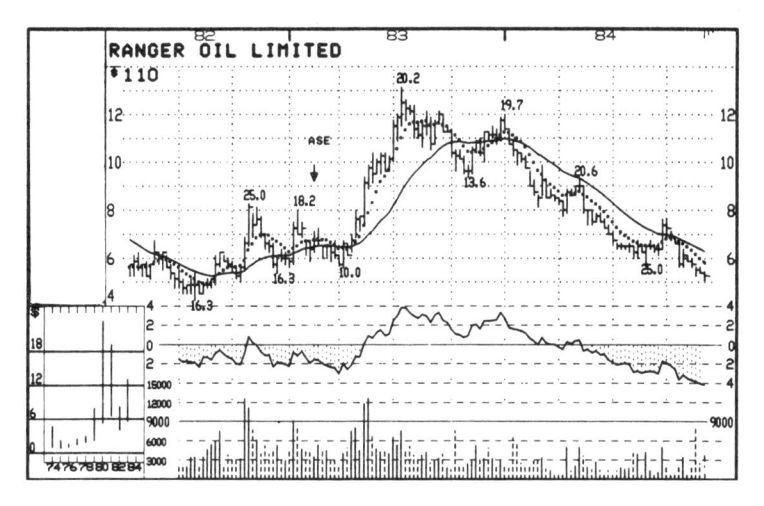

TCKR: RGO
HIGH: 12
LOW: 4⅞
PRICE: 5¼
EARN: 0.23
P/E: 23
DEBT: 82.1
YIELD: —

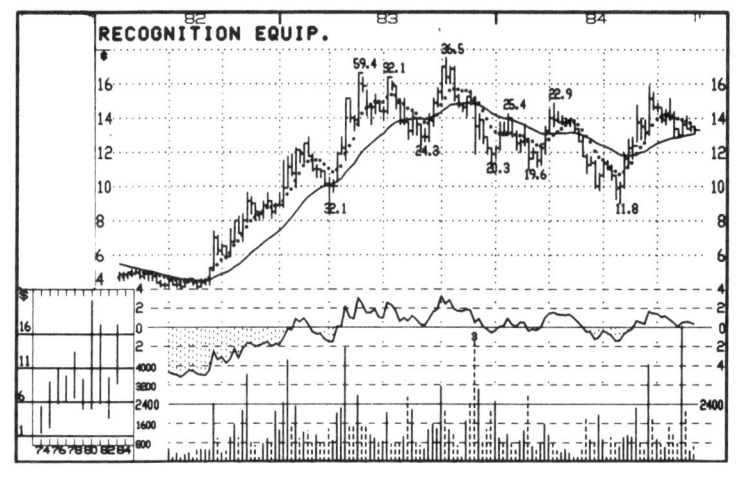

RECOGNITION EQUIP.

TCKR: REC
HIGH: 15⅞
LOW: 9
PRICE: 12½
EARN: 0.76
P/E: 16
DEBT: 21.5
YIELD: —

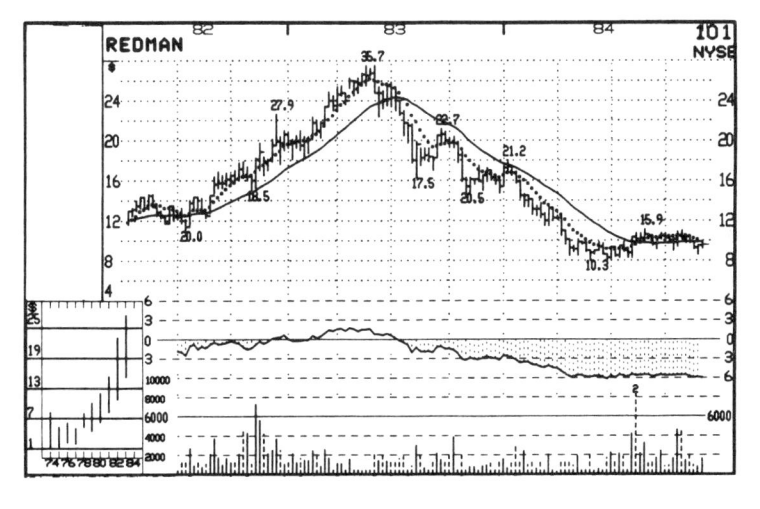

REDMAN

TCKR: RE
HIGH: 18
LOW: 8
PRICE: 8½
EARN: 0.68
P/E: 12
DEBT: 12.0
YIELD: 3.5

REVLON, INC.

The change in Revlon's product mix has been more than cosmetic — diversification has been going on for some time at this company, started with $300 by Charles Revson early in the Depression. The new stress is on diagnostics, pharmaceuticals, and vision care. Its more traditional products include fragrances and make-up marketed under the Charlie, Ciara, Jontue, Moon Drops, Natural Wonder, Norell, Princess Marcella Borghese, and Ultima II names. Aquamarine, Flex, and Milk Plus 6 shampoos, as well as Mitchum antiperspirant and Tums antacid are other revenue sources. Revlon was a veritable rumor mill last year concerning a possible takeover.

REYNOLDS METALS

In this energy-intensive industry, domestic aluminum producers have to deal with high energy costs. And the strong dollar has made aluminum imports from Australia, Brazil, and Canada even more attractive buys. The prices aluminum producers have been getting for their product have been low: At the end of 1982, aluminum ingot was selling at an unhealthy $.45 or so a pound, and two years later it was hovering at the same level. So why is Reynolds, the nation's second largest producer of this useful metal, making any money at all? Economy of scale has a lot to do with it. It is in every aspect of the business, from bauxite ore to the foil in which you wrap your fried chicken. In fact, the world gets a full 10 percent of its aluminum from Reynolds. The operation is lean; one-fifth of their salaried employees have been trimmed since the industry's dark days in the early 80s. In 1984, $450 million was spent on capital improvements, and in 1985 Reynolds will open its new Quebec smelter, which will run on inexpensive hydroelectric power.

ROHM & HAAS

This company is into big molecules in a big way. Rohm lives off the cornucopia of polymer chemistry: plastics (with a specialty in acrylics) and chemicals for agriculture and industry. Farmers use Rohm insecticides and fertilizers, and the company's products are also found in the construction and petrochemical industries. Deflation in commodities prices has helped decrease the cost of the raw materials that are grist for Rohm's various mills. Recently the company bought Hydronautics and Plaskon Electronic Materials. Rohm's cash flow, in the foreseeable future, should be excellent.

REVLON INC

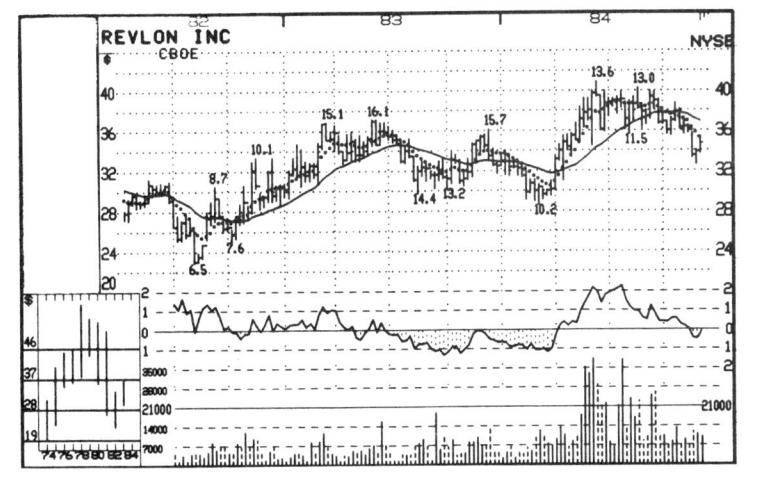

TCKR: REV
HIGH: 40⅞
LOW: 28⅝
PRICE: 34⅝
EARN: 3.15
P/E: 11
DEBT: 369
YIELD: 5.3

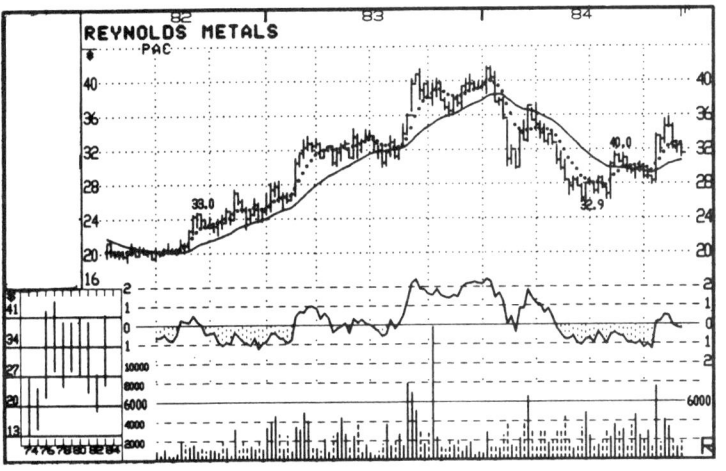

REYNOLDS METALS

TCKR: RLM
HIGH: 41⅝
LOW: 26
PRICE: 31
EARN: 5.25
P/E: 6
DEBT: 1102
YIELD: 3.2

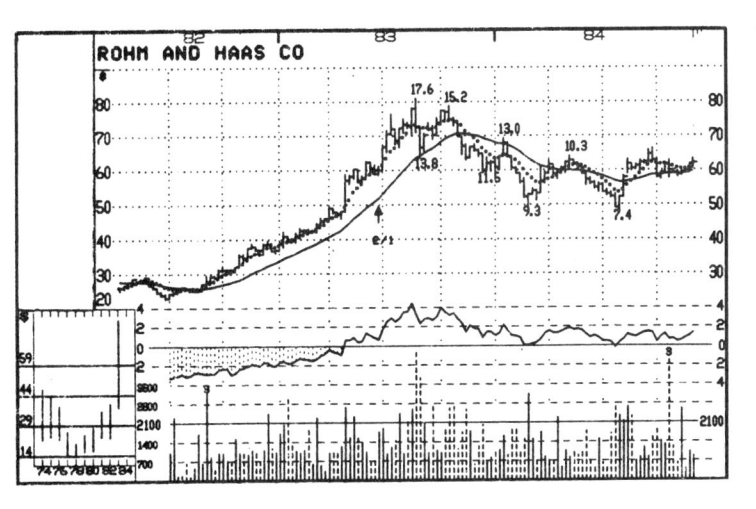

ROHM AND HAAS CO

TCKR: ROH
HIGH: 69¼
LOW: 48⅛
PRICE: 61¾
EARN: 6.81
P/E: 9
DEBT: 172
YIELD: 3.2

RYLAND GROUP

Ryland makes the product whose market many young Americans feel they have been priced out of: the single-family house. Its operations are concentrated in the Middle Atlantic states, Florida, and the Southwest. Business has been good for several years now, although interest rates are, of course, always something that bears watching in this industry. Ryland provides more than sympathy on that front for the prospective home owner: Ryland Mortgage helps almost three-quarters of the building company's customers finance their purchases. Ryland entered the modular housing business in 1982 with one plant in Maryland producing those units and another scheduled to begin operations this year.

SABINE CORP.

Sabine's operation is smaller and tighter than it once was, with the divestiture of their Canadian interests and the spinning off of their oil and gas royalties into Sabine Royalty trust. The pared-down core of the company is now ready to concentrate on the business of exploring for and producing oil and gas. As of last year, Sabine had in reserve about 8.5 million barrels of oil and approximately 119 billion cubic feet of gas. Management is currently in the market for new oil-producing properties, but only at a very good price. The $45 million spent on such assets last year manifests their cautious approach to acquisitions.

SAFEWAY STORES

No U.S. supermarket chain is bigger. Safeway has approximately 2,000 units in this country and more than 550 abroad (over 50 percent of these in Canada). It has opted for the economies of scale and a wider product mix (including more nonfood items) and is gradually replacing older and less profitable smaller units with new "superstores," each averaging over 35,000 square feet. Among several types of specialty stores Safeway owns, there are about 100 Liquor Barns. Safeway operations in some areas are carried on in an atmosphere of severe price competition. So far the company has been able to deal with that by holding down labor and other costs. Last year Safeway bought Weingarten stores and spent more than $600 million on capital improvements.

RYLAND GROUP — NYSE

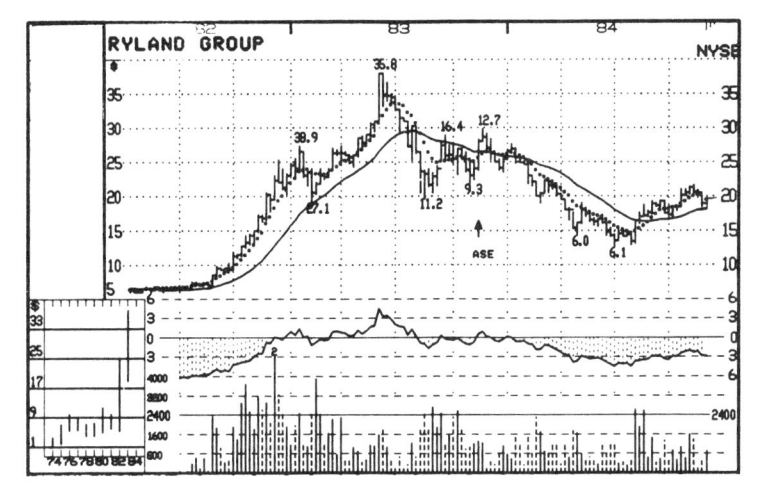

TCKR: RYL
HIGH: 27⅝
LOW: 12½
PRICE: 19⅞
EARN: 1.70
P/E: 12
DEBT: 13.1
YIELD: 3.0

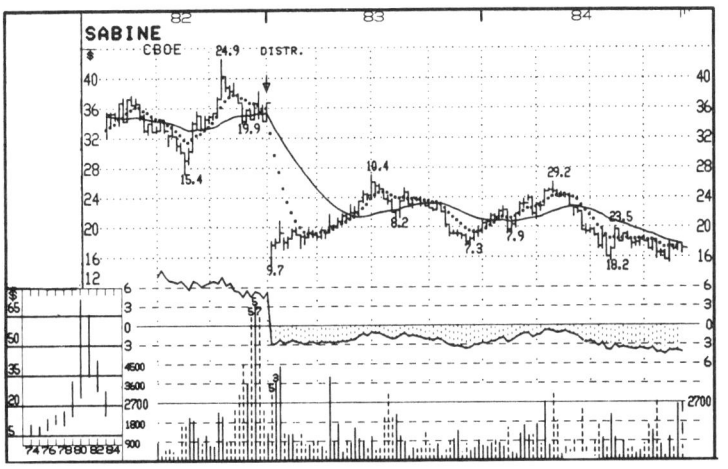

SABINE — CBOE

TCKR: SAB
HIGH: 26
LOW: 15¼
PRICE: 16
EARN: 0.85
P/E: 19
DEBT: 26.1
YIELD: 0.3

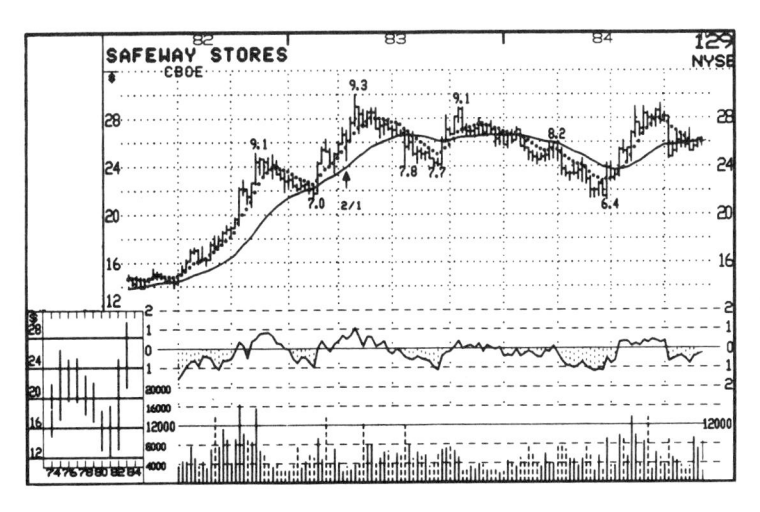

SAFEWAY STORES — CBOE / NYSE

TCKR: SA
HIGH: 29¼
LOW: 21¼
PRICE: 28⅞
EARN: 3.13
P/E: 9
DEBT: 1289
YIELD: 5.5

SCHLUMBERGER LTD.

Wireline services is Schlumberger's game—that involves betting on oil, not horses. If you dig a hole with hopes of raising a gusher, "Slumberjay," as it's known in the business, will come out to the dig and scientifically determine what you've got down there. It also drills under contract, builds rigs, and helps shore up wells. Through Sangamo and Weston, it provides equipment that measures and controls energy flow. Schlumberger, which was founded in France, is incorporated in Curaçao, and is headquartered on New York's Park Avenue. It also owns Fairchild Semiconductor. The company is cash rich (last year to the tune of $3.5 billion).

SCIENTIFIC-ATLANTA

Scientific-Atlanta is involved with a number of hot industries: cable television, energy control, home security devices, and satellite telecommunications. It also produces a variety of electronic measuring devices for government and industry through its Spectral Dynamics company, which has been getting an increasing amount of attention from the parent firm. In telecommunications, Scientific-Atlanta is supplying CBS with earth stations to receive and distribute signals that have been bounced off satellites. Scientific-Atlanta has done well with its popular cable television converter, but the technology involved and the nature of the cable TV business itself are both still evolving, so the company will have to stay on top of things if it is to continue to prosper in this area.

SCOTT & FETZER

Management claims that a takeover offer would be welcome. If you made an offer that couldn't be refused, what would you get? A potpourri of products spanning the known world—for example, *The World Book Encyclopedia* and other educational books and products. You would also be getting Kirby vacuum cleaners and other floor-care products; and there would be cutlery, various kinds of pumps, compressors, welding equipment, hoists, winches, and pressure-measurement devices used in heavy industry. You would also be acquiring facilities for making paint sprayers, but you would not get the life insurance business, which was sold two years ago. Meanwhile, business is good and cash abundant.

SCHLUMBERGER LTD

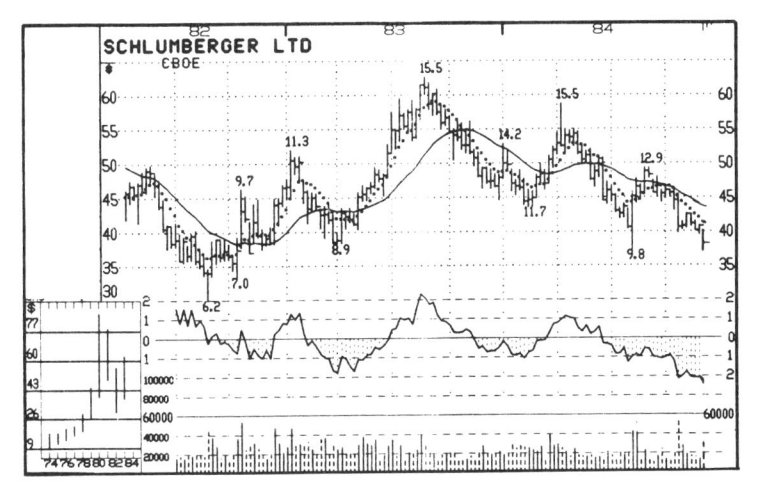

TCKR: SLB
HIGH: 55
LOW: 37¼
PRICE: 38⅝
EARN: 3.92
P/E: 10
DEBT: 600
YIELD: 3.1

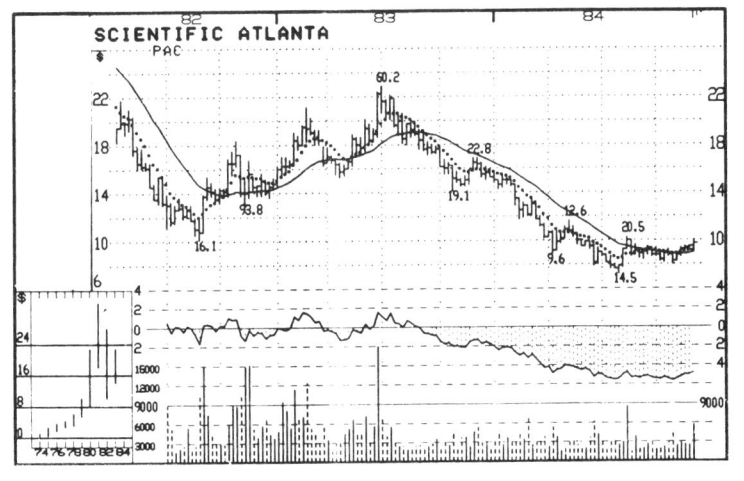

SCIENTIFIC ATLANTA

TCKR: SFA
HIGH: 16⅛
LOW: 7¼
PRICE: 10⅛
EARN: 0.54
P/E: 19
DEBT: 7.86
YIELD: 1.2

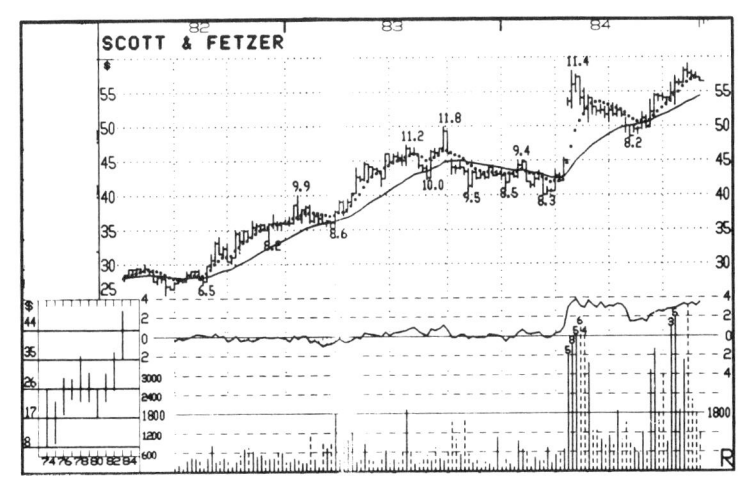

SCOTT & FETZER

TCKR: SFZ
HIGH: 59⅛
LOW: 39⅞
PRICE: 58⅝
EARN: 5.98
P/E: 10
DEBT: 34.9
YIELD: 3.1

SEARS, ROEBUCK

Your great-grandmother wouldn't recognize the place! Granted, it's still the world's biggest mail-order general store—but now the company is headquartered in the world's tallest building, and its sights are set just as high when it comes to future growth. Sears currently operates more than eight hundred stores, six hundred of which are scheduled to be redesigned by 1989 into "Stores of the Future" stressing soft goods, where the profits are. Financial services are robbing floor space from overalls: Savings and loan associations are currently tops on the company's acquisitions shopping list. The Allstate insurance company accounts for 25 percent of Sears's income, and a few years ago Sears acquired the real estate brokerage firm of Coldwell Banker. Lowered interest rates could boost retail credit sales over the 50-percent mark, and could also promote the sale of stocks, thus increasing profits at Sears's Dean Witter, which had a rough time in the bear market of the early 80s.

SIGNAL COMPANIES

Two years ago Signal merged with Wheelabrator-Frye, a company rich in construction technology. Signal brought to this match strength in the technology for processing petrochemicals and other organic chemicals. Currently, aerospace products, which Signal produces through Garrett Corp., are bringing in the most profits; Garrett also builds power plants. Ampex makes tape recorders and computer peripherals, while Kellog-Rust serves the gas, oil, petrochemical, and paper industries. Signal also has investment and real estate interests. Its holding in Mack Trucks, which was substantial, is now down to 10 percent.

SOUTHEASTERN PUBLIC SERVICE

Notwithstanding this company's name, the majority of its sales are in the textile business. But the lion's share of profits is generated by the services division: keeping wayward trees from disrupting utility lines, installing and maintaining utility wiring, and doing maintenance work on concrete structures such as bridges and dams. Southeastern also makes and sells ice and provides warehouse and cold storage service. It explores for and produces oil and gas, as well as selling liquified gas. The company also owns just under 50 percent of Chesapeake Financial, which specializes in reinsurance. A majority of Southeastern stock is owned by the ubiquitous Victor Posner and his group.

SEARS ROEBUCK & CO — CBOE

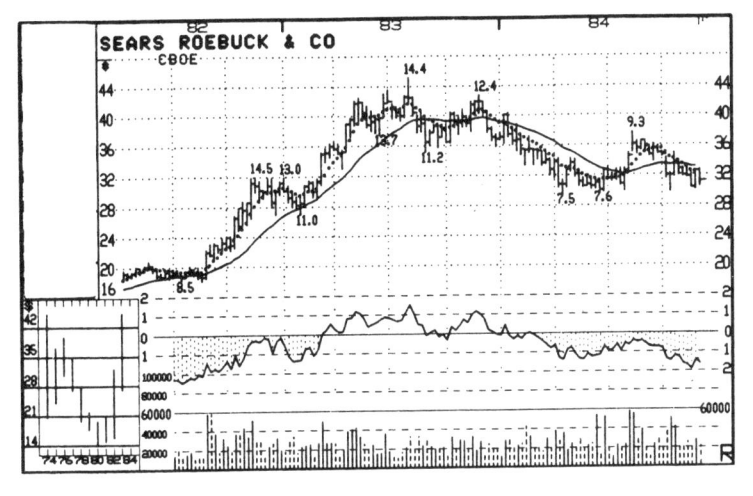

TCKR: S
HIGH: 40⅜
LOW: 29½
PRICE: 31½
EARN: 4.12
P/E: 8
DEBT: 7878
YIELD: 5.6

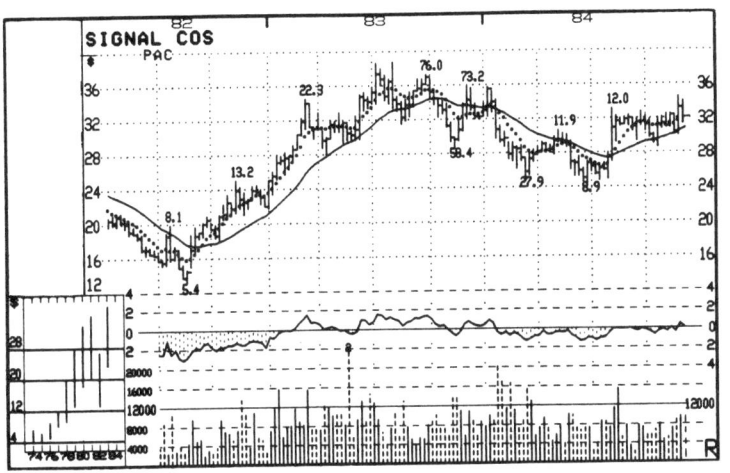

SIGNAL COS — PAC

TCKR: SGN
HIGH: 35¾
LOW: 24½
PRICE: 32¾
EARN: 2.39
P/E: 14
DEBT: 384
YIELD: 3.1

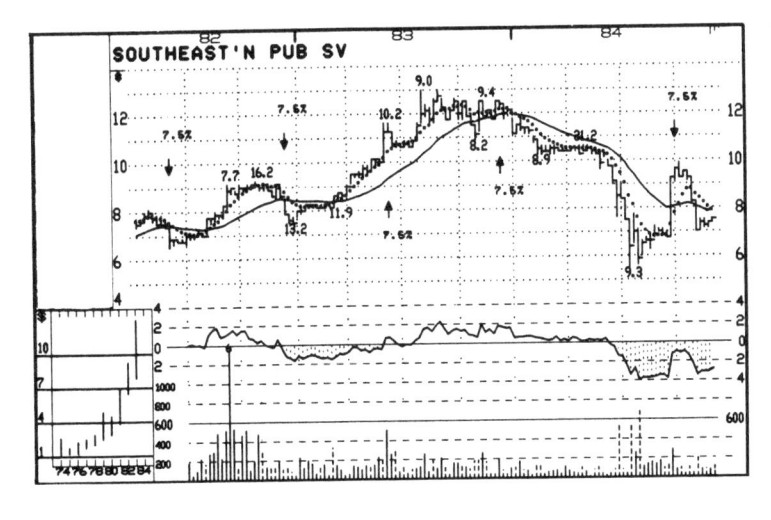

SOUTHEAST'N PUB SV

TCKR: SPV
HIGH: 13¼
LOW: 5⅞
PRICE: 7⅞
EARN: 0.53
P/E: 15
DEBT: 95.1
YIELD: 21

SOUTHLAND ROYALTY

This company explores for oil and gas in many land and offshore locations in North America. Their proven reserves most recently totaled 70,000,000 barrels of oil and 600,000,000 cubic feet of gas. Southland is also in the production end of the business, where their gas operations have been faring best. Since 1980, a substantial proportion of Southland Royalty's producing assets have been lodged in two royalty trusts that were spun off to shareholders: San Juan Basin Royalty Trust and the Permian Basin Royalty Trust. Southland also owns 25 percent of a Fort Worth, Texas, skyscraper.

SOUTHMARK CORP.

Its mode of operation is complex deals worked out in pages of fine print, but its product is really down to earth. This former real estate investment trust, now operating as a corporation, deals in real estate through all kinds of leases, partnerships, and outright ownership. Texas and Georgia are their stomping grounds, and direct sales and syndication produce the bulk of revenues. Southmark is nothing if not acquisitive. Recent purchases include Dominion Mortgage and Realty Trust, North American Mortgage Investors, Novus Property Co., Pacific Standard Life Co., San Jacinto Savings Association, Security National Investment Corp., and Univest, Inc. And all that has not caused indigestion. The company is doing well.

SOUTHWEST FOREST INDUSTRIES

Paper products account for half the sales of this company, which has access, under various arrangements, to approximately 600,000 acres of forest. Wood products for the residential construction industry are also important, and the company sells lumber and items such as cabinets through retail outlets. Southwest's paper mills in Arizona and Florida together can turn out 250,000 tons a year each of pulp and newsprint, and more than 400,000 tons of linerboard. Southwest also has a small land development operation. The Irish paper company Jefferson Smurfit Group appeared to be close to taking over Southwest last year, but eventually pulled away. Lumber prices have been down, and interest rates are of prime concern for gauging the future prospects of a company tied closely to residential construction.

SOUTHLAND ROYALTY

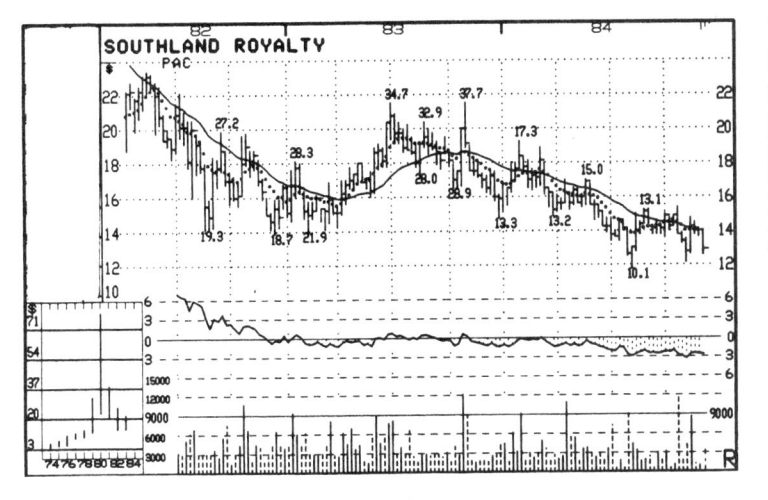

TCKR: SRO
HIGH: 19¼
LOW: 11¾
PRICE: 13⅜
EARN: 1.16
P/E: 12
DEBT: 330
YIELD: 0.06

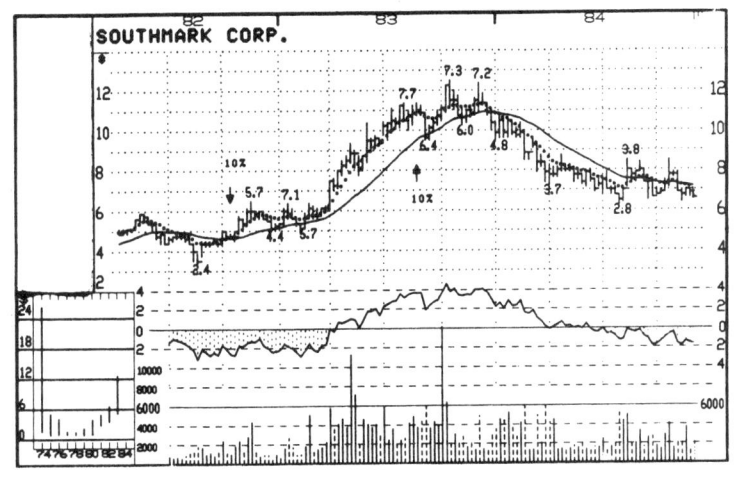

SOUTHMARK CORP.

TCKR: SM
HIGH: 11⅜
LOW: 6¼
PRICE: 6½
EARN: 1.68
P/E: 4
DEBT: 560
YIELD: 3.1

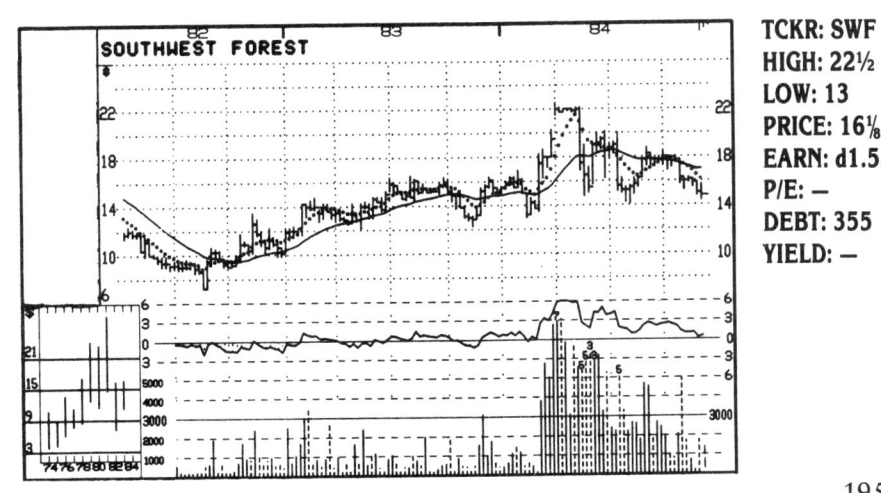

SOUTHWEST FOREST

TCKR: SWF
HIGH: 22½
LOW: 13
PRICE: 16⅛
EARN: d1.52
P/E: —
DEBT: 355
YIELD: —

195

STANDARD OIL OF INDIANA

There's nothing confusing about this company's product mix. All but a few percent of its profits comes from oil and gas. The company has always had a good nose for new deposits and in recent years has substantially broken away from its former dependence on outside oil sources. Standard was in an expansive mood as we moved into the middle of the decade—last year alone it budgeted $5 billion for exploration and production and completed the modernization of its domestic refineries. Most American consumers buy Standard's products under the Amoco sign, but about 40 percent of the company's profits are generated overseas.

STANLEY WORKS

Stanley, the biggest hand tool company in the world, works best when the housing industry is working. Aside from industrial sales, its aim is to keep you doing it right, so Stanley also markets do-it-yourself equipment for the around-the-home putterer. It makes automatic door openers, hardware such as door hinges, and a variety of steel products and equipment used in concrete construction. Last year Stanley bought the Proto tool company and HED Corp., a firm that makes equipment for the construction industry. Stanley's Vidmar company produces inventory systems.

SUN BANKS, INC.

The second biggest bank holding company in the Sunshine State has over 35 units and close to 300 branches. More than $4.5 billion in assets makes Sun Banks tops in Florida in that category. The biggest earning assets are investment securities, and time deposits are the largest source of money. But the big story is not in what they've got but in what they are likely to be, which is part of Sun Trust Banks, Inc., the product of their merger with the Trust Company of Georgia—assuming the U.S. Supreme Court okays the deal or Congress legislates its approval by permitting regional banking. If the go-ahead is given, the summer of 1985 will see the beginning of operations. Meanwhile, the banking business in Florida is balmy.

STANDARD OIL IND
CBOE

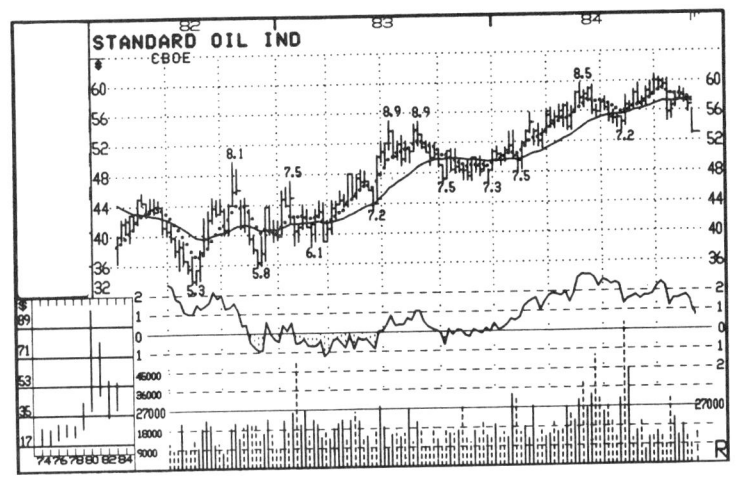

TCKR: SN
HIGH: 60⅝
LOW: 46⅝
PRICE: 55⅝
EARN: 7.55
P/E: 7
DEBT: 3566
YIELD: 5.4

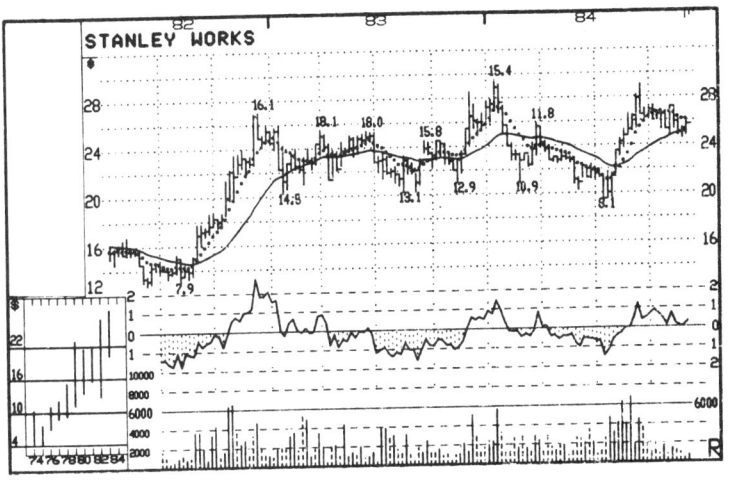

STANLEY WORKS

TCKR: SWK
HIGH: 29½
LOW: 19½
PRICE: 24⅝
EARN: 2.54
P/E: 10
DEBT: 82.0
YIELD: 3.9

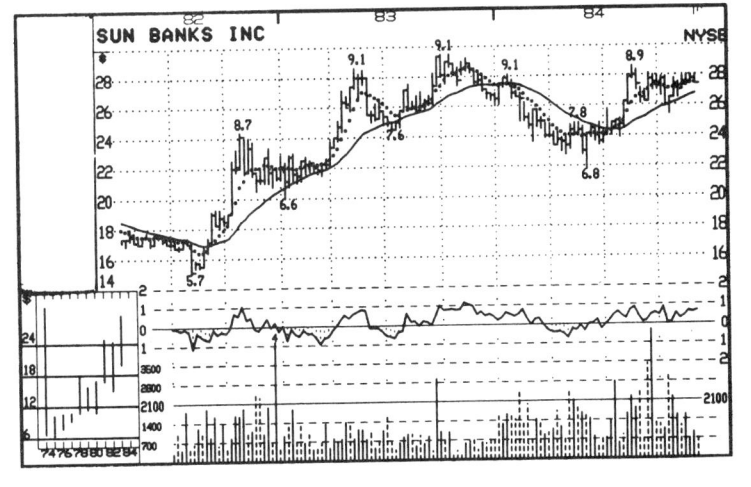

SUN BANKS INC

TCKR: SU
HIGH: 28⅝
LOW: 21¾
PRICE: 27⅞
EARN: 3.18
P/E: 9
DEBT: 138
YIELD: 4.3

SUNSHINE MINING

It digs in Idaho, and it's not for potatoes. Its silver mine in Kellogg, in the Coeur d'Alene district, is the second biggest in the country. When going full blast, 1,000 tons of ore can be processed per day. Reserves of this precious metal, whose price has not been terribly encouraging recently, were over 30,000,000 ounces at the beginning of last year. Sunshine owns a controlling interest in a Nevada mine as well, with reserves there of close to 6,000,000 ounces of silver and 30,000 of gold. It is also developing substantial processing facilities. The company had grandiose ideas last year—with Hecla Mining it planned to take over Rancher's Exploration & Development. But the offer was withdrawn, and Sunshine and Hecla arrived at a complicated settlement of various interests and issues between them. Sunshine has lately been selling coins to investors; it also owns a commodity trading company in Great Britain.

SYNTEX CORP.

Syva, a Syntex medical diagnostics company, has lately been troubled by competition and a decline in hospital admissions. The company's skin and beauty care business has also been down. But Syntex's pharmaceutical products, which account for two-thirds of its sales and about nine-tenths of its profits, have done well. Syntex makes Naprosyn, a profitable anti-arthritis drug, and Anaprox, a prominent analgesic for menstrual pain. It's also done well with oral contraceptives.

TALLEY INDUSTRIES

This company is up in arms, into handouts, and has its finger on the red button—which is not to say that management doesn't have its feet planted firmly on the ground. In truth, the company is up to its elbows in diversification. Talley makes clocks (Big Ben, Seth Thomas, and Westclox) and related equipment. It also makes dispensing machines and fighter aircraft escape systems and propellants. The apparel division specializes in sportswear and there's a real estate investment operation as well as compenents for automobile air-bag safety systems. Recent Talley acquisitions include Dimetrics, Inc., a welding equipment firm, and operations that have become Talley Metals Technology, a steel fabricating division.

SUNSHINE MINING

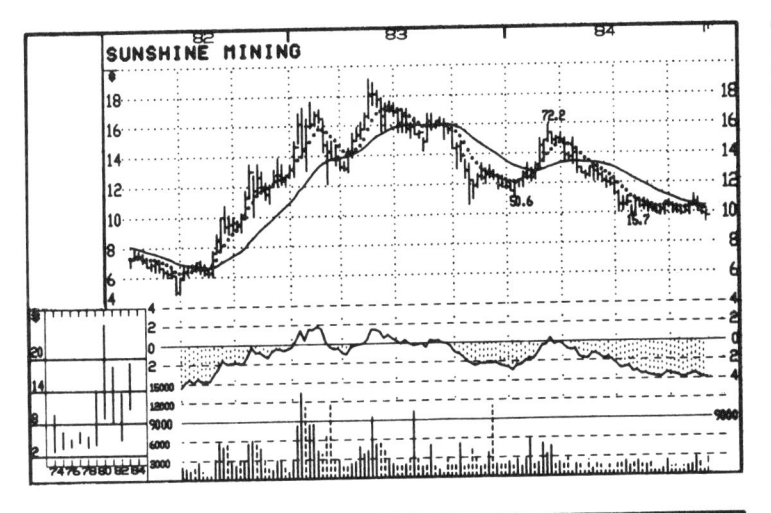

TCKR: SSC
HIGH: 15⅞
LOW: 8¼
PRICE: 8¼
EARN: 0.64
P/E: 13
DEBT: 75.3
YIELD: —

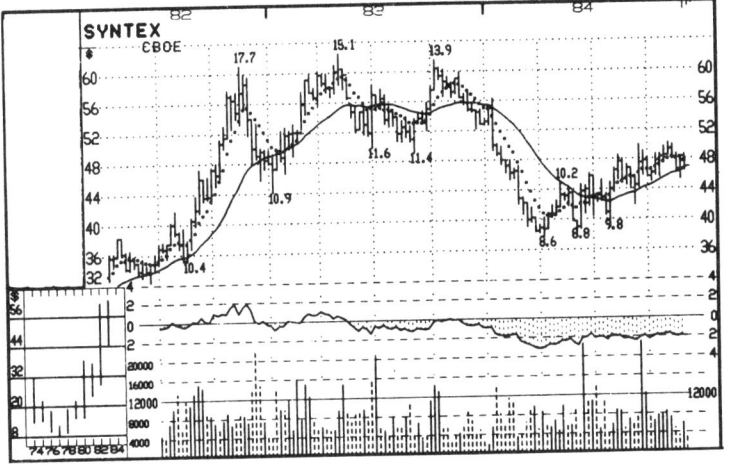

SYNTEX (CBOE)

TCKR: SYN
HIGH: 56¼
LOW: 37¾
PRICE: 48½
EARN: 4.08
P/E: 12
DEBT: 172
YIELD: 3.3

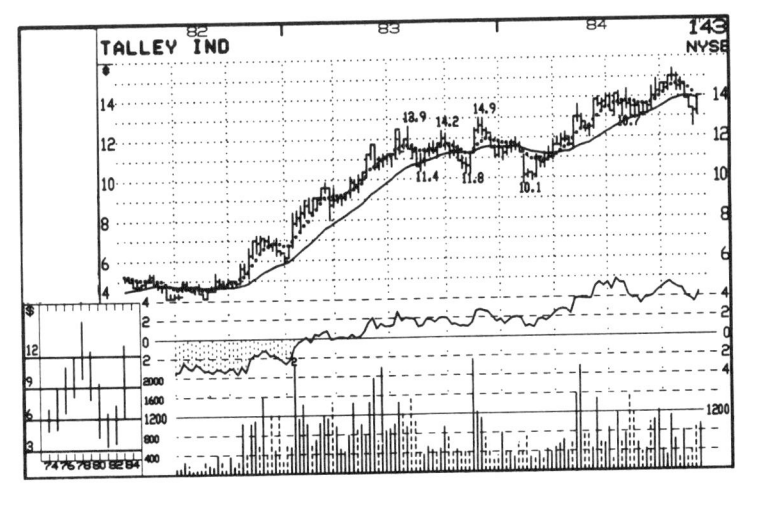

TALLEY IND (NYSE)

TCKR: TAL
HIGH: 15⅜
LOW: 9¾
PRICE: 13
EARN: 1.25
P/E: 10
DEBT: 67.7
YIELD: —

TANDY CORP.

The public knows this company as Radio Shack, a national chain that serves the electronic hobbyist with a variety of inexpensive parts and cheap electronic appliances and telephone equipment. But the reason that Tandy, with its more than 8,000 Radio Shack stores, showed its first quarterly loss last year can be summed up in one word: computers. Radio Shack's first model was on the scene a bit before Apple in the late 70s; until two years ago a newer machine maintained a respectable share of the personal computer market. But when times and the market changed, Radio Shack didn't. It insisted on selling only its own brand of software for its machines, and it assumed that its large distribution network could insulate it from price competition. The rude awakening has come.

TEKTRONIX, INC.

Specialties are oscilloscopes and computer terminals for graphics applications, and both are under pressure from Japanese competition. Measuring and testing instruments account for half of Tektronix's profits, and foreign sales produce about 40 percent of total revenue. The company also makes computer equipment and various kinds of semiconductor components. It is dabbling in artificial intelligence and getting into the Computer Aided Engineering (CAE) field, although it lags behind in software development. The company also makes some products for the television industry. Tekronix is currently being propelled along by the explosive growth in the electronics industry and its consistently increasing demand for the company's measurement and testing devices.

TELEDYNE, INC.

Teledyne is a diversified corporation whose activities span a broad range of industrial and consumer products. Fifty percent of the piston engines used in the U.S. come out of Teledyne-owned plants as well as a variety of combustion engines. Other products include machine tools, specialty metals, AR stereo speakers, and the Water Pik. Profits from Teledyne's insurance business are invested in stocks and bonds. The company owns more than half of Curtiss Wright and one-fourth of Litton Industries. Last year Teledyne sold some stock of other companies, and then offered to buy back 5 million of its own shares. It ended up purchasing 8.7 million at $200 a share.

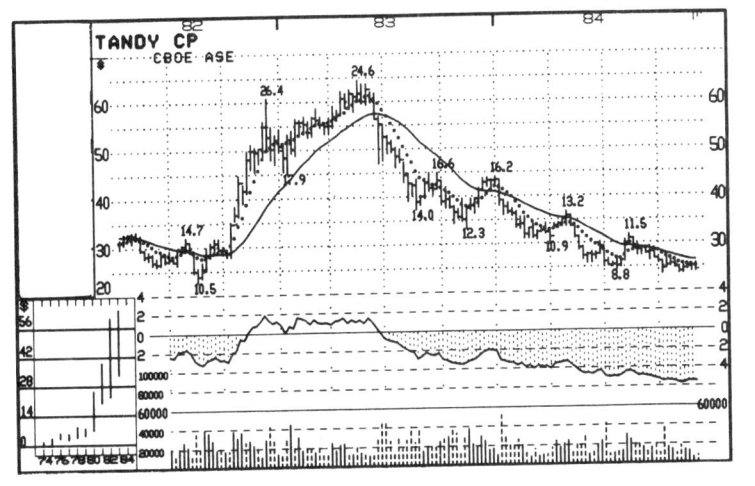

TCKR: TAN
HIGH: 44
LOW: 23¼
PRICE: 24
EARN: 2.60
P/E: 9
DEBT: 355
YIELD: —

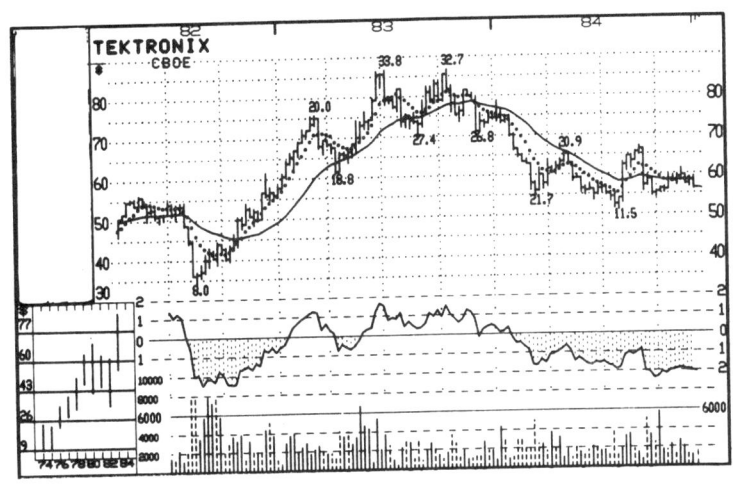

TCKR: TEK
HIGH: 78¾
LOW: 51⅛
PRICE: 55½
EARN: 6.36
P/E: 9
DEBT: 142
YIELD: 1.8

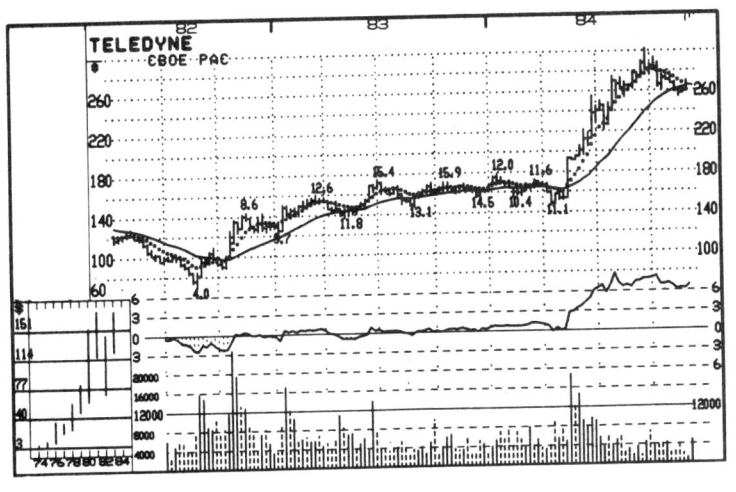

TCKR: TDY
HIGH: 302⅜
LOW: 147¼
PRICE: 259
EARN: 17.26
P/E: 15
DEBT: 1168
YIELD: —

TELERATE, INC.

Telerate is a holding company whose *raison d'être* is to hold Telerate Financial Information Network. This service supplies institutions with up-to-the-minute data about a wide variety of markets — e.g., government securities and precious metals — via computer terminals. Currently more than 8,000 customers are on line in this country and there are upwards of 3,000 abroad. (The service will soon be available to individual subscribers with personal computers.) Much of Telerate's data comes gratis from banks and brokers, to whom it is advantageous to have their information displayed. Overseas, the service is marketed through AP-Dow Jones/Telerate. Last year Telerate, more than 50 percent of whose outstanding shares are held by British Exco International p.l.c., increased its sales by 50 percent over the preceding year. The company's sole competitor is Reuters.

TELEX CORP.

"IBM-compatible" is the name of the Telex game. It makes terminals and computer peripherals that mate with IBM's products and the products of others who seek to emulate the leader of the pack. Last year Telex bought Raytheon Data Systems (now Telex Data Systems), whose terminals division put Telex solidly in the airlines reservations terminal business and gave them a stronger profile abroad. Telex sells high-tech workstations through Advanced Systems Group and flat terminal screens through Plasma Graphics. The company also makes tape recording equipment aimed especially at the education market.

TESORO PETROLEUM

Tesoro refines and markets so it can explore and produce — at least that's the way the company has been allocating cash flow to expenditures lately. There's a refinery in Alaska and wells as far-flung as Trinidad and Indonesia. Last year Tesoro pocketed $1.3 million from the sale of its Texas refinery and twenty-five gas stations in the western U.S. The oilfield services division is not currently profitable. Tesoro's reserves totaled more than 9 million barrels of oil in 1984, with Indonesia contributing the greatest amount, and 140 billion cubic feet of gas, almost three-fourths of it in Bolivia. Tesoro has been trying to sell the Trinidad operation to the government because of legal restrictions on activity there. And the Bolivian operation is in trouble — the unstable government is in arrears in its payments to the company.

TELERATE INC

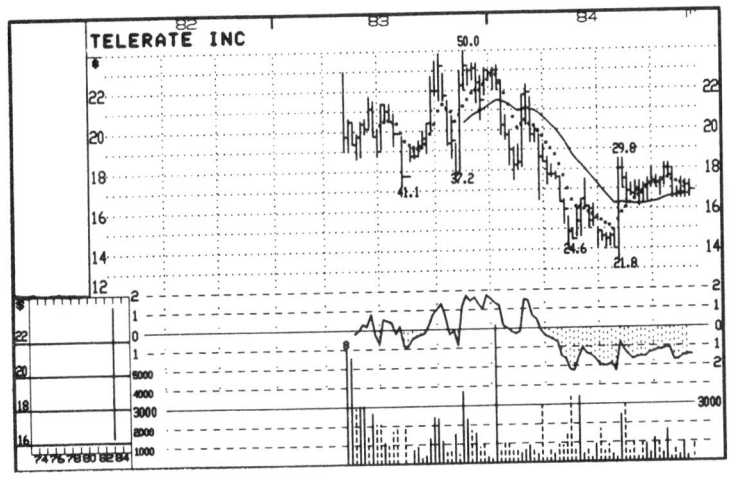

TCKR: TLR
HIGH: 23¼
LOW: 13½
PRICE: 17
EARN: 0.61
P/E: 28
DEBT: —
YIELD: 1.9

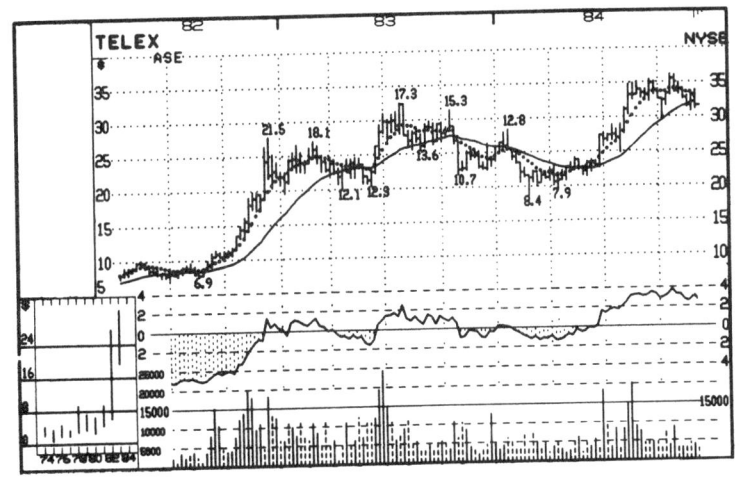

TELEX

TCKR: TC
HIGH: 36⅛
LOW: 18⅝
PRICE: 31⅞
EARN: 2.92
P/E: 11
DEBT: 28.8
YIELD: —

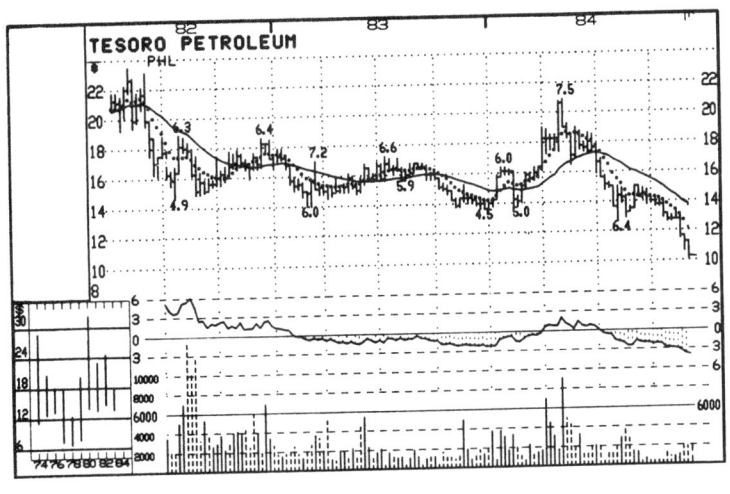

TESORO PETROLEUM

TCKR: TSO
HIGH: 20⅞
LOW: 10
PRICE: 10½
EARN: 1.76
P/E: 6
DEBT: 105
YIELD: 3.8

TEXACO, INC.

When you run short of oil, you call the oil company and ask for a delivery. So when Texaco saw its reserves dwindling, it called Getty Oil — and bought it for a cool $10 billion. Acquiring Getty's reserves was a lot cheaper than drilling for the stuff, although the ultimate cost will be higher than the original estimate because interest rates rose after Texaco hatched its plans. But divestiture of some of Getty's non-oil interests will help pay the bill. Further complicating matters is a lawsuit from Pennzoil, which also wanted Getty. Texaco's oil-related (predominantly shipping) business has been off of late.

TEXAS INTERNATIONAL

Its current posture is one of controlled shrinkage to cope with the uncontrollable weakness in its oil and gas exploration business. Debt has been restructured, but at the price of selling off some productive assets and cutting back on capital spending. Texas International explores in Canada, Egypt, and the United States and exploits its deposits exclusively through drilling services, with no capital currently sunk in rigs. Company reserves are about 14 million barrels of oil and over 150 billion cubic feet of gas.

TNP ENTERPRISES

Once called Community Service, then Texas-New Mexico Power, TNP is a holding company that looks for profitable ventures beyond its present line, which is the distribution of power produced by other utilities in Texas and New Mexico. Most revenue comes from Texas, and most of that is earned in the Gulf Coast area. TNP's customers are industrial, residential, and commercial, in that order. The company buys more of its power from Houston Lighting & Power than from any other source. Capital expenditures were just under $40 million last year. In the future, cogeneration plants figure to be an area of interest for this company.

TEXACO INC

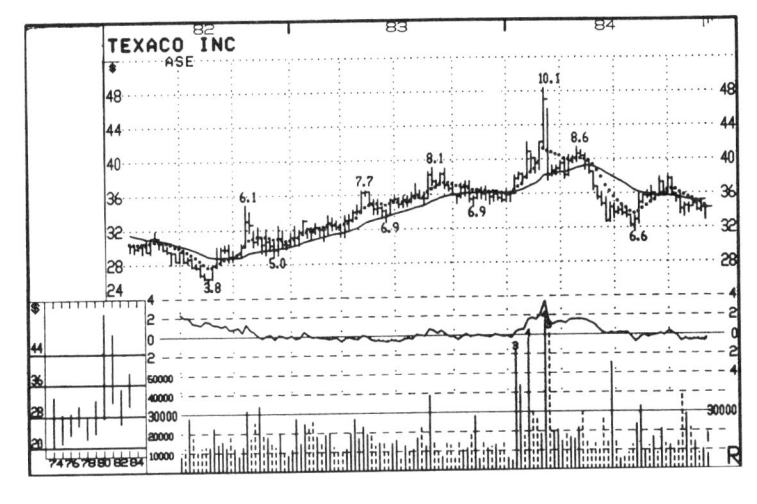

TCKR: TX
HIGH: 48 3/8
LOW: 31 1/2
PRICE: 33 5/8
EARN: 4.39
P/E: 8
DEBT: 14750
YIELD: 8.9

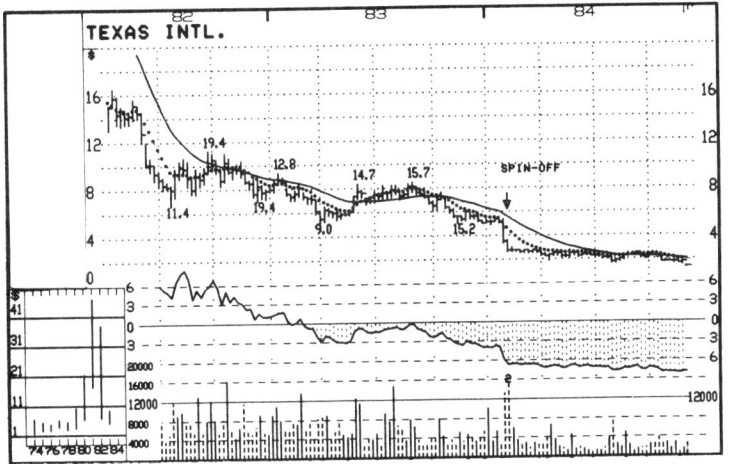

TEXAS INTL.

TCKR: TEI
HIGH: 5 3/4
LOW: 1 3/8
PRICE: 1 3/8
EARN: d1.78
P/E: d
DEBT: 346
YIELD: —

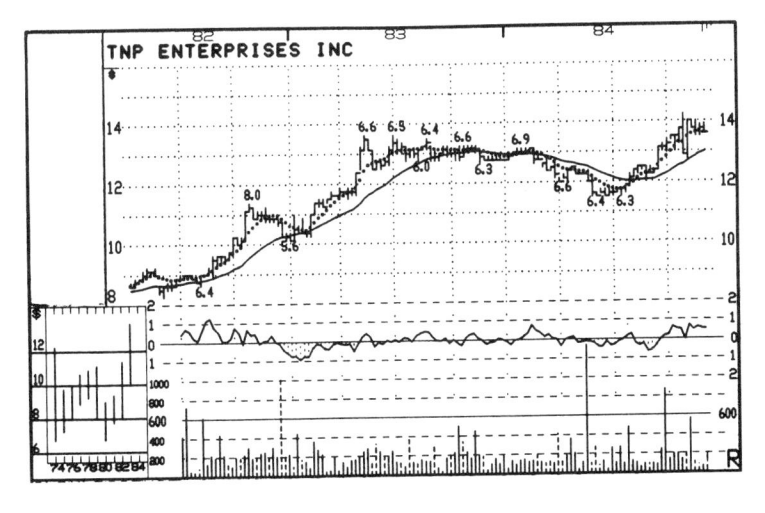

TNP ENTERPRISES INC

TCKR: TNP
HIGH: 14 1/4
LOW: 11 3/8
PRICE: 13 5/8
EARN: 3.74
P/E: 4
DEBT: 99.0
YIELD: 8.7

TOWLE MANUFACTURING

This company sets a nice table with some sterling products that are often given as gifts. Towle, in fact, makes all manner of flatware, as well as china, cutlery, and pewter. It also makes artificial flowers and real candles and candlestick holders. When you think about it, there are few things that might grace your table (other than food) that it doesn't make. Marketing is its forte: an in-house art department produces some very attractive catalog pages. Recent gifts that Towle has purchased for itself include Galway Crystal Ltd., H.E. Lauffer, National Silver Industries, Oxford Hall, and Seiden Brass & Giftware. But last year's profits were somewhat tarnished by a decline from the previous year. A slippage in service may be partly to blame, with order fulfillment often lagging behind as the company rapidly grew.

TRAVELERS CORP.

Travelers' assets make it the seventh biggest U.S. insurance company. The company's group insurance business accounts for more than half its revenues. Approximately 100,000 companies insure their employees through Travelers, which also manages pension assets in excess of $16 billion. Travelers recently ran into the same dip in revenues from its property-casualty insurance business that has affected other insurance companies, but gains in other parts of its broadly diversified product line balanced those losses. Currently, life and health insurance are strong fields for Travelers, which is also actively pursuing entry into the diversified field of financial services.

TRIANGLE INDUSTRIES

"Put another nickel in" might have been this company's slogan thirty years ago. But today it would take at least a quarter to operate their vending machines, which include jukeboxes and money changers whose tune is the jangle of coins pouring out in exchange for your bill. Triangle also distributes arcade video games and makes a variety of wire products for the construction industry and other businesses. In 1984, Triangle bought Trafalgar Industries, which produces machines that sell hot drinks, and Philip Moss & Co., a vending machine distributor. Triangle's income was up last year, thanks mainly to its wire business. The price of the stock also rose, chiefly in response to takeover rumors.

TOWLE MFG

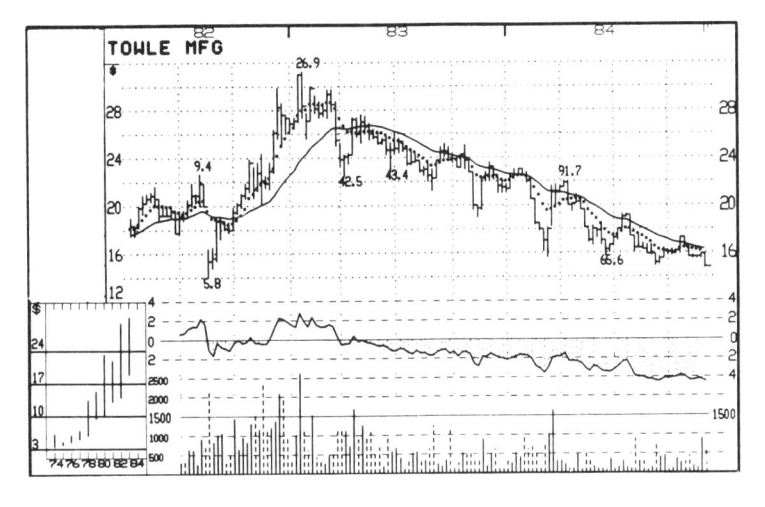

TCKR: TOW
HIGH: 23
LOW: 13¼
PRICE: 14
EARN: d0.30
P/E: d
DEBT: 89.1
YIELD: —

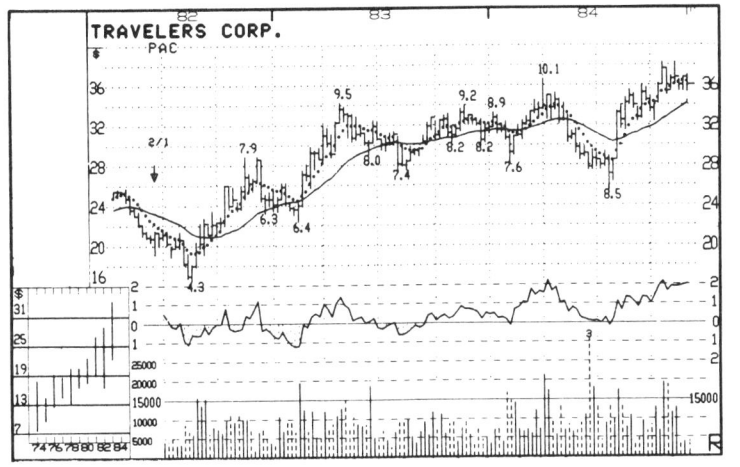

TRAVELERS CORP.

TCKR: TIC
HIGH: 38¼
LOW: 25½
PRICE: 35¼
EARN: 3.96
P/E: 9
DEBT: 64.0
YIELD: 5.4

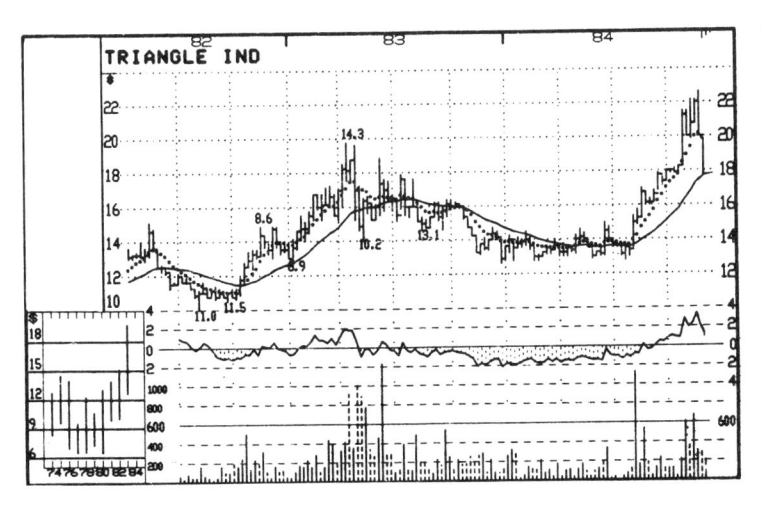

TRIANGLE IND

TCKR: TRI
HIGH: 22⅝
LOW: 12⅝
PRICE: 17¼
EARN: 0.10
P/E: 173
DEBT: 187
YIELD: 2.3

TRW, INC.

It was founded by executive refugees from Hughes Aircraft, who built it into a major corporation and one of the Pentagon's most important suppliers. Two years ago, in fact, 40 percent of everything TRW sold was bought by the U.S. government. Electronics and aerospace products account for half of TRW's profits, and last year half of the company's $375 million in capital expenditures went into those divisions. Energy and automotive products are other important areas. In 1984 TRW sold its hand tool division and bought Firestone's auto seat belt operation. TRW's profits have increased annually for the past decade. Name recognition has also increased with the stready repetition of the television commercial identifying it as "A company called TRW..."

TUCSON ELECTRIC POWER

This cost-efficient company has set 1988 as its target date for switching over to completely coal-based power. Residential customers in Tucson and nearby Pima County buy about a third of TEP's power, but the primary customers are businesses related to the mining and processsing of copper. That industry—and many high-tech firms as well—are experiencing burgeoning growth in the Tucson area, which has meant expansion for Tucson Electric Power. The company's growth has been largely financed through the sale of tax-exempt bonds. This year it anticipates capital expenditures of about $250 million. Tucson Electric also has a subsidiary that invests in securities, many of which earn tax-free income.

TWA

TWA hasn't paid a common stock dividend since Richard Nixon's first year in the Oval Office. The skies have not been friendly to *this* company, which struggled into the 60s under the often strange direction of Howard Hughes, then was run by lawyers and bankers, and finally was spun off by Trans World Corp. last year. TWA was one of the more prominent victims of the fare competition that came with airline deregulation and higher fuel prices, and it fought back by cutting down on staff and routes (starting in the mid-70s). TWA has also made St. Louis the hub of its domestic operations, which bring in almost twice the revenue of its overseas flights.

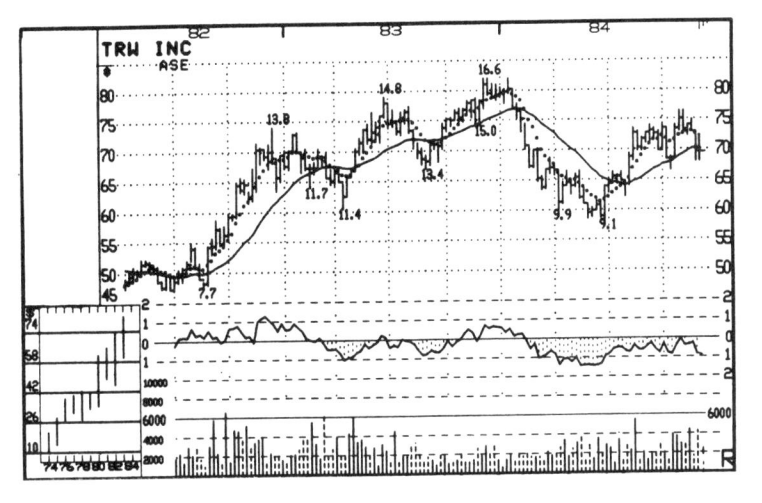

TCKR: TRW
HIGH: 82
LOW: 58 3/8
PRICE: 70 1/4
EARN: 6.96
P/E: 10
DEBT: 205
YIELD: 4.3

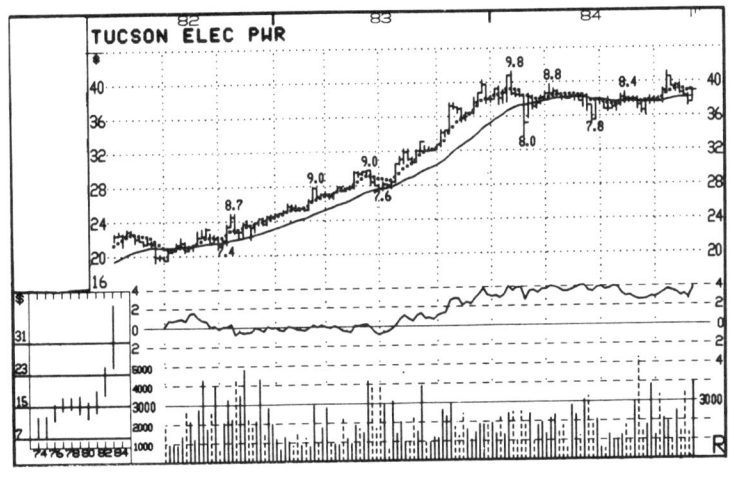

TCKR: TEP
HIGH: 41 1/4
LOW: 33 5/8
PRICE: 39 3/8
EARN: 4.62
P/E: 9
DEBT: 1034
YIELD: 6.6

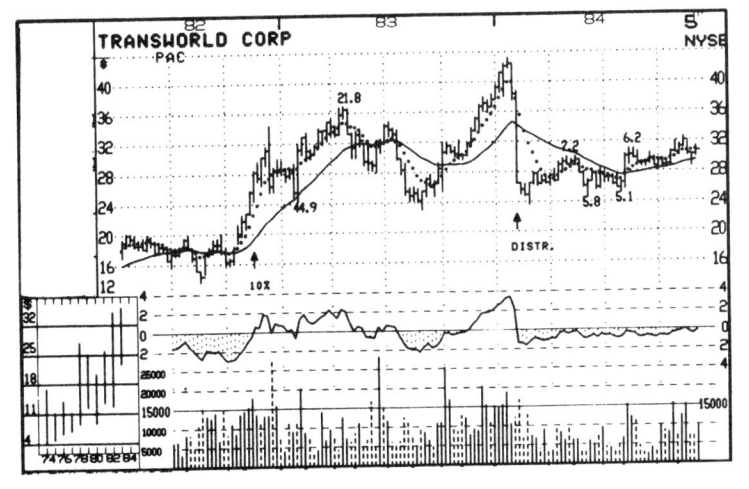

TCKR: TWA
HIGH: 32 1/2
LOW: 23 5/8
PRICE: 30 1/8
EARN: 1.76
P/E: 1.7
DEBT: 1170
YIELD: 1.3

TYCO LABORATORIES

Tyco has been unloading nonoperating assets and looking to enrich its collection of companies, which are concentrated in packaging, fire protection, and electronics. Ludlow Corp. makes packaging material, and does quite well at it. Grinnell Fire Protection Services produces smoke alarms and sprinklers, a business dependent on commercial and industrial construction. Tyco's Simplex Wire & Cable sells underwater cables and associated equipment to the Navy and civilian telephone companies. Simplex has also been getting into fiber optics — one of its most important customers in that line is AT&T. Last year Tyco sold its interest in Heinecke Instruments and bought Multi-Circuits, Inc., which produces circuit boards.

UNION CARBIDE

This third biggest of the nation's chemical producers is trying to get away from raw chemicals and put more of its capital into high-tech production and services, emphasizing electronics. That part of the operation now provides one-fourth of the sales. Union Carbide brand names include Eveready, Gladwrap, Prestone, and Simoniz. The company aims to increase its production of silicon, the vital substance in semiconductors, in response to the recent decline of battery sales abroad. But in light of the recent poison gas release at a Union Carbide factory in India — in which over 2,000 people lost their lives — declining battery sales become the least of this company's foreign problems.

UNIROYAL, INC.

For years its trademark was a little pajama-clad boy holding a candle and a tire, accompanied by the slogan "Time to Re-Tire." It's big enough to rank fourth in the country in tire production — also big enough to have lost $120 million in 1979. The next few years were also difficult ones. But Uniroyal's product mix has changed, and with it its fortunes. About 70 percent of tire output used to be earmarked for General Motors, thus making Uniroyal heavily dependent on the whims and success of GM. That figure is now down to 20 percent. More important, tire sales no longer account for the bulk of Uniroyal's profits. Chemicals, plastics, and rubber have come on strong, as have engineering services; and management now appears to be treading a profitable path.

TYCO LABORATORIES

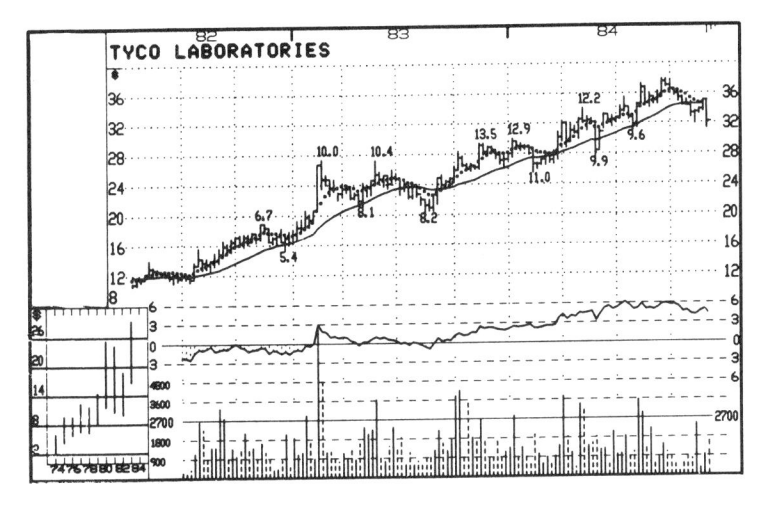

TCKR: TYC
HIGH: 37⅞
LOW: 25½
PRICE: 32
EARN: 3.67
P/E: 9
DEBT: 58.8
YIELD: 2.5

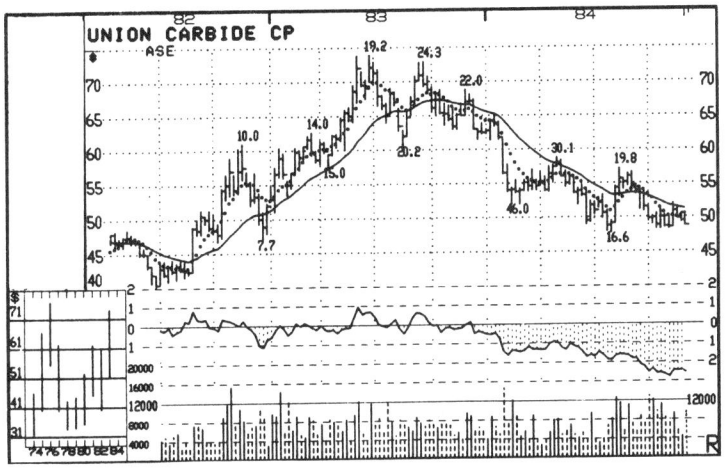

UNION CARBIDE CP

TCKR: UK
HIGH: 65¼
LOW: 32¾
PRICE: 35¼
EARN: 4.80
P/E: 7
DEBT: 2307
YIELD: 9.6

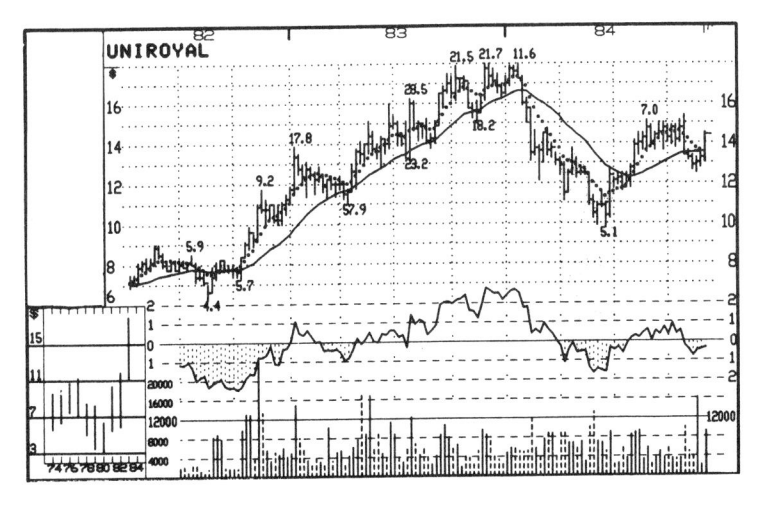

UNIROYAL

TCKR: R
HIGH: 18
LOW: 9¾
PRICE: 13⅛
EARN: 2.47
P/E: 5
DEBT: 314
YIELD: 0.2

UNITED BRANDS

Yes, they still have bananas — United Fruit is at the center of United Brands, and bananas are at the center of United Fruit. This fabled and controversial company has toppled Central American governments in the past ("banana republic" is a term generated by their operations). Aside from Chiquita, other banana name brands include Bananos, Chico, Fyffes, and Petites 150. The company also distributes a variety of other produce. United Brands sells meat through John Morrell & Co., with pork products the leading item. But fruit and livestock prices fluctuate a good deal, and United has been seeking stability. So the company has been putting its money in plastics, livestock feed, and telecommunications.

U.S. SHOE

That moniker is a little misleading, although possibly useful for public relations at a time when many people are sensitive to the loss of U.S. jobs because of competition from goods made abroad. (In fact, U.S. Shoe imports some of its products.) The company makes and sells shoes for both men and women. Brands incude Amalfi, Bandolino, Bill Blass, Capezio, Cobbies, David Evans, El Dorado, Evan-Picone, Freeman, French Shriner, Garolini, Joyce, Liz Claiborne, Papagallo, Red Cross, Selby, and Texas. Last year it added the Calvin Klein label to its shoe operations. U.S. Shoe runs 500 of its own shoe stores and also operates specialty apparel stores, including Casual Corner, J. Riggings, Little Folks, and Ups 'n Downs. Its discount stores have had it rough lately, and its stores in shopping malls have experienced lower sales.

U.S. STEEL

This company has made Pittsburgh and Andrew Carnegie's ghost more than a little uncomfortable in recent years. Other materials (such as aluminum and plastics) have replaced steel in many applications, and foreign competition has worn down the market share of this, the nation's number one steel producer. U.S. Steel's response has been twofold. It has sharply pared down its steel operations (obsolete plants that were closed down constituted one-third of its steel-making capacity) and has determined that the company was not iron-bound to stay solely with its eponymous product — hence its purchase of Marathon Oil.

UNITED BRANDS — FOOD-MEAT PACKERS

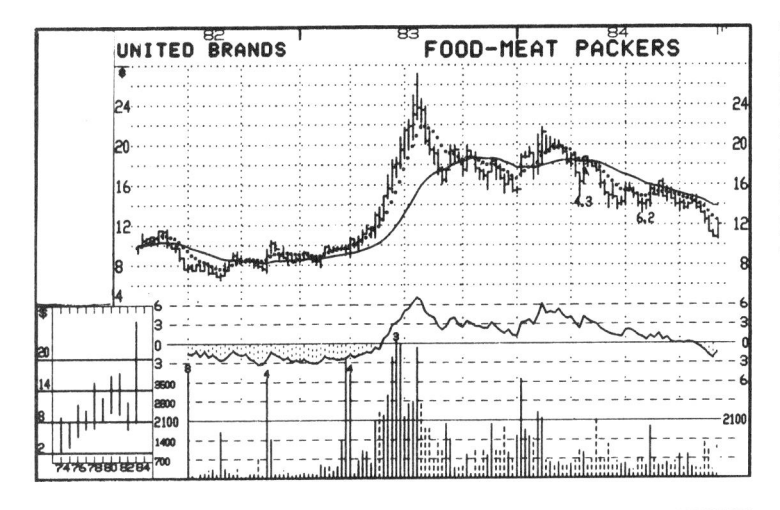

TCKR: UB
HIGH: 21¾
LOW: 10¼
PRICE: 12
EARN: 2.10
P/E: 6
DEBT: 381
YIELD: —

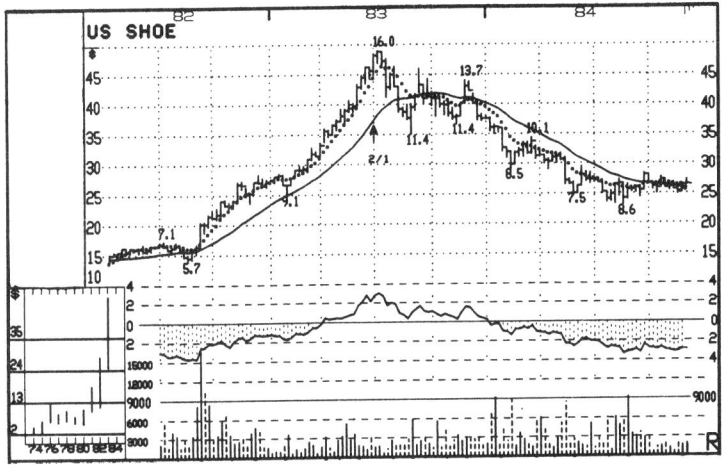

US SHOE

TCKR: USR
HIGH: 40⅛
LOW: 23
PRICE: 26½
EARN: 2.88
P/E: 9
DEBT: 42.2
YIELD: 3.2

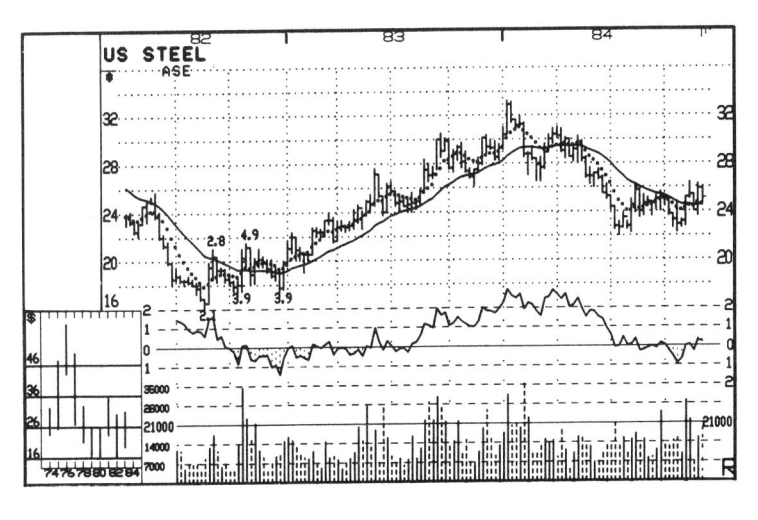

US STEEL ASE

TCKR: X
HIGH: 33¼
LOW: 22
PRICE: 24⅝
EARN: d6.60
P/E: d
DEBT: 6636
YIELD: 4.1

213

UNITED TECHNOLOGIES

The perfect name for a conglomerate of the 80s: It suggests everything and reveals nothing—particularly about recent charges of alleged buggings in the executive suite. The keys to its success are weaponry, commercial construction, and building automation. Under its banner are the defense-oriented Pratt & Whitney, Sikorsky, and Norden (of bombsight fame) companies. Carrier and Otis keep you cool and take you to where you want to get off. United has gotten solidly into building automation (energy use and telecommunications controlled by computer), and its Mostek semiconductor company leaves it well positioned in that field. United Technologies is also penetrating the automotive electronics market.

UNITRODE CORP.

This company has been sailing along under blue skies for ten continuously profitable years. This is partly the result of tight and effective management, but it has as much to do with the fact that Unitrode has been where the action has been—namely in electronic components, half of which are sold to customers in the defense and aerospace industries (computer and telecommunications companies are its next best customers). Power semiconductors and ceramic capacitors are Unitrode's mainstays. Other products are analog/digital conversion devices and a host of electronic parts.

VARCO INTERNATIONAL

"Iron Roughnecks" sounds like an appellation for the sturdy men who work with Varco's oil drilling equipment. However, it happens to be the name of one of the products of Varco Oil Tools. Varco's Marine Tools supplies the marine construction industry as well as companies engaged in offshore drilling; Best Industries makes devices used to control the flow of oil in pipes; and Varco Electronics is the company's entry in that field. Varco has been around since 1908, the year William Howard Taft became president. No doubt those were better times for the firm. About three-fourths of their revenue is derived from foreign sales, and the strong dollar hasn't helped there. Nor has the oil glut that overtook the industry a few years ago. Last year Varco was selling off plant and equipment and aiming to cut employment rolls by 10 percent. Preferred stock holders got no preference in 1984: Their dividend was skipped. And technically, the company was in default.

UNITED TECH

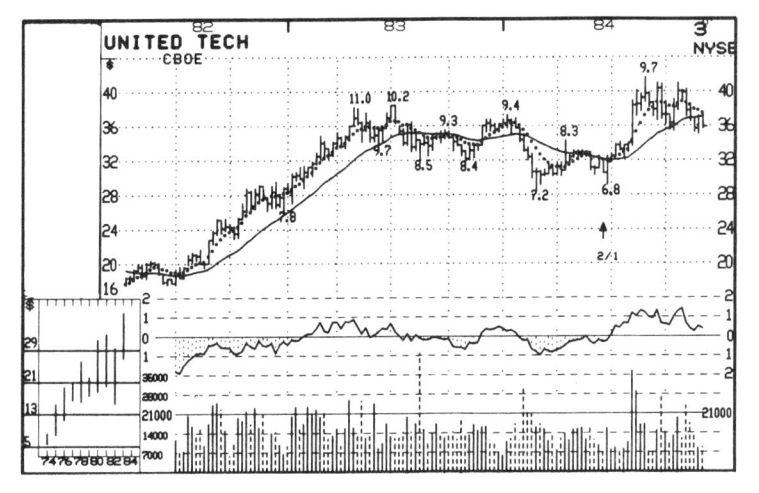

TCKR: UTX
HIGH: 41⅝
LOW: 28½
PRICE: 35⅞
EARN: 4.83
P/E: 7
DEBT: 837
YIELD: 3.9

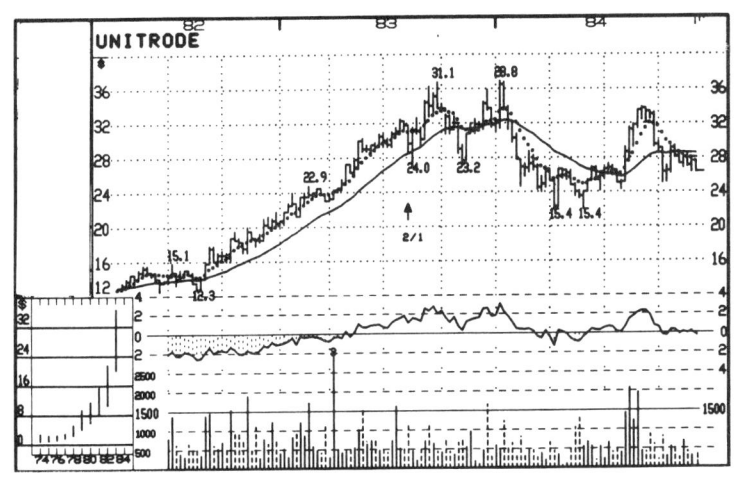

UNITRODE

TCKR: UTR
HIGH: 36⅞
LOW: 22
PRICE: 23¾
EARN: 1.51
P/E: 16
DEBT: 12.3
YIELD: 0.8

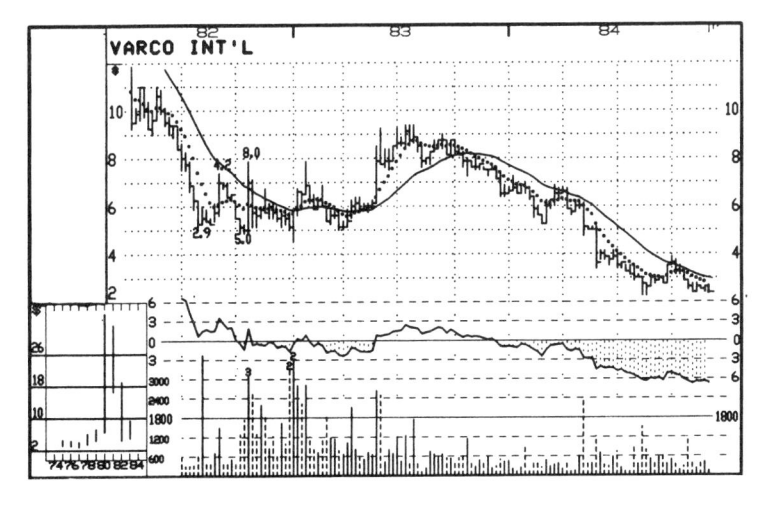

VARCO INT'L

TCKR: VRC
HIGH: 7⅜
LOW: 2¼
PRICE: 2½
EARN: d1.98
P/E: d
DEBT: 8.08
YIELD: —

WEBB, DEL E.

Del Webb was once co-owner of the New York Yankees, an outfit so conservative that its operatives were required to wear pinstriped suits even when they were playing games. Webb has long since passed from the scene, and the construction company he left behind has become daring enough to enter the gambling business. It owns three hotels in Nevada (now being upgraded) with substantial casino operations, and it also manages the Claridge in Atlantic City. Business and residential community construction still account for the lion's share of activity, with the spotlight on close to 10,000 Arizona acres known as Sun City West. The company almost excavated itself into a deep pit in 1981, and the chips have lately been falling on some wrong numbers in Nevada. But the Claridge pays off steadily.

WESTERN AIR LINES

For a while, Western, which ranks ninth among U.S. carriers, was flying on a wing and a prayer. Today it's still up in the air—but in more ways than one. Reduced labor costs (and a bit of luck) may help them get back on course. Salt Lake City is the hub out of which Western serves a primary area in the triangle formed by Alaska, Mexico, and Hawaii. The cutthroat deregulated competition of a few years ago has eased somewhat, but it left the line in need of a pretty good debt juggling act. And it still has to deal with Continental, Frontier, and Southwest airlines, whose routes overlap some of Western's.

WESTERN CO. OF NORTH AMERICA

The name only tells you where Western operates. This company sells oil field services and performs a considerable amount of offshore contract drilling through Western Petroleum Services and Western Oceanic. Its services division is horizontally integrated: It uses Western-made equipment. Working operations have spread as far as the Appalachians. Contract drilling was a busy area in 1984, with rigs operating at 96 percent of capacity, although rates were off. Natural gas activity has picked up, but profit margins are narrow due to competition and the specter of Canadian gas.

WEBB DEL E

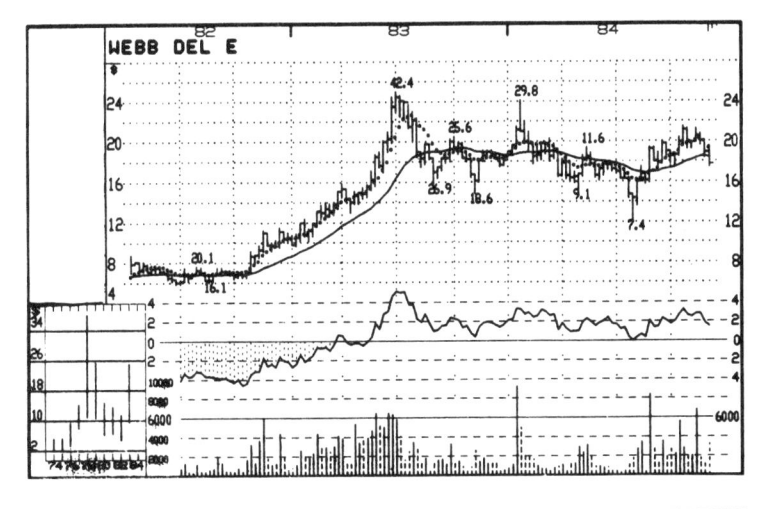

TCKR: WBB
HIGH: 24⅛
LOW: 12⅛
PRICE: 18½
EARN: 1.50
P/E: 12
DEBT: 95.7
YIELD: 0.8

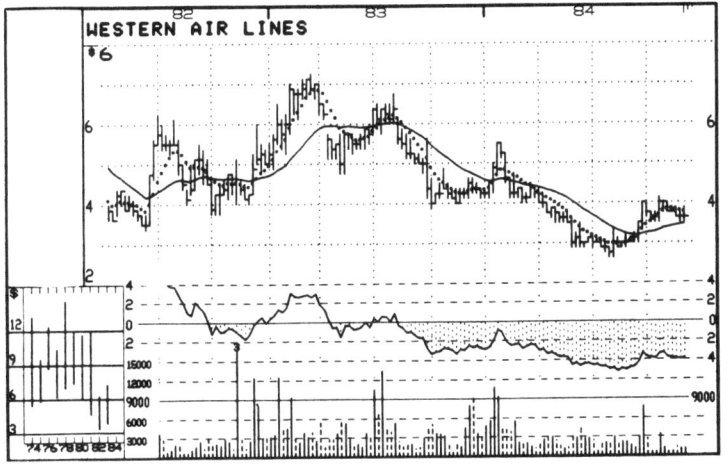

WESTERN AIR LINES

TCKR: WAL
HIGH: 5½
LOW: 2⅝
PRICE: 3½
EARN: d2.56
P/E: d
DEBT: 422
YIELD: —

WESTERN CO NORTH AMER

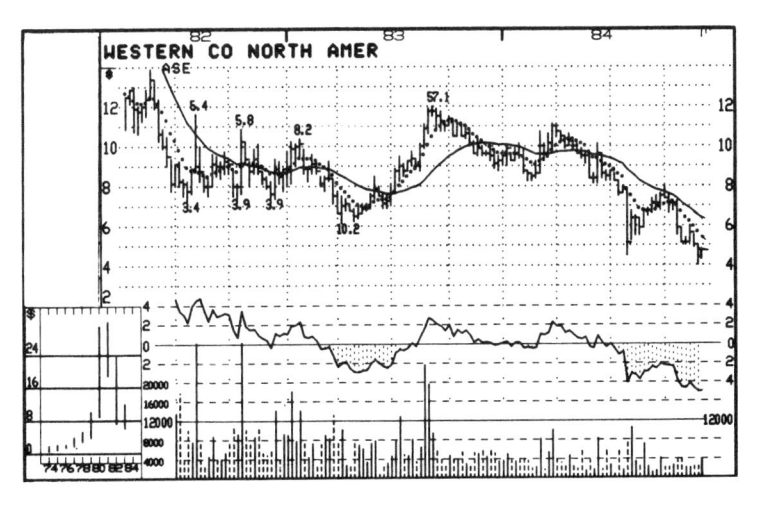

TCKR: WSN
HIGH: 28⅜
LOW: 16¼
PRICE: 17¼
EARN: d0.85
P/E: d
DEBT: 619
YIELD: 2.6

217

WESTERN UNION

The very name conjures up a yellow telegram with good or bad tidings, or the 1941 movie of the same name in which Robert Young and Randolph Scott helped unite the West by telegraph wire. But these days, spurred by intense telecommunications competition, this holding company is just as likely to use one of its five satellites (with another due up this year) or microwaves to deliver the message. Traditional Telex and telegraph business has been sluggish of late, although their Telex system is installed in well over 100,000 offices. Soon-to-be-instituted increases in phone rates for access to the system are another negative factor. Western Union's TWX transmits data as well as messages. Currently, the company's prospects look best in their Easylink electronic mail service, which allows customers with personal computers to gain direct access to Western Union's telecommunications network.

WESTINGHOUSE ELECTRIC

You used to be able to be sure if it was Westinghouse. In the 70s, however, doubts arose—especially when the company built a nuclear power plant on the side of an active volcano. But a revitalized top management seems to have pushed all the right buttons lately. Longines and Wittnauer watches are now Westinghouse products, and the company has entered the office furniture field. It owns Teleprompter, and cable television operations are healthier since they pulled out of satellite news transmission. Still number two in electrical energy, Westinghouse has positioned itself well in the products and services that support high-tech industry, including robots. Westinghouse stock was split two-for-one in 1984.

WESTVACO CORP.

Its main activity is beating raw material to a pulp—and although that's sometimes the finished product, more often it's different kinds of paper: paperboard, kraft paper, shipping containers, cups, and envelopes. In fact, the U.S. Envelope operation is one of the major producers in its field. Westvaco owns well over a million acres of timber, providing 50 percent of its raw material needs: the goal is to make that 75 percent. In the past two years, Westvaco's capital budget has approximately doubled. Rigesa, Ltd. is its Brazilian paper company. Westvaco also operates a small chemical business, and last year it bought the St. John Chemical Corp.

WESTERN UNION

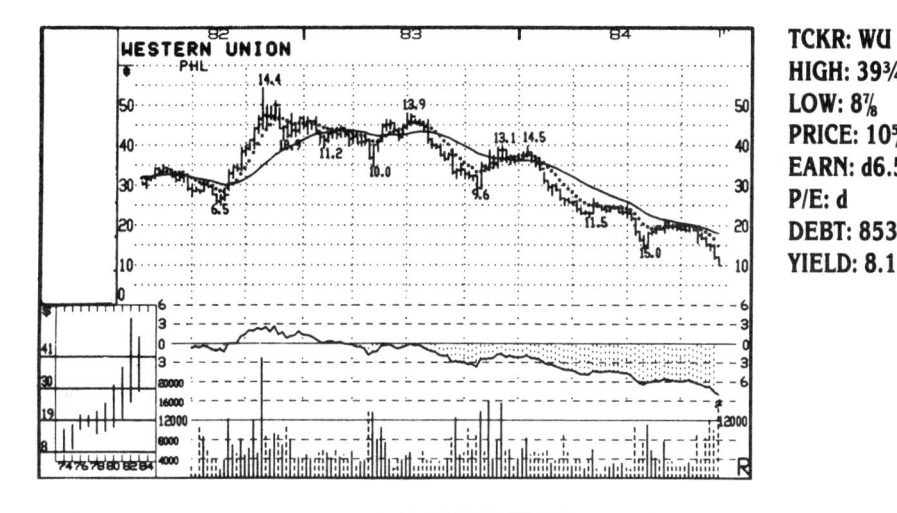

TCKR: WU
HIGH: 39¾
LOW: 8⅞
PRICE: 10⅝
EARN: d6.50
P/E: d
DEBT: 853
YIELD: 8.1

WESTINGHOUSE EL

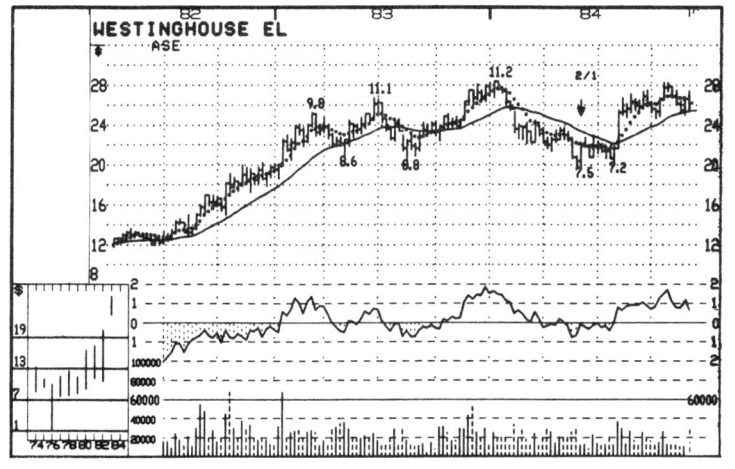

TCKR: WX
HIGH: 28⅜
LOW: 19¾
PRICE: 25¼
EARN: 2.91
P/E: 9
DEBT: 545
YIELD: 4.0

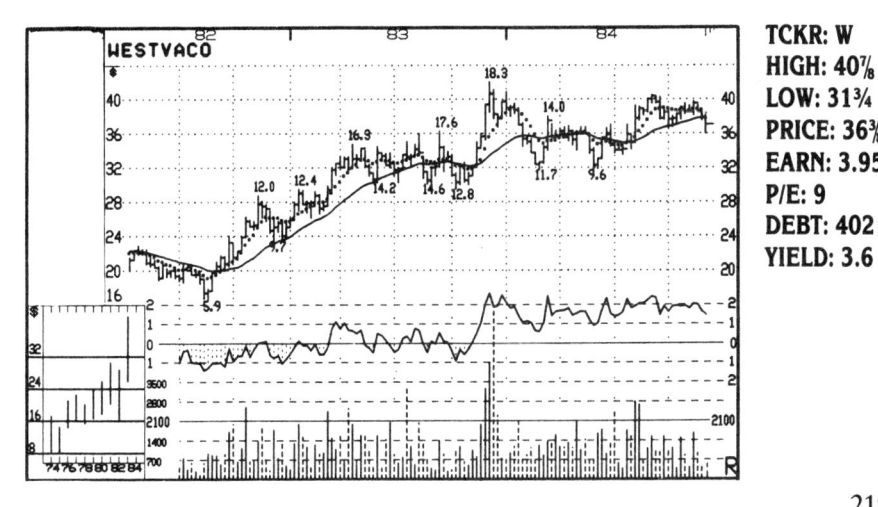

WESTVACO

TCKR: W
HIGH: 40⅞
LOW: 31¾
PRICE: 36⅜
EARN: 3.95
P/E: 9
DEBT: 402
YIELD: 3.6

WHITTAKER CORP.

Hydraulic equipment and upscale pleasure boats are major products of this diversified company. Chemicals and metal products for the oil and gas business are also important. More important still is the health care division, where future growth is likely to take place. However, that growth will not be happening in Saudi Arabia, even though Whittaker's contract to provide health services there had been their best profit generator. The contract, which expired last year, was lost to an underbidder. Now the pressure is on that division to get the company moving, because the rest of Whittaker's operations have not been doing too well, either. Whittaker could start to get out of the woods by getting out of the water (the boat business is up for sale.)

WILLIAMS ELECTRONICS

In recent years, this arcade and home video game company had to jump quicker than Pac Man trying to avoid a ghost as the industry all but dropped off the screen. One direction Williams jumped was toward the gaming tables in Puerto Rico, where it bought two casino-equipped hotels, one of which has been temporarily closed for renovations. (An interest in the Atlantic City Sands was sold last year.) Not that Williams has abandoned the electronic game world. It has licensed some of its software to Atari (which with any luck will remain solvent) and in 1984 brought out a laser disc game. Williams also makes pinball machines and is now producing musical programming for television.

WOOLWORTH, F.W.

There's still life in the old five-and-dime. With the elimination of its domestic Woolco stores and the divestiture of its British subsidiary, Woolworth is prepared to concentrate on its specialty retailing operations in the U.S., which now include 3,000 Kinney Shoes stores and the Anderson-Little, J. Brannam, Little Folk, and Richman clothing chains. The 1,200 or so Woolworth stores in this country are being renovated at the rate of 100 a year. The merchandise mix will be customized for each local market, with the emphasis on the traditional health and beauty products, which already produce two-thirds of the store's sales. The company also operates 500 stores in Canada and Germany.

WHITTAKER ASE

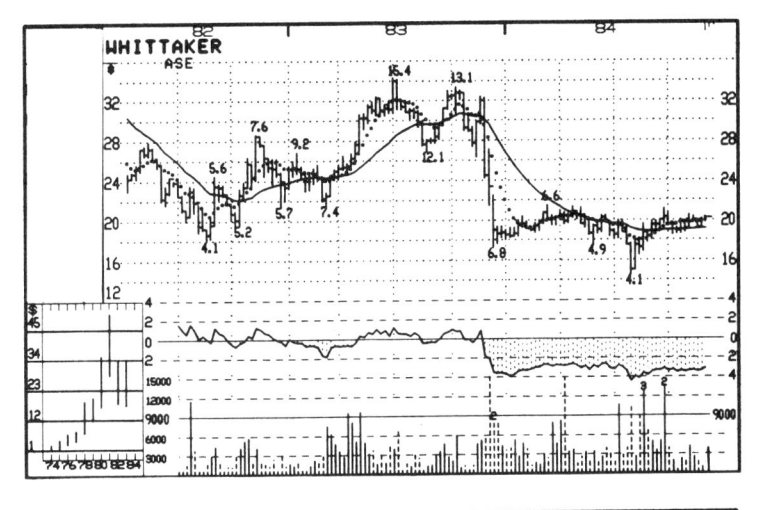

TCKR: WKR
HIGH: 21½
LOW: 14½
PRICE: 20
EARN: 3.51
P/E: 6
DEBT: 139
YIELD: 3.0

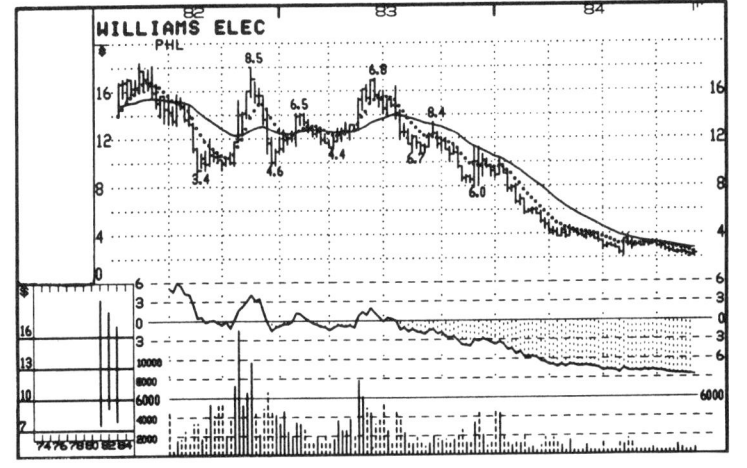

WILLIAMS ELEC PHL

TCKR: WMS
HIGH: 10⅜
LOW: 2
PRICE: 2⅛
EARN: d0.75
P/E: d
DEBT: 45.3
YIELD: —

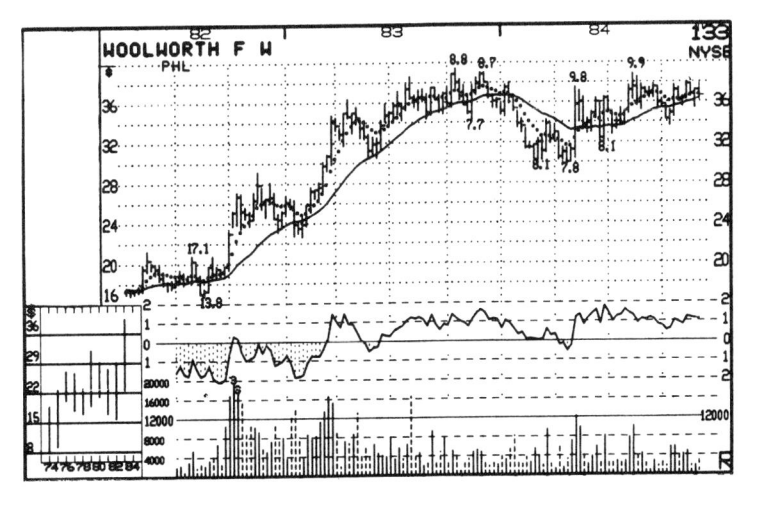

WOOLWORTH F W PHL

TCKR: Z
HIGH: 38⅞
LOW: 29⅞
PRICE: 36¼
EARN: 3.93
P/E: 9
DEBT: 389
YIELD: 5.0

XEROX CORP.

About 90 percent of Xerox's profit comes from its copying operations. This copy king was not a copycat, though — it started the business. Its early domination of the industry led to the use of its name as both a verb and a generic noun, something the company has tried to discourage. Recently, many competitors have entered the field with the aim of helping Xerox to dissuade customers from "Xeroxing" anything. The company's electronic printing division has prospered. But Xerox's workstations, data-processing operations, and Ethernet local computer network have done less well. Xerox's property-casualty insurance company, Crum and Foster, has shared the tough times recently typical of that industry. Taking another step in its quiet entry into financial services, last year Xerox bought the investment banking firm of Van Kampen Merritt, Inc.

ZAPATA CORP.

Zapata is a contract oil driller whose profits seemed to have gotten lost in a deep hole in fiscal 1984. About half their revenues comes from offshore drilling, and another third from servicing other companies' rigs. It also owns some small oil and gas reserves. Last year Zapata purchased three semi-submersible units to pursue oil deposits at greater depths. It is also involved in the Menhaden fishing industry, augmenting activities there a year ago with the purchase of Seacoast Products. Fishing and fish processing now make up about 10 to 15 percent of Zapata's revenues, but only 1 percent of its profits.

XEROX CBOE PAC

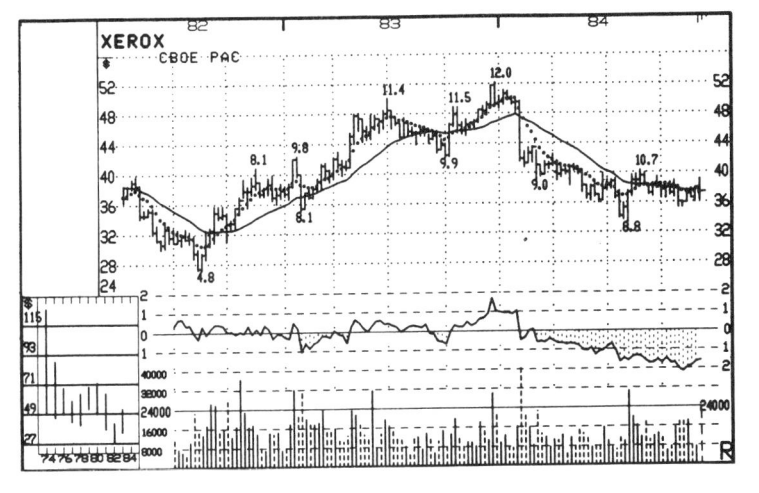

TCKR: XRX
HIGH: 52 1/8
LOW: 33 1/4
PRICE: 37 1/4
EARN: 3.43
P/E: 11
DEBT: 1581
YIELD: 8.1

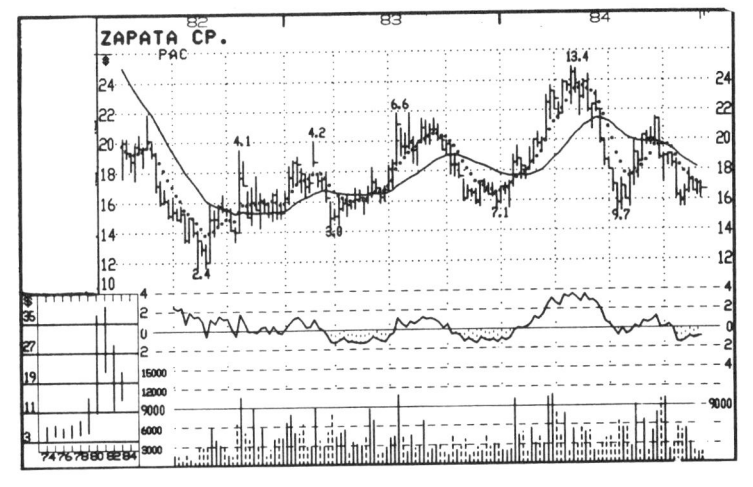

ZAPATA CP. PAC

TCKR: ZOS
HIGH: 24 7/8
LOW: 15 1/4
PRICE: 16 5/8
EARN: 1.42
P/E: 12
DEBT: 579
YIELD: 5.1

223

8
Vital Statistics

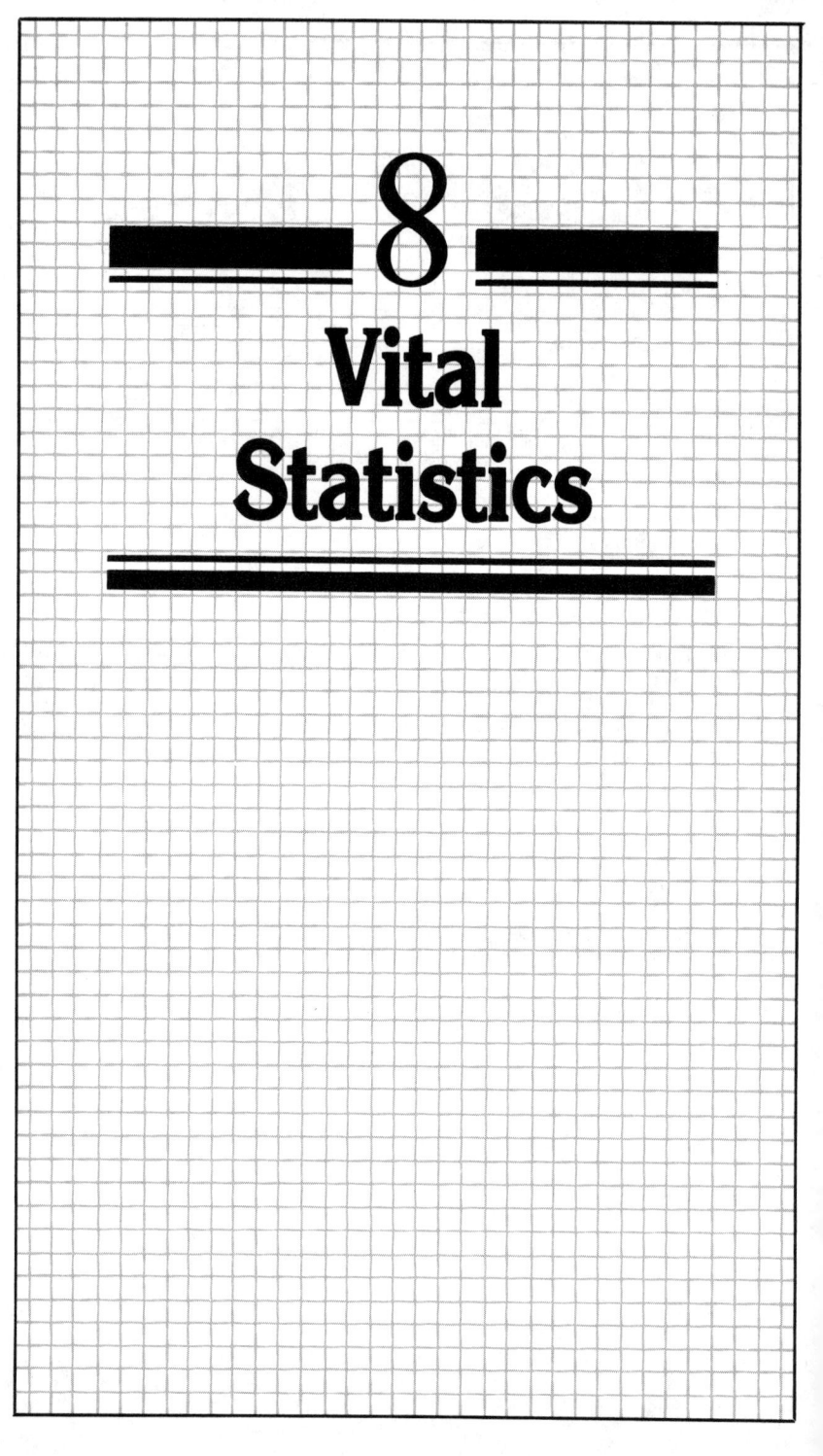

Some investors carefully transcribe every one of their transactions and track every indicator in journals of gold lamé. Others jot notes on mustard-stained napkins, which are then stuffed in their pockets and sent to the dry cleaner.

Beat the Market offers a third alternative with twin advantages.

1. You've already paid for it.
2. You can individualize it.

The following pages consist of the most commonly used stock market forms and graphs, and can serve as masters for duplication on a copying machine. With the touch of a button and the crunch of a stapler, you can have at your disposal a customized stock market log.

The choices range from comparison-shopping questionnaires for choosing the best mutual fund to market statistics logs, from blank graph paper (for charting your favorite stocks) to transaction record forms. In every seasoned investor, there is a bit of the gambler—now, too, a bit of the bookmaker.

DAILY MARKET LOG

Date								
NYSE Comp.	Close							
	Change							
DOW Ind.	Close							
	Change							
DOW Trans.	Close							
	Change							
DOW Util.	Close							
	Change							
NYSE Volume								
NYSE	Stocks Up							
NYSE	Stocks Down							
NYSE	New Highs							
NYSE	New Lows							
AMEX Comp.	Close							
	Change							
OTC (Nasdaq) Comp.	Close							
	Change							

STOCK TRANSACTION RECORD

Order Placed

Date _____

Time _____

Broker _____

Account Number _____

☐ Buy
☐ Sell _____ Shares of _____ At $_____

☐ Market Order
☐ Day Order
☐ G.T.C.

Order Confirmed

☐ Trade Never Executed

☐ Trade Executed at $_____ per Share

Confirmed by _____

Date _____

Time _____

PORTFOLIO RECORD

Date Purchased	Price	Quantity	Stock	Date Sold	Price	Profit/Loss

STOCK MARKET/MUTUAL FUND DIRECTORY

Organization

Representative

Phone Number(s)

Account Number

Name on Account

Special Notes

STOCK EVALUATION SHEET

Company

Ticker Symbol

High

Low

Current Price

Earnings (12 months)

P/E

Cash

Assets

Liabilities

Long-Term Debt

Book Value

Principal Business

Graph Evaluation

Additional Notes

Overall Rating

MUTUAL FUND EVALUATION SHEET

Name of Fund

Address

City, State   Zip

Phone

Fund Objective

Degree of Risk

Percent Change/10 Years   %

Percent Change/5 Years   %

Percent Change/1 Year   %

Commission (Load)   %

Minimum Initial Investment $

Minimum Additional Investment $

Listed in Daily Newspaper?   ☐ Yes   ☐ No

Check-Writing Option?   ☐ Yes   ☐ No

Exchange Privileges?   ☐ Yes   ☐ No

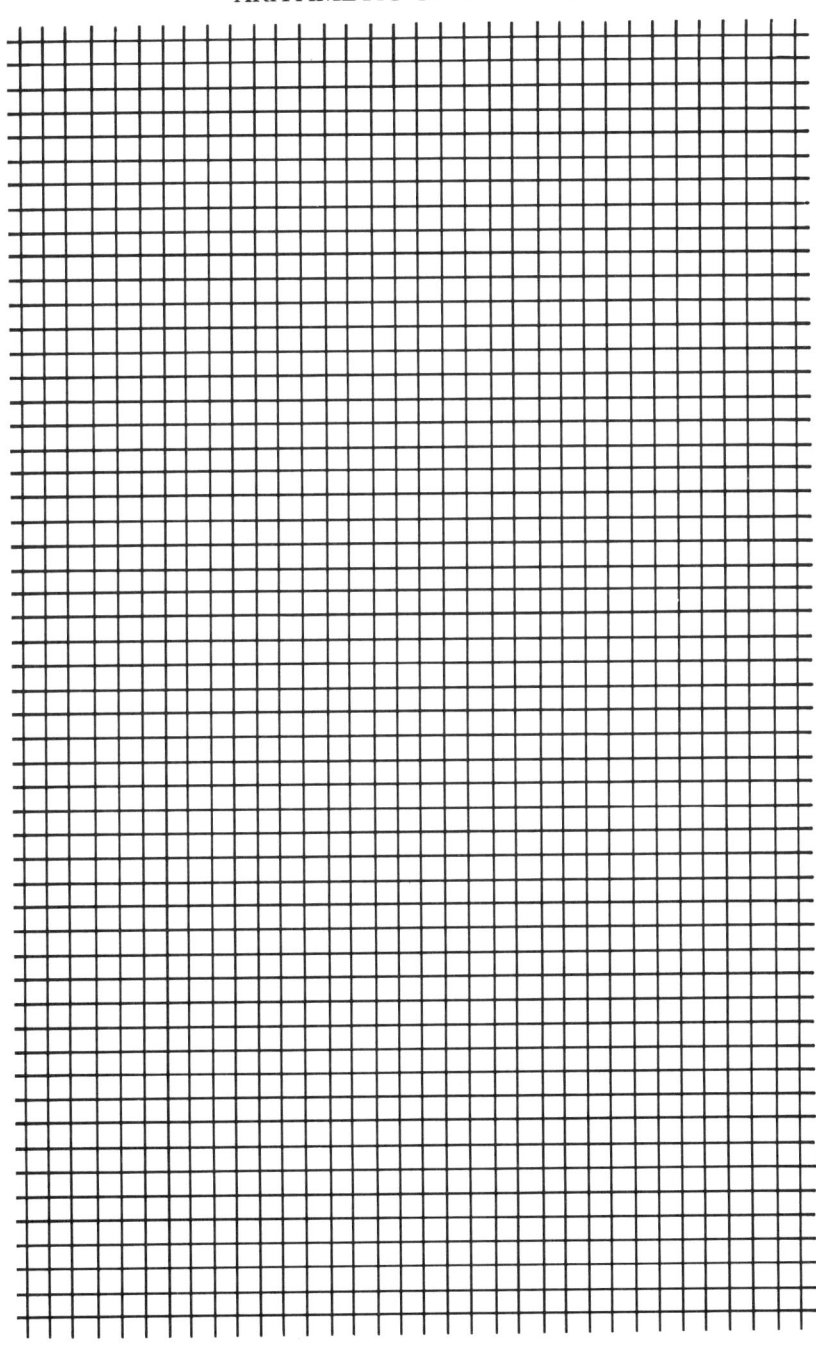

ARITHMETIC GRAPH PAPER

LOGARITHMIC GRAPH PAPER

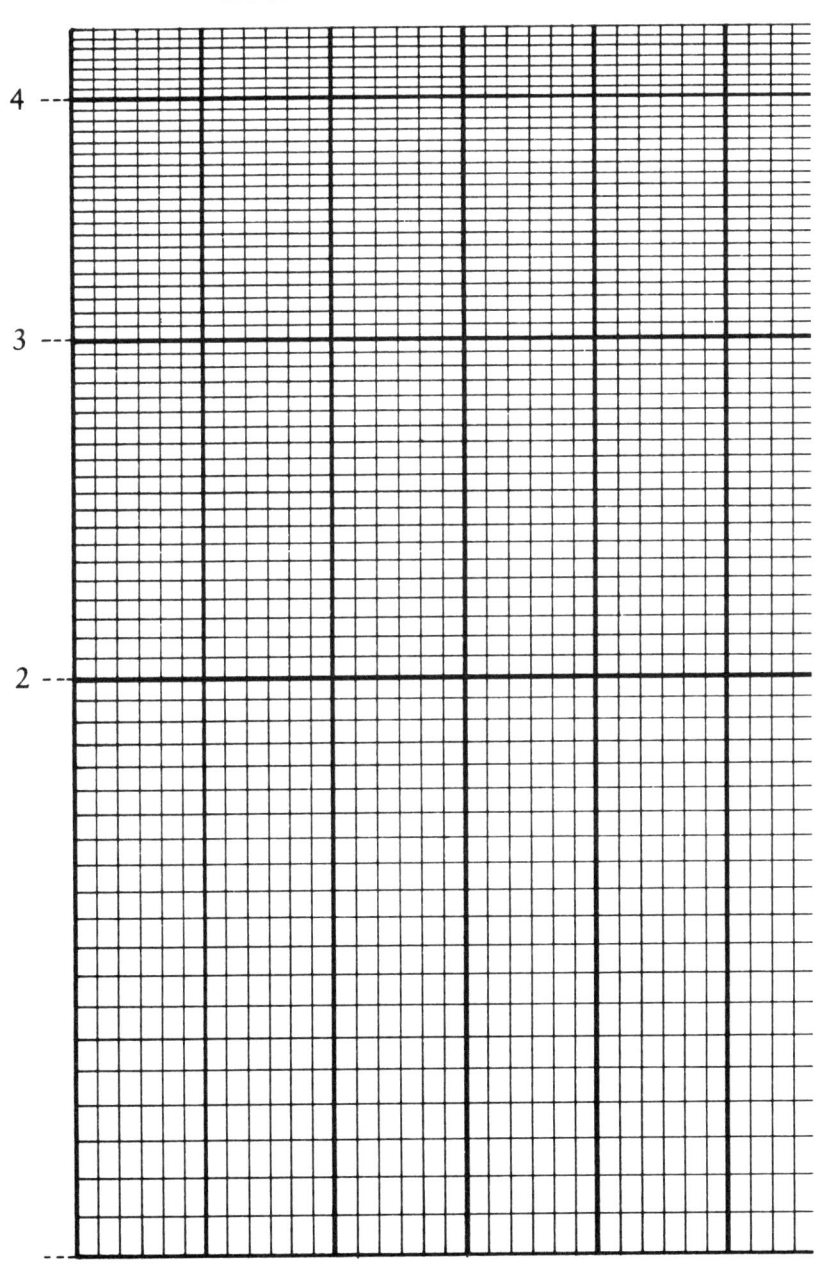

9
The Rules of the Game

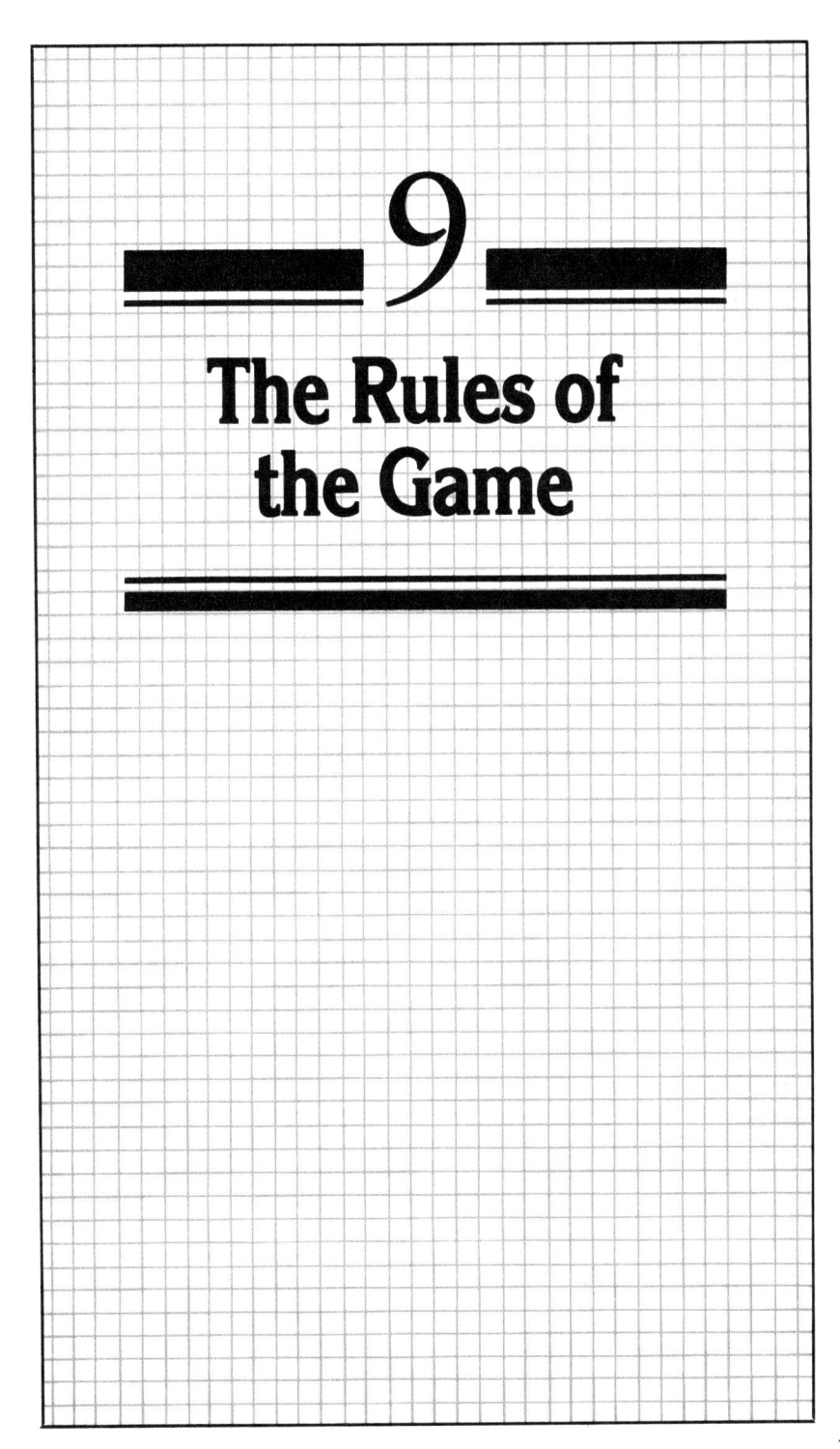

THE *BEAT THE MARKET 1985* STOCK MARKET GAME

Here is your opportunity to try your hand at building your own stock market portfolio. Stock selection is up to you. You may choose as few as 5 and as many as 10 of the 200 stocks listed in *Beat the Market 1985* in which to invest an imaginary $25,000.

Timing is as important an element in the Stock Market Game as it is in real life. You determine when your "investment clock" begins to tick. Choose the 6-month time span in which you think your chosen stocks will put in their best performance.

Read the Official Rules carefully before entering. Follow all instructions. Print clearly. Mail early. Choose wisely.

The *Beat the Market 1985* Stock Market Game is a chance to test your mettle and technique, to play in an investor's paradise in which the jackpot is grand — 25 grand, to be exact — and where a downside simply doesn't exist.

Potential reward with nary a risk.

We welcome you to the finest game in town.

Official Entry Form
THE *BEAT THE MARKET 1985* STOCK MARKET GAME
No Purchase Necessary to Enter

Please print clearly:

I. Name _____
   Address _____
   City _____ State _____ Zip _____

II. Investment time period (check one only):
   ☐ 4/1/85–10/1/85   ☐ 9/3/85–3/3/86
   ☐ 5/1/85–11/1/85   ☐ 10/1/85–4/1/86
   ☐ 6/3/85–12/2/85   ☐ 11/1/85–5/1/86
   ☐ 7/1/85–1/2/86   ☐ 12/2/85–6/2/86
   ☐ 8/1/85–2/3/86   ☐ 1/2/86–7/1/86

III. **Clearly print the names of securities you would pick** to invest $25,000 in to aggregately appreciate the greatest over the 6-month time period you have selected above (you must select at least 5, but no more than 10 stocks; the names of securities selected must be from among the 200 securities discussed in *Beat the Market 1985*):

   1 _____   6 _____
   2 _____   7 _____
   3 _____   8 _____
   4 _____   9 _____
   5 _____   10 _____

IV. Mail your completed entry to: Beat the Market 1985
                                     P.O. Box 4192
                                     Blair, NE 68009

For eligibility, an entry must be received no later than one (1) day prior to the beginning of the 6-month time period indicated on the submitted entry form. To be reasonably sure that your entry will be eligible, we recommend that you mail it at least 10 days prior to your chosen Starting Date.

See Official Rules for complete details and means of obtaining an additional Official Entry Form and complete listing of the 200 securities discussed in *Beat the Market 1985*.

All federal, state, and local laws and regulations apply.
Offer void wherever prohibited by law.

THE *BEAT THE MARKET 1985* STOCK MARKET GAME

Official Rules
No Purchase Required

1. In the spaces provided on an Official Entry Form, hand-print your name, address, and guess as to which 5 to 10 stocks of the 200 securities discussed in *Beat the Market 1985* you would pick to invest $25,000 in to aggregately appreciate the greatest over a 6-month investment time period, and in what time period: 4/1/85–10/1/85, 5/1/85–11/1/85, 6/3/85–12/2/85, 7/1/85–1/2/86, 8/1/85–2/3/86, 9/3/85–3/3/86, 10/1/85–4/1/86, 11/1/85–5/1/86, 12/2/85–6/2/86, or 1/2/86–7/1/86.

Mail your completed entry to: "Beat the Market 1985," P.O. Box 4192, Blair, Nebraska 68009. For eligibility, an entry must be received no later than one (1) day prior to the beginning of the 6-month time period indicated on a submitted entry form. To be reasonably sure that your entry will be eligible, we recommend that you mail it at least 10 days prior to your chosen Starting Date. Enter as often as you wish, but each entry must be on an Official Entry Form and sent separately via first class mail.

Additional Official Entry Forms and a complete listing of the 200 securities discussed in *Beat the Market 1985* can be obtained by sending a self-addressed, stamped envelope (state of Washington residents need not affix return postage) for each entry form/security listing you wish to: "Beat the Market 1985" Entry Form, P.O. Box 4220, Blair, Nebraska 68009. Requests for entry forms/security listings received after November 30, 1985 will not be honored.

2. A single $25,000 cash prize will be awarded to the individual whose submitted entry lists the portfolio which has aggregately increased in value the greatest from amongst all submitted entries. In the event of ties, prize will be divided equally among all those individuals submitting entries listing the portfolios that have aggregately increased the greatest. Limit: one prize distribution to an individual or family. Splits, mergers, leveraged buy-outs, and takeovers will be accounted for in accordance with the announced terms of such. Final value of stocks which are no longer traded or have become delisted during an entry's indicated 6-month time period will be valued on the basis of last listed trade price during that period. In the event a listing does not occur during that period, stock will be considered worthless.

Determination of increases or decreases in portfolio values will be based on the closing New York Stock Exchange market prices of securities listed on the first and last date of the particular 6-month time period indicated on an entry form.

3. Prize winner selection will be under the supervision of the D. L. BLAIR CORPORATION, an independent judging organization whose decisions are final. Winner(s) will be notified by mail and be required to execute an Affidavit of Eligibility within 30 days of notification. In the event of noncompliance within this time period, an alternate winner will be selected. Taxes on prize are the sole responsibility of the winner(s). Chances of winning are determined by the total number of entries received.

4. Sweepstakes participation is open to all residents of the United States except employees of Cloverdale Press Inc., Viking Penguin, Inc., their agencies, affiliates, and their immediate family members. Offer is subject to all federal, state, and local laws and regulations, and is void wherever prohibited by law. Winner's entry and acceptance of prize offered constitute permission to use winner's name, photograph, or other likeness for purposes of advertising and promotion on behalf of Cloverdale Press Inc. and/or Viking Penguin, Inc., without further compensation to the winner.

5. For the name of the winner(s), send a self-addressed, stamped envelope to: "Beat the Market 1985" Winner, P.O. Box 4264, Blair, Nebraska 68009.